MASTER YOUR
MONEY
TYPE

*Using Your Financial Personality to
Create a Life of Wealth and Freedom*

JORDAN E. GOODMAN

A Cooper/Sonberg Book

WARNER
BUSINESS
BOOKS™

NEW YORK · BOSTON

This publication is designed to provide competent and reliable information regarding the subject matter covered. However, it is sold with the understanding that the author and publisher are not engaged in rendering legal, financial, or other professional advice. Laws and practices often vary from state to state, and if legal or other expert assistance is required, the services of a professional should be sought. The author and publisher specifically disclaim any liability that is incurred from the use or application of the contents of this book.

Warner Business Books
Warner Books

Time Warner Book Group
1271 Avenue of the Americas, New York, NY 10020
Visit our Web site at www.twbookmark.com.

The Warner Business Books logo is a trademark of Warner Books.

Printed in the United States of America

First Edition: January 2006

10 9 8 7 6 5 4 3 2 1

Library of Congress Cataloging-in-Publication Data

Goodman, Jordan Elliot.
    Master your money type : using your financial personality to create a life of wealth and freedom / Jordan E. Goodman.—1st ed.
        p.   cm.
    Includes bibliographical references and index.
    ISBN 0-446-57801-0
    1. Finance, Personal.   I. Title.
    HG179.G6755 2006
    332.024'01—dc22   2005022209

Book design by Giorgetta Bell McRee

*To my wife, Suzanne, whose astute psychological insight
served as an inspiration during this project, and my teenage
son, Jason, whose generation I hope will benefit from
understanding their Money Types better
than their parents did.*

ACKNOWLEDGMENTS

Master Your Money Type would not have been possible without the generous and skillful contributions and extremely hard work of many talented people.

Foremost among these contributors are the team of Lynn Sonberg and Roger Cooper, who originally conceived of the idea of harnessing the power of your financial personality. Lynn skillfully guided the work from the original proposal through the research, writing, and editing process, always staying on top of the many details and maintaining a high standard for accuracy and clarity in the work. Roger was also instrumental in framing the book's direction and was the key player in getting the book distributed to the wide audience that is benefiting from its message.

The writing and research team also did a remarkable job of combining psychological insight and real-world financial savvy. Connie deSwaan artfully wrote the text, weaving in the stories of the volunteers of all the Money Types with a keen psychological awareness, combined with an understanding of the financial steps people need to take to improve their situation. Roberta Yafie showed a great deal of skill and persistence by interviewing hundreds of people across the country in many situations to arrive at the most poignant stories to illustrate each

Money Type. Cheryl Winokur Munk did exhaustive research to find the most relevant resources and worksheets to help readers put all of my advice into action. Meg Schneider, CSW, a therapist in private practice, and author of several psychological self-help books, was an invaluable resource as a psychological consultant for the project.

The team at Warner Books was also instrumental in making this project a reality. Editor Rick Wolff immediately embraced the concept of Money Types and championed the project from beginning to end. Jamie Raab, publisher of Warner Books, was extremely supportive of the book from conception through publication. Flamur Tonuzi, art director, created the wonderful cover design. Robert Castillo was responsible for overseeing the production of the book, and Fred Chase undertook the meticulous copyediting of the manuscript. Herman Estevez skillfully took the photograph for the cover.

I want to thank the hundreds of people who generously revealed their Money Type personalities and the financial details of their lives for this book. They've all made this book so much richer and personal. While their stories are real, we have changed names and identifying features to protect their privacy. Finally, great thanks to the thousands of subscribers to my Web site, www.moneyanswers.com, and the many thousands of people who, over the years, have contacted me for ongoing financial information and advice.

My hope is that readers of *Master Your Money Type* will come to understand their financial personality much better and be empowered to act to make the most of their financial opportunities as a result.

Jordan E. Goodman
January 1, 2006

CONTENTS

MASTER YOUR
MONEY
TYPE

CHAPTER 1

The Money Type Promise

People always ask me where the money is.

The other day, after signing off from my phone-in radio show, I opened an e-mail from a young Tennessee woman with just such a request. Her story struck me as both poignant and typical of what so many people are going through in their efforts to better handle their money. It went like this.

"It's been one of those rough years," Holly wrote. "I've had a shopping problem that my husband and I attacked head-on and have, for the time being, been able to control. I leave my credit and debit cards with him so I only buy what we absolutely need on a day-to-day basis. Unfortunately, he didn't get hold of my cards before I ran us into serious debt. Now we are trying to dig out of the $10,000 I owe plus pay off some costly repairs on our roof. I feel like I've laid my head on a chopping block and now the ax is swinging. How can we deal with debt? Who can help us catch up? Frankly, I'd just like to run away. I'm terrified."

I was particularly struck by this e-mail for one reason. Holly's "rough year" sounded all too familiar. I felt as if I'd heard about it, or variations on the theme, many, many times before from people all over America who also seem unable to manage their resources. Naturally, the details are different, but the urgency, and the sense of feeling lost about money issues, were the same. Consider:

- Peter from Florida, running a small, successful real estate firm who is consumed with worry about how to save for his children's college education.
- Frank and Ellen from New Jersey, who are living so close to the vest they can hardly make it from payday to payday while sitting on a pile of savings they are too afraid to touch.
- Maria, a devoted government employee from Alabama, living well within her means but feeling frustrated by her unrealized dreams.
- Sam, a California freelance graphic artist who is in demand but can't figure out where all the money he takes in is going.

One thing is true: People everywhere work hard and want to live better. Often, they can overextend themselves in their desire "to live the dream" and then get caught with bills they can't pay. Or they are doing well but live with the fear that they may lose it all—and may not have any idea how to manage what they have to improve their lives.

In more than two decades as a financial commentator on radio and TV, a lecturer, author, and Wall Street correspondent for *Money* magazine, I've spoken to and advised thousands of people—some successful, some struggling—on how to solve money questions. But no matter where these people fell on the continuum between haves and have-nots, I realized that I was speaking to many of the same individuals over and over again, people who were asking me for the same advice for the exact same financial problems.

Obviously, they were not following my advice, yet they kept contacting me! What was going on? I had to be missing something. At first, I thought it was simply a matter of answering their question "What do I do now?" with more clarity and greater attention to detail.

Determined to help, I would enthusiastically explore the details of their situation and offer carefully considered financial advice tailor-made for that person's income, holdings, responsibilities, and needs. Truly, it seemed to me, all these people needed was sound advice from an attentive financial expert for them to make some significant changes with their finances. But I know now that expertise alone isn't the answer. I finally realized that the "What do I do now?" to which I'd been responding with such optimistic fervor was actually only the first half of the question. The second half is, "... *given how I feel about money.*"

I realized that for people to put into effect the best financial advice specific to them, they—and I—had to recognize and understand their complicated feelings about money.

I began listening even more closely to the questions I was being asked and became aware there was an intense emotional subtext behind every comment or request for advice. Rarely were these words uttered exactly, but I could hear the emotional subtext—loud and clear.

- "I don't want to end up on the street."
- "I know if I take one more chance, I'll hit the jackpot and have everything I've ever wanted."
- "I feel comfortable financially, but I keep thinking ... is this all I dare wish for?"
- "I don't know a thing about managing money, and whenever I try, I feel like a moron!"

It occurred to me that people ask the same questions about money because they tend to keep dealing with money the same way—the only way that feels familiar. That made sense, in its way. People also operate from experiences and messages given to them in their past and what they learn along the way. These influences clearly hinder how they deal with money now. This also made sense, and I suddenly knew I'd hit on my answer at last: *Everyone's money behavior falls into definable patterns.*

Everyone, including you, has some kind of "financial personality"—a style of handling money that reflects everything from the deepest fears to the most heartfelt desires to basic practical dealings on a day-to-day basis. The problem with the people asking those same questions was that they weren't looking at what they *felt* about money—those very powerful emotional connections just below the surface that drive their decisions. And so they continually make the same mistakes, unable to break away from their usual way of money management to find the prosperity or sense of security—or both—they all craved. Furthermore, this was why they couldn't follow or create a financial plan that might actually work.

I considered the complexity of the money-and-emotion equation, and knew I had to find a way for you to better understand your "financial personality." When you did, your fears about money would lessen and your strengths and creativity with money could grow. What could I do to make these goals happen for you? People came from diverse backgrounds and had different feelings, different values, and different personal histories. Clearly there wouldn't be just one solution.

I wanted to create some sort of simple process wherein I could help you, no matter what your background, beliefs, or present financial situation. I wanted to reconcile money information (*what you need to know about managing money itself*) with your money attitudes (*what you need to know about your feelings and fears about money*) so that you could emerge feeling secure and more confident about money, for now and for the future. This became my mission.

This book grew out of my determination to find effective answers to your money questions in a way that would be meaningful. The result is this guide to mastering your Money Type. The key to real life-changing financial success for you can lie within these types. I'll show you how very shortly.

First let's talk about money and what it means to you.

TAPPING INTO YOUR RELATIONSHIP WITH MONEY

Everyone gives money all sorts of meanings beyond the value of the goods or services it can buy. Why do some people idolize money while others reject it? Why are yet others afraid of money or believe that wanting it is an unworthy or even shameful goal? Why do some people kill for money or kill themselves if they lose it all? Why do close relatives, spouses, or friends become enemies over one's "rightful share" of the money?

The answers are within every life story—the way *your* answers can be found within your story. Maybe your parents were stingy with you or generous to a fault. Perhaps you were told that life is tough, money is limited, and that you should be grateful for the money you get. Then again, maybe you were raised to believe that the world was bountiful and that the bounty would have your name on it.

Whatever you were told and whatever you believe, no matter how contradictory, one thing is true for all of us: Money is never just money but a repository for our deepest fears, doubts, insecurities, anxieties, aggressive impulses, and even sense of self. All these feelings can influence and even dominate how you manage money. There is *always* an emotional component to money. When you think about money, how do *you* feel? Deserving, powerful, confused, secure, happy, insatiable, entitled, guilty, corrupt, fearful?

More important, your *attitudes* about money can affect and drive your financial aspirations. If, for example, *you have a strong conviction that you will always have money*, you'll do everything you can to earn more or take the kind of investment risks that will provide financial prosperity. I recently spoke to a woman who said she figured out that she had "ten pockets" from which she could either put in or take out money. That is, she had a job, but she also invested in a friend's business for a share, rented out the family cottage for the summer, as well as having a trusted broker who guided her investment pockets, and so on. For her, security was all-important, and she made every effort to build it.

Perhaps you feel the opposite. You believe your fate is to struggle and never have enough. In this case, you may be in debt and have a *poverty mentality that keeps you broke.* I got an e-mail from a family man in his forties who said he "hated money matters" and that he couldn't figure out how to make his salary stretch. He said he wanted to "pursue the American Dream," but for him, "it turned into a Financial Survival Nightmare." For this man, the quest for more money will always go hand in hand with hating the details of acquiring and keeping it.

Or perhaps a sense of personal powerlessness stands in the way of financial planning, thus leading to a disastrous retirement fund. I get so many letters that tell me how much you want to know about saving for a specific goal, but you feel intimidated by the information—and most of all, fearful that you cannot learn how to do it. When you believe that money management is elitist or arcane and beyond your scope, well, as the saying goes, "If you *believe* you can't, you're right!" Believe you *can.*

In this book, I'll help you uncover your dominant money values, attitudes, and behavior and pinpoint what emotional baggage is standing in the way of you improving your finances. Identifying your emotional baggage helps you understand the motivation and emotions behind your money behavior. This involves *self-awareness*—what is *really* happening in your money life, not what you want or don't want or can't admit is happening. It is about making peace with the past and finally letting yourself master how money works and can work for you.

WHY SELF-AWARENESS COUNTS IN MAKING MONEY WORK FOR YOU

As psychologists tell me, *awareness* of the emotional impact of an event is the first step toward healing. Denial keeps you where you are and promotes inaction. It takes a little courage to look back, but it has a big payoff: You're relieved of a life-long burden that is of no use to you. You need to go back and track your emotional history and, hopefully, identify the defining moment or trauma that you keep reliving.

Awareness makes it safer for you to explore practical financial strategies you might not have been able to attempt before. Once you understand your traits, you can *take optimal action to improve your entire Money Type profile.* You can set goals *based on your strengths with money* that will help you realize your dreams and learn to manage your core weaknesses so that they do not trip you up any longer. When you *get your money weaknesses under control*, you can consolidate your debts and pay them off efficiently, start building a growth portfolio, understand retirement and estate planning, work with a financial planner, choose the best mortgage to make the most of your real estate dollar, and accurately assess your risk tolerance (I have a quiz you can take to learn more about this in Chapter 8) and learn how to control a long-term financial and investment plan, and much, much more.

A little more success with finances builds your confidence with money and extends your reach just enough to realize some dreams. You and your money are going to have a lifelong relationship, and to make any relationship flourish, you need to know your strengths, weaknesses, undeveloped talents, and also which traits are so fundamental to your core personality that you'll need to make peace with them.

What you feel and how you show your feelings to the world pretty much show up in your Money Type.

INSIDE MONEY TYPES: MASTER YOUR TYPE AND CHANGE YOUR FORTUNE

So, let's get to the nitty-gritty: What makes a Money Type, and what makes it yours?

As I began to analyze how people deal with money, I saw

that certain groups of traits clearly defined a financial personality, which is what I mean by a Money Type. These are the dominant traits that drive people to prosperity, to ruin, or down a more secure path. If I've learned anything in doing the extensive research for this book, it is that everyone has a set of attitudes, fears, behaviors, and values that, when put together, fit into a distinct personality or Money Type. Dozens of traits make up the Money Types.

With thousands of cases to evaluate, I formulated sets of behaviors and beliefs that reveal how you care about, use, spend, invest, lose, and earn money. For example, one profile of a Money Type stresses striving for more. Another tends to deny the impact of money on their lives, while yet another takes excessive risks with money or simply prefers to coast along, intent on maintaining the status quo. Maybe you're tightfisted about money and don't like spending, borrowing, or giving to others. These traits are reflected in, for example:

- How you feel about money in general. Perhaps you think money is more important than anything else, or, conversely, is given too much importance.
- How your background affects the way you deal with money now. Perhaps you grew up with very little, and now do what you can to ensure you don't duplicate your parents' money struggles.
- What your fears and fantasies are related to money. Perhaps you fear poverty, and being out on the street, and therefore, you cannot spend money.
- What your financial situation is now. Perhaps you're doing okay, but you inherited some money you want to invest. You don't know where to put it to keep it secure and have it grow.
- Where your ultimate financial goals lie. Perhaps you'd like to buy a beachfront home to retire to and not worry about running out of money to live on.

Then I had another revelation: The best way for me to help people effectively was by tailoring my advice for the best fit within your dominant personal financial style. I could match a person's emotional experience of money with individualized practical financial advice. This was the key to effective change. In working out the types, I found that almost everyone falls within one dominant Money Type but has a characteristic or two from other types. As you read through the chapters devoted to each Money Type, you'll see how your complete financial personality is revealed to you more clearly.

Here, then, are brief profiles of the six basic Money Types. You'll probably see yourself in one or more of the types, *but start out by focusing on the behaviors and money habits that most dominate your finances now.* Be sure to read every chapter. There are true stories, confessions, revelations, and real financial turnarounds to inspire your own efforts!

Start with:

The Strivers

For you, the starting point is about acquiring, achieving, and letting *others* know how much you have. Since money and what it can buy are measures of success, Strivers find a way to play the part of the success story before they've attained the role. At their best, Strivers have energy and drive to make things happen. You make great entrepreneurs, who are willing to take a chance on new ideas, and invest in yourself. Strivers get into trouble when the focus is on overspending—and in forgetting how your income matches up with your expenses. Striving to live up to standards beyond your means tends to get you into debt and interpersonal troubles.

Money mastery for Strivers: If anyone can meet the challenge of gaining control of money by cutting back on nonessentials, it's you. You should still be able to afford some luxury items, but most importantly, you'll learn how to put money aside for the future and make your money grow.

The Ostriches

Ostriches define themselves as being baffled, intimidated, or embarrassed by money. Does this mean Ostriches are unworldly or not used to making a lot of money? Quite the opposite! You're in *every* profession, including law, teaching, medicine, blue-collar or middle-management jobs, or the arts. Whoever you are, I'm always struck by your fortitude and contradictions. You believe you'll always survive—even though it's hard for you to deal with money on a day-to-day basis. Some Ostriches are proud of their indifference to money while others ignore it until there's a crisis. Most of all, you feel confused or even angry about how you deal with your finances—a state of mind that arises from the misguided belief that you *can't* learn to master money basics. But of course, you can.

Another aspect of the Ostrich is a variation I call the White Knighter. Here, you hope that one event or person—a symbolic white knight—will rescue you from money problems. Winning the lottery or hoping for an unexpected inheritance keeps you dreaming and thereby neglecting your finances.

Money mastery for Ostriches and White Knighters: After understanding what steps you can take to help yourself, you'll never again believe that you're "just not a money person." You'll finally be inspired to snap out of inertia mode and take charge of your finances.

The Debt Desperadoes

Whether in debt because of overspending or being underfinanced, Debt Desperadoes are always coming up short. The spending addicts (or shopaholics) among you prefer the thrill of buying to the security of *having*. Then again, some of you are underfinanced because of having lost your jobs. Or you're left with no assets after some personal catastrophe, and you max out your credit cards and borrow to pay for staples.

Many Debt Desperadoes hit a wall, and the out-of-control spenders finally go cold turkey to stop the spendaholism. It's not uncommon for your type to bury yourselves deeper. You create more debt by borrowing to pay other outstanding debts and use still active credit cards to charge more stuff.

Money mastery for Debt Desperadoes: Can you finally work your way out of debt and prove to yourself that you can manage money? Yes! I'll show you how with a financial plan that's easy to follow. Remember: It's your money, and you deserve to have it work for you, not against you!

The Coasters

This Money Type is the most financially stable—you're someone who's coping and thriving. Coasters are, in general, probably doing better than most Money Types and may not be aware of it. Although there's no money crisis, you don't have a huge distance to go financially, but a few changes can make a huge difference.

At their best, Coasters are organized, responsible, and focused on stability. You are more likely than most types to have decent insurance coverage and have done some retirement planning. Your weakness shows up when, because you're not facing any big financial problems, you're too complacent about money. You stop at the status quo, freeze in time, and coast along with the same investments and savings. You may even pass by opportunities for the future. So, while you're financially healthy and happy, you could be a lot more prosperous.

Another aspect of the Coaster is a variation I call the Optimist. A little spoiled by having been brought up without many financial woes, Optimists are most known for leaving jobs to work at, for example, companies your generation virtually invented: the dot-coms and Internet businesses. If you're an Optimist, you can get into trouble by believing you'll always be bailed out and *always* get what is rightfully yours—and that it's what you deserve.

Money mastery for Coasters and Optimists: If you are more of a Coaster than an Optimist, I'll show you how to meet the challenge of taking a few small steps away from the status quo and shaking things up for yourself, a little at a time. You'll be inspired to set new financial goals with money that can ultimately pay off. If you're an Optimist, you're a bit more confident about the here and now, so your challenge is to plan more smartly for the future. You're hard workers, so I'll motivate you to make some important changes to make your money work better for you.

The High Rollers

For you, money is about the grand gesture infused with bravado and a belief in the long shot. You're the High Roller, who is likely to be found gambling around a table, gambling on a dream to build a business, or playing the stock market on margin. Your type tends to think you're smarter, faster, and shrewder—and invincible. And when entering a high-risk deal or tossing the dice at a casino, you think, either, "Out of my way, I'm coming through," or, "This is my lucky night."

At their best, High Rollers do everything right and risk taking pays off grandly. The truth is, in the world of money, you have to take some calculated risks to attain your goals. But weaknesses? High Rollers get into trouble when they habitually take risks without a safety net. You seek the rush of daring the universe to take you down. Often, with the throw of the dice, unlucky nights are more frequent.

Money mastery for High Rollers: Your surest bet is in learning how to manage your money without completely squelching your risk-taking impulses. You can do it. I'll show you how to make peace with limiting big risks and find peace in what you do earn.

The Squirrels

Motivated by a fear of loss, Squirrels are, sadly, cheating themselves. You have a secret fear of losing everything and believe that the resources you have are never enough. This fear, when it takes hold, can turn those of you who are comfortable into hoarders who live way beneath your means.

At your best, your Money Type lives with your assets in a fairly safe, if financially insular world. At your worst, Squirrels cannot enjoy what they have or give to others with any sense of generosity. You tend not to see a balanced picture of money opportunities, nor are you willing to understand how you can actually be *losing* money by not making an attempt to improve your financial situation.

A close cousin of the squirrel is the Bag Lady, a personality who's more anxious about accumulating assets than any other Money Type. Bag Ladies fear imminent destitution and loss of control over their lives, worrying that they'll never have enough money—no matter how much they may actually have socked away.

Money mastery for Squirrels and Bag Ladies: Since your types are so good at saving money, I hope to inspire you to *manage* it more wisely. I show you how you can make a difference in what you have by learning to invest safely and smartly.

Okay, now that you have an idea of what your type may be, here's how knowing your Money Type can make the difference for you:

HOW BEST TO USE THIS BOOK

The book is set up so that you can systematically understand your dominant Money Type and find other traits that are part of other, less influential types for you. For instance, you may be an Ostrich/White Knighter by inclination, and you would say this is your dominant type. But you may have shades of being a Squirrel or a Coaster/Optimist, too. Take in all the information!

Every chapter opens with a profile of a different Money Type and its concomitantly distinct strengths and weaknesses. I follow with true-life cases of that type, which will clarify your type's issues for you in ways with which you can identify. You'll read about the money problems these people are grappling with *because* they are Ostriches or Strivers or High Rollers or whatever the type. That is, they are stuck repeating negative behavior typical of their type. I analyze what they're doing and point out how the behavior might have become second-nature. Next, I provide suggestions for lessening the effect of negative behavior patterns in the Emotional Path section. Finally, in the Financial Path for your type, you see how your Money Type can make significant changes that build, rather than destroy, your financial future.

The payback in mastering the Money Type process is that *you do not need to change your core money personality.* What's important is that you examine your money behavior honestly by reading the suggestions I make for you in the Emotional Path. Then, make enough effort to unblock progress and take action to change what's holding you back, as found in the Financial Path.

Too many of you are stuck or feel limited because of how you're living. I hear from you thousands of times a month, and I understand that you want change for the better. I'm unable to bestow change upon you, but I can give you something even better: effective guidance you take for yourself that touches you both emotionally and financially and makes a real difference.

Before we move on to the next chapter—which is a series of quizzes that will help reveal your belief systems and intimate feelings about money—let me assure you of one important point:

I don't expect you to disavow or deny your Money Type, and I hope you don't feel insecure about what your type turns out to be. Nothing is as critical to your financial and emotional well-being as working within your type to become more financially secure. For example, if you're a Squirrel and you have all your money tied up in low-interest CDs (certificates of deposit), I wouldn't suggest you sell them and go completely into high-risk futures. What's best for you is to loosen up a little so you can help your money really grow and learn to enjoy it more.

The power behind the advice in this book is that:

- You can work on the margins of your type to make better decisions with your money.
- You can learn how to operate from your strengths so you do not continue to limit your options.
- You can finally increase your level of comfort with money, and you can learn to make decisions that normally may be unusual for you.

Your new journey to financial mastery begins now!

CHAPTER 2

You and Your Money: An Emotional Partnership

Money is clearly quantifiable. It's something we can negotiate to the penny. It can be lost or won, and at the end of the day we have a number. What could be more black-and-white, more rational? But the problem is *we* are not always rational, and no matter how we try, this fact immediately alters the world of our personal finances.

In other words, when it comes to money, two plus two might equal four, but when we add in our emotions, this equation may not hold. To see what this equation may mean to you, for example, complete this sentence: "If I had a lot more money, I would . . ."

How did you respond? There are so many possibilities:

"I'd never walk into an office again, or take any job."

"I'd give some of it to medical research, do an extreme make-over on myself, and start a business."

"I'd leave my spouse and start fresh somewhere else."

"I'd get Martin Scorsese's phone number and invest some of the money in his next movie."

"I'd move to Vegas and play the tables every night."

"I'd buy a house for my parents and a new house nearby for myself."

"I'd sock away 90 percent of it and give my kids some money to play with."

I have asked this question so many times of my clients, and it never ceases to amaze me how idiosyncratic the answers can be. Some reflect a desire to change lifestyles or even partners. A few responses reveal generosity and philanthropy. Other answers mirror a deep desire to realize a dream or simply take care of loved ones. And then, of course, I often hear about the need to feel safe and secure. On the surface, these replies can seem so different. But they do share one quality: deep feelings.

Money, quite simply, is an emotionally charged topic.

When people think about having a lot of money, they think about how it can bring them happiness and fulfillment—and an exciting new definition both to their lives and their very sense of self. It's not the actual numbers that make the difference. You will note that my hypothetical question doesn't include a specific amount of money. Few people ever even ask if I have a number in mind. The definition of "a lot more money" is different for everyone and is reflected in what people want to do with it.

What counts is the fears, dreams, and needs stirred by the prospect of having—or not having—money.

You may believe that how people manage money is based on a combination of experience, reason, background, and social trends. And you'd be right—but only partially so. The simple fact is that before a conscious decision based on a real understanding of finances is made, another influence is actively exerting a significant force on our rational thinking. It is *our feelings about money.*

WHY MONEY IS ALSO ABOUT FEELINGS

Whenever I talk about the emotional component of getting a financial life in order, I learn that most of us are ready to acknowledge that people can feel anger at loss, pride at gain, fear or defensiveness under a threat, and exhilaration at having made it. I can't say I disagree with that. But to stop there misses the most important point about money and feelings: *How you feel about money affects how you make financial decisions*—no matter how big or small, whether for today or tomorrow, or for yourself or your loved ones.

You can have everything you need to succeed—expertise, luck, and the right connections—but still unwittingly make a decision that destroys a business deal that could have been profitable for you. Why? Perhaps you're stuck believing that you don't deserve success, or that you haven't worked hard enough for your good fortune, while others you love are still struggling mightily. Maybe your parents fought for every dime as you were growing up and you don't want to outshine them. Guilt could easily squelch your grabbing an opportunity and passing up a good deal so that you are not "better than . . ."

Or consider this. Perhaps you grew up in a home in which the experience of a financial trauma changed life as you knew it. You were a have, and then a have-not, almost in the blink of an eye. Today, money is a profound symbol of what you think you can gain or lose: status in the eyes of others. You're determined never again to be a have-not. While you fear losing it all, paradoxically, you may be spending most of your income on maintaining an upscale lifestyle. Recently, your upkeep is beginning to cost you too much, financially *and* emotionally.

In both of these cases, emotions are ruling your behavior, not rational thinking.

Which leads me back to my opening question: "If I had a lot more money, I would . . ." What does the money really mean to you? Is it power or security that you're after? Is it your idea of freedom? Is it the stuff you think you have to own to impress others? People behave emotionally and sometimes to the extreme about money. If hoarding money is at one end of the spectrum, then holding up banks, killing for money, or jumping out a window because you've lost it all is at the other end.

When you think about money, do you feel deserving, confused, stable, unstable, excited, entitled, guilty, optimistic, fearful, powerful, relieved, philanthropic, greedy, or corrupt? This is one of the key questions you need to answer. The more you know about yourself, the more your financial decisions will be ruled by your rational self and not by any emotional burdens that could cloud your thinking.

Don't worry about how much money you do or do not have right now. Don't worry about what Money Type you are or what you're going to do about your situation. Right now the task at hand is to explore your money behavior from an emotional and personal historical perspective. What beliefs and feelings are you bringing to the party, when did they first occur, and how are you playing them out in your current life?

This chapter is designed to be a kind of launching pad from which you can begin to discover your very personal (and emotional!) financial style. This is your opportunity to examine your past and present experiences, feelings, disappointments, dreams, and even misconceptions about money. It's a chance to glimpse what might unconsciously be behind many of the financial decisions you make, both positive and negative. As you go through this chapter, answer the questions as honestly as you can and they will add enormously to your self-knowledge. Always keep in mind how your feelings relate to your possible financial type. Of course, you may have a number of characteristics from a few Money Types, but there will be clues in your answers as to your most dominant style.

EMOTIONAL BASICS: WHAT MONEY MEANS TO YOU

Understanding the emotions and beliefs behind your money behavior involves self-awareness. It means facing the most basic beliefs that rule your present money decisions, understanding how these beliefs evolved, what the emotions are that fuel these beliefs—and making peace with the past, where a good many of your feelings about money inevitably began to take shape. Uncovering your emotional relationship with money is the best way to formulate a new plan that defuses your weaknesses, embraces your strengths, and in doing so, frees you to make new plans and decisions that result in your prosperity.

It begins by looking at what you think money represents. These are classic beliefs that could easily keep you stuck with the same money problems, again and again.

Money Equals Self-Worth

You believe that money is a measure of your worth as a person. The source of the money is irrelevant: You can earn it, marry it, inherit it, or win it. What matters is that you have your version of "enough." You feel, "Unless I bring in x amount of money and have another x amount in savings and investments, I'm no one." It is likely that you have forgotten that money can be lost by forces way beyond your control. Are you honestly willing to bank your self-worth on an unpredictable world?

Money Equals Security

You tend to plan like this: "We can't afford a vacation now, but if we save, we can take three weeks off in five years," or, "If I don't worry about money, no one else will—and then where will we be!" If your feelings about money focus on saving rather than investing or spending, and on long-term goals and on long hours at work—nearly to the exclusion of a fulfilling family life or social life—your inner peace is strongly dependent on financial security. You might not realize that sometimes the security you think you need has become so distorted that the pursuit of it places everything you really need in life at risk.

Money Equals Love

You tend to feel, "Gifts from my spouse/partner/children/
parents/friends are proof they care about me." Or, "I can never
spend money on myself until everyone else is taken care of."
Few connections in life are as emotionally loaded as the money-
equals-love belief. Real nurturing—affection, attention, support, and protectiveness—require less material evidence and far
more expressions of profound feelings. It may be that you are
more comfortable extending money than time and attention
to those you love, and thus may be missing out on more than
could ever be quantified.

Money Equals an Opiate

If you feel sad, lonely, angry, abandoned, or temporarily spiri-
tually empty, and spending money provides temporary relief,
you likely use money as a kind of medication. You believe that
money can ease emotional pain, smooth the difficult moments
in life, and most significantly, buy pleasure. Buying an expensive car to soothe an injured ego or depression, for example, is
a temporary fix. Sometimes, days after purchasing the car and
feeling on a high, that person's mood has crashed, and he or she
is driving tearfully around town.

Money Equals Prestige

You believe a show of what money can buy brings you the
respect and the admiration of others. You tend to feel, "If I
look rich, people will give me respect." Or, "I deserve a certain
lifestyle, and I'll do what's necessary to achieve and maintain
it." Because you are affected by what others think, you don't
want them to believe you are only getting by financially. You

tend to appraise what you own as if from an outsider's perspective, wondering, for example, "What will the neighbors think if I drive around in a four-year-old car?" But that can become an exhausting pursuit. It may be hard for you to remember that the only way off the pedestal you want to live on is down. And that there is always someone coming up the pike with a bigger car . . .

Money Equals Power

You think, "Money rules. The richer I am, the more I can call the shots," or conversely, "Money rules. If I had a lot of money, I'd be free, and then I could use money to sponsor a meaningful cause." In some ways these notions are true. Some people with money, especially those you work for, do rule the roost. It can be a wonderful feeling to realize you are no longer dependent on others to enjoy a good quality of life. Then, too, power is intoxicating—both striving for it and having it. The yearning for financial power can become your new master, although, ironically, your first impulse is to think, "At last, I have no master." But chances are you're wrong, and you're answering to a force called "money is everything."

Money Equals Happiness

You feel, "If I just had enough money for the things I want, I'd finally be happy," or, "If I had the money, I could have gone to Paris or film school (fill in your sincerest desires) and made my dreams come true." Being in desperate financial straits is bound to make you feel distressed or depressed. But its opposite—having enough money—will not necessarily guarantee happiness. If you envy others because they have more money or believe that you can enjoy life only by using or having money, you are sadly mistaken. Happiness comes from inside. Money can be used to provide pleasure. Happiness and pleasure are two different concepts. Happiness is a state of mind. The other is an experience. And sometimes, just a short-lived one.

A CLOSER LOOK AT YOUR FEELINGS ABOUT MONEY

Understanding the emotions behind your money behavior can be a surprising journey. Most of us don't stop to think about why we like to hoard, take risks, spend, or even ignore our money. Often, we don't wonder why we suddenly panic or are fearful that we're about to lose it all (sometimes, for no reason!). But it's time to heighten your self-awareness and start tracing back why you feel and think as you do about money. Doing so will let you understand your past, place it in a new perspective, free yourself from some of its most toxic messages, and move on. When you're finally aware of why you're having the same money problems, you can make astonishing changes. There's a whole new world out there filled with money management options that will help you achieve the prosperity you crave.

Looking Back: Finding Clues to Your Feelings About Money in the Past

The topic of money behavior is wide-ranging, so I've done a lot of reading on the subject and talked to a number of psychologists on what you might ask yourself. I've narrowed the areas down for you, and provided a number of questions that I urge you to answer. If the questions make you uncomfortable, press on. You've probably hit a sore spot about money that needs to be healed and resolved.

I always find important clues to money issues by exploring messages that travel across generations. I'm convinced that a lot of financial decisions are made based on ingrained, automatic responses to how parents, and even grandparents, dealt with money.

Your answers to the following questions will help you begin to understand how your family history contributed to your values about money today. There are, of course, endless questions you might ask yourself related to the role money played in your family. The questions here are meant to serve as a kind of warm-up. Perhaps some don't quite apply but will inspire you to ask yourself the questions that do. For instance, your parents may indeed have been generous with money. But taking it a step further, you might want to ask yourself, "Were there strings attached?" Allow these questions to get you thinking, to dig deeper, to really figure out the genesis of who you are today when it comes to money. Let's begin here:

Your Grandparents and Their Money

Your parents' attitudes about money were shaped by *their* parents' attitudes. You may or may not have known your grandparents, but their influence regarding money lived on in some measure in your parents. So, your answer to one of these multi-generational probes may be, "My mother told me that my grandfather was stingy and impossible to live with. Strangely enough, she wound up being very much like her own father—tight with a dime. She could never quite shake it, though I'm not sure how hard she tried." So think back to what your parents used to say about your grandparents, and consider these general questions:

- Did they worry about making ends meet, or was there enough for necessities?
- Did your parents often feel as children that they did without?
- Did your grandparents feel like haves or have-nots?

- Did your grandparents speak angrily or resentfully about money?
- Did they sacrifice a lot to make sure your parents had everything?
- Did they enjoy prosperity with an air of entitlement?
- What were the messages in their home about money in general? Was money good or the source of evil? Could it be spoken about openly or was it a secret? Was it something to be enjoyed or accumulated?

Your Parents and Their Money

A friend of mine confided that her mother told her, "The way you spend money, you'll be broke by the age of twenty-one." She was thirteen years old at the time and had bought herself a pair of shoes with her baby-sitting money. She said the remark shocked her, as did the judgment. It haunts her to this day. "I'm fifty-one now, and I'm still afraid of going broke." Other messages from parents can sound like these: "There are no free rides. If you want something, you have to earn it." Or, "You can have anything you want." What were *your* parents' messages?

- Were they proud of the money they made?
- Did your parents talk enviously about others?
- How did your parents describe themselves when you asked the question, as most children have at some point or another, "Are we rich?" Or, "Are we poor?"
- Did your parents seem content with the life they created?
- Did your parents ever predict how much money you would or would not have with comments like, "You'll never amount to anything"?
- Looking back, would you say your parents emphasized achievement of goals and commitment to family over ambition, competition, and acquisition of material goods?

- Did a relative ever go to an extreme because of wanting, losing, or keeping money—one that had a lifelong effect on you? For example, did a relative commit suicide over money; cheat another relative or associate out of money and say, "It's only business"; commit a crime for money; or gamble compulsively, wreaking havoc in the family?
- Do you think you're like your parents in their attitudes about money, or did you rebel and become their opposite?
- Did either or both parents use money as a reward or a weapon? Was there a promise of money or what it could buy if you were "good," or a threat to remove or not provide what you wanted or needed if you weren't? If you complied, excited about getting "the reward," did they make good on their promise or renege on it?
- Did a parent ever threaten to leave you with no money?
- Did your parents tell you that money was a corrupting force and make you feel guilty or ashamed about wanting it?
- Did they tell you that money was the great equalizer and that you should get as much as you can?
- Did they tell you that the value of money is less important than how you value yourself?
- Did they stress the influence of money and say, "Marry money"?

How Did You Feel About Money During Your Childhood?

A colleague recently told me about her mother, a woman who had apparently gone through hard times during the Depression of the 1930s. She said, "My mother did something interesting which she thought would make me love her more, but wound up making me angry with her. She used to wait until I was alone in the room I shared with my sisters, and say, 'Here's $10—don't tell your father.' I grew up thinking my father didn't want me to have anything beyond the barest survival." Another woman, whose story you will read about in detail in the Squirrels chapter, reported that her father used money as a way to control the family. "He was always threatening to leave us, and then give all his money to an animal shelter. I grew up fearing that I'd wind up on the street." So, now think back:

- Did you feel you had enough of what you wanted—clothes, toys, trips, what you needed for school, and so forth?
- When you were growing up, did anything happen with money in your home that you swore you would never do or have happen to you? What did it say to you about the power or effect of money on people?
- If you answered yes to the previous question: Has the effect of this incident crept its way into how you feel about or manage your own money today? Has it come back to bite you?
- Did you feel loved when your parents gave you money?
- Did your parents use money as a way to control you? Did they make promises to buy you something or take you somewhere, if you did as they asked?
- As a child, did you think your parents were poor, rich, or middle-of-the-road?
- Were you jealous of any friends or other children about your age because they had more or better things than you?
- Did you save money as a child and enjoy counting it from time to time?
- Did you ever fear your family could be poor and out on the street?
- If you needed something reasonable, was it bought for you without debate or was it handled as if you had requested the Hope Diamond? Or somewhere in between?

What You Learned About Money in Your Early Adolescence and Early Adulthood

When you start earning your own money, usually about the age of twelve or so, you start making financial decisions—small as they are—for yourself. At this point, you start learning about getting paid for work done, see a little about how business operates—and you meet other people with other ideas about money. A colleague told me, "I started working at the age of fifteen, lying and saying I was eighteen. I worked all year, part-time at a department store as a salesgirl to save for college. I never thought beyond that goal. Another salesgirl and I were talking while doing inventory, and she asked me if I would marry for love. I told her yes. She said, 'You're a fool. The only thing that matters is money.' I expected to hear a comment like that from my mother but not from an eighteen-year-old girl. I still wonder where she is and if she got her wish. I didn't!"

- What were your feelings about earning your own money?
- As soon as you started making money, were you a spender?
- Were you allowed to enjoy the money you earned as a teenager?
- Was there a turning point when you understood you had to learn how to manage money?
- Did you enter the workforce with a strong successful role model in your life, or was your role model someone you feared being like?
- Were you proud when you got your first job? Were your parents proud?
- As you gained experience in the world, did the beliefs about money you were raised with start to come true?
- Were your beliefs in any way proved untrue? For example, did you decide that work, marriage, an inheritance, luck, or some other factor would most shape your financial future? Or a combination of these possibilities?

How You Live Out Your Feelings About Money

I was speaking to Jonathan Rich, Ph.D., a psychologist and the author of *The Couple's Guide to Love and Money*, about the complex emotional components of money. I was interested in how people take on their feelings about money and how we can change the ones that are causing us problems now. "All your experiences have been incorporated into your life's script," Dr. Rich said. "If your beliefs about money bring you personal and financial gain, there's no real reason to change how you think— your beliefs work for you. If there's a loss in both areas, then the decision to change is clear enough—your beliefs are working for you. We have problems because an assumption about money that worked for us in the past no longer applies to our current situation."

My primary goal in this book is to show you how to maximize your assets and grow your money. But if you are stuck in any way—that is, your beliefs don't work for you anymore— you won't be able to fully take advantage of money opportunities. Damaging beliefs are in the way and they need to be disabled and out of the emotional picture. To do that, you'll need to make what I call a shift in thinking.

CHANGING YOUR MONEY BELIEFS FOR THE BETTER: A BLUEPRINT FOR A SHIFT IN THINKING

No matter what your dominant Money Type turns out to be, your emotional sore points will hold you back unless you make a cognitive switch, or a shift in thinking. The results of making a shift can be life-changing for you! Here's what I mean. Every Money Type has a number of specific examples of emotional traps common to it. You'll read about them in the section "The Emotional Path," which I present in every chapter. I analyze the internal mechanisms that keep activating the sore points or traps. Then, I show how *a shift in thinking can change the emotions* that previously undermined your ongoing prosperity. This is the key to change: Relinquish damaging financial beliefs about yourself that serve no purpose. Next, turn those beliefs around by substituting helpful, positive beliefs, to feel more confident about financial gain.

What follows is a detailed exercise that shows you how an emotional sore point affects your money picture and how a shift in thinking sets you on the road to change. You'll help yourself even more if you refer back to this blueprint for change when you read the shift-in-thinking sections in the Emotional Path.

To start out, I've borrowed Jonathan Rich's suggestion. This involves a simple written exercise where you take an old belief about money that is holding you back, then associate it with where you first learned it and made it a part of your thinking. Next, ask yourself if you want to change the thought. Then— and here's the breakthrough—write down a positive substitute thought. My suggestion is to add two more key questions to Dr. Rich's exercise, for a fifth and sixth dimension. My questions are: How does the old belief make you feel? Is there a benefit to holding on to the outmoded belief that keeps getting you into trouble?

To show you how this exercise breaks down, I'm using Patti's case as an example. Try the exercise on one of your own self-sabotaging money beliefs!

Money Is an Emotional Fix

After a lot of "agony and patience," as Patti described it, this thirty-seven-year-old department store buyer finally dug herself out of $35,000 in unsecured debt, a lot of it from credit cards and student loans. She just wrote to me, saying that she's determined to be debt-free. Patti has become more careful about money, pays bills on time, and knows what she owes at any given moment. However, she added, "I still to some degree like 'buying stuff'—shopping is my fix. I don't go completely nuts with money or credit the way I used to, but there are times when I binge and buy things I don't need. Part of me believes that being in debt is how people get by. I don't want to live this way again, and it scares me!"

Finding a Solution to an Emotional Fix

My sense is that this generally reformed spender (someone who likely fits pretty well into our Debt Desperado type) *can* achieve her goal of living more securely and eventually prosper. She's taken the first step, and it's an important one. Patti has identified one of the beliefs that fuel her emotionally driven shopping binges: *Being in debt is okay. This is how millions of people get by*. She needs help, and she knows it—and faces it. Now she can work with the belief this way.

All the answers are Patti's, as she would answer them.

Outmoded belief: Money troubles, like just scraping by or being in debt, are normal. I may as well spend the money and get some fun out of life. I can always figure out how to pay the money back later.

Where did the belief originate? My parents always complained about money. When I was a kid and asked for anything, whether I needed it or not, my father said, "No. Money doesn't grow on trees." Then my mother usually added some version of why they didn't have the money for it, such as, "Your father doesn't make a good living."

I swore that when I grew up, I'd give myself whatever I wanted and never have to ask anyone for anything.

How does the belief make you feel? The belief makes me feel frightened. I know that I'm kind of out of control. But I have to buy stuff. The thing I just bought gives me pleasure for an hour, maybe a day, and then I feel sick that I bought it. I felt guilty about wanting anything when I was young, even if it was a pair of galoshes in the winter. Whenever anything to do with money came up, I waited for my parents to refuse me. My stomach was in knots. I was never sure they loved me.

Do you want to change the belief? Yes.

What are your new beliefs? I'm my own boss. I won't deprive myself of something I need or go through somersaults to get them. I don't have to be in knots about reasonable purchases anymore.

I will feel better by not bingeing on stuff to make myself "feel better." Overspending is a short-term fix that doesn't really work, and I know it.

I feel deserving and I can buy what I want for myself—but only if it is within my budget. My ability to pay back that $35,000 proves to me that I can control my money and keep my future secure. I can feel greater satisfaction by investing the money, or at least banking it instead. I can do it.

My self-worth is not dependent on how my parents did or didn't spend money on me in the past. My parents demonstrated their love for me in the only way they knew how. I accept that and freely move on! I can begin to stop reliving the past.

Patti's is not an atypical story. Spending binges, also called "money drunks," are a kind of heady emotional connection to money that are destined to create financial disaster. Many people who don't come from money or don't have experience managing a lot of money keep spending until going broke or bankruptcy stops them. The truth is that your emotional connection to money will always be the first reason you do or do not spend. The best thing you can do for yourself is to know how you feel and why you feel it—and then change your thinking.

But can Patti change her feelings? Could you? Will you? Change is never simple or easy, but when it is change for the better, it's worth the effort—and the aches. Giving up a bad money habit can never hurt as much as the pain it continues to cause you.

This is why you may need to make changes slowly and in small steps. For instance, Patti may not be able to totally stop the fear and yearning she feels when she sees something she wants. Perhaps she'll set herself a goal. She will allow herself to give into an impulsive purchase once a month and it can't exceed a certain dollar amount. In this way, Patti will begin to learn that saying no to herself doesn't have to send her back to the unhappy past—a time when she felt so profoundly that her needs were being disregarded.

Here's another test you can give yourself about whether to shift your thinking to a more positive belief system. First, identify the circumstances under which you commit certain self-sabotaging behavior around money. If you're still unsure about whether you should change, ask yourself this question:

Is there a benefit to holding on to the outmoded belief that keeps getting me into trouble?

What is the cost of holding on to negative and, ultimately, financially undermining beliefs? Is the cost tolerable or intolerable? Take Patti again. Being in debt and/or spending excessively as an emotional fix puts her back in the past, in that room with her parents denying her what she wanted. There, she was a dependent child with no earning power and under the control of parents who had a hard time parting with a dime. Then again, her old habits are a way of staying close to home. Many of us would rather repeat the mistakes that were visited upon us as children than face the hurt head-on and say, "I was made to feel terrible. My parents hurt me tremendously." We may often try to fix the mistakes by righting them as if we were children. This is Patti, buying indiscriminately. The familiar somehow feels safer—even when the result couldn't be further from the safety she's seeking. It's easier to act than to feel. It's easier for Patti to impulsively buy than it is for her to deal with her feelings of disappointment and hurt.

Patti has to decide whether the fear of "leaving home" and creating her own way in the world is greater than going back into debt and potentially being completely broke.

Patti's self-esteem was tied up with feeling that she wasn't worthy of having much and that she was unloved by begrudging parents. So if the beliefs "money is an emotional fix" and "getting into debt to have my fix" provide personal and financial gain, there's no reason to change. But when there's real loss in one or both areas, then a shift in thinking makes sense: The beliefs aren't working for you anymore. Are you paying too high a cost to feel good on a short-term basis or paying too high a cost to stay stuck grappling with money troubles?

Facing the issues that cause you money troubles moves you closer to emotional *and* financial well-being. Some people say they have an epiphany about why they feel and act as they do, and can never go back to destructive money habits. I wish the same for all of you!

Let's begin now.

CHAPTER 3

The Strivers

Do you believe that if you look successful, you will be successful?

Do you believe that people only respect someone whose image says, "status"?

Do you take the same pride in your possessions as you do in your achievements?

"Everybody wants money. That's why they call it money," actor Danny DeVito explains to a friend in the movie *Heist*. Of course he's right at the simplest level—having money is better than not having it. We can also hear in his joking remark the implication of something deeper, a belief shared by millions of people: Everybody wants money for its ability to buy power, the finest material goods, and, of course, one's idea of rank. That is, he's saying that everyone wants to live rich—and is a Striver.

After all, living in luxury feels good—owning the newest status symbols can elevate you in your social circle, while money in the bank and smart investments can provide security. So yes, the Striver's lifestyle in its ideal state with all its trappings of success can be emotionally and financially gratifying. But as I've seen again and again, it's gratifying only when you know you can truly afford it. Too often Striver Money Types fall in love with status possessions and sacrifice long-range savings and investment opportunities to spend for today. Not an ideal state at all.

Did you answer yes to any of the questions at the start of the chapter? If so, you may have a need to be a Striver. But if you're tired of juggling funds and not having security for the future, I'm here to show you how you can put your hard-earned money to work to maximize its returns and still have some left over for living rich but within your means.

My purpose is not to completely change your Striver tendencies. Rather, I'll offer real solutions by guiding you through simple exercises to help you know your Money Type intimately. This knowledge will enable you to set realistic money goals and put them into action. The benefits? You get your finances under control, build capital for the future, master your emotional hot spots related to money, and ultimately feel a real sense of peace. And you become the kind of achiever you want to be, not just look like one.

First you must understand your Striver personality with its strengths and weaknesses and the kinds of problems you face. Then you'll discover how to work with your Money Type to get the best from yourself.

THE STRIVER REVEALED

If you are a Striver, money is a powerful symbol that transforms you by what it can buy. For you, the thrill is about status and living as if you earn more than you do. You get into trouble when you can't afford what tantalizes you. Your need to spend has a deeper meaning—the money you pay out allows you to keep score and compare yourself to others: "I have the big house" or "the wardrobe" or "the boat." Thus you can feel, "I'm as worthy as anyone else." As food can provide psychological comfort to an overeater, so buying upscale goods and associating with moneyed people stoke the internal dynamics of your type.

Would you believe me if I told you that I've met people who live in $1 million homes who've put all their money into maintaining the property so it looks great from the curb? Walk inside and you'll find, literally, nothing but a bed, a dresser, a TV, and a few chairs in the otherwise empty rooms. The owners say that's acceptable because a great house gives them hope and the motivation to earn more. Yet they're worried about money, if not in a bit of a panic and fearful about losing it all! They may own a lavish wardrobe but have no emergency fund, no health insurance, and haven't even begun to think about retirement. They say they're okay with the situation, but is it any wonder that they don't sleep at night?

In real life, truly "living rich" is something only about 4 percent of Americans get to enjoy. I find that fact astonishing! Of the other 96 percent, about half are doing okay, while about 45 percent of Americans are struggling to make it through the month. In my many years of being a financial advisor, one chief element of being a Striver hasn't changed: Not having the means doesn't stop many of us from continuing to *over*estimate our earnings and *under*estimate our spending. If you are a Striver, you are likely to be out of touch with why you're spending so much money, rather than investing it or putting it away for retirement. The good news is that because your type is smart and ambitious, you *can* mend your ways to make your money work for you.

So, how do all these qualities add up in real life for you and for other Strivers?

The Striver: Your Strengths

Most, though not all, of you who prefer the Striver style have energy and drive to make things happen. You're imaginative, original thinkers who work best when you've got the upper hand or work for yourself. You like being in control and can be ace entrepreneurs. When you spot a good investment, you find a way to buy in. If you have any outstanding qualities in common with other Striver types, it's being good at sales and marketing and selling yourself. You can talk your way into a deal or direct your energy into selling others a product, a philosophy, or a way of life. It's probably how you make your money.

I sometimes marvel at how your type is able to draw others into helping you fulfill your dreams. Since you're passionate about what moves you, you can convince others to follow your lead. Your Money Type usually doesn't wait for someone to hand you what you want—you're willing to put in the work, feel great pride in your accomplishments, and take the lumps with dignity if you lose. However, among the several Money Types, you have the biggest stake in appearances. You need to look as though you've arrived and look good for others' approval. Above all, you want to appear as if you've attained social success. When you thrive in a living-rich lifestyle, you know how to get your talents, strengths, and expertise into alignment. This also implies that you've learned how to deal effectively with your weaknesses. Shortcomings are the part of the equation that can put prosperity in jeopardy. Identifying your weaknesses and taking action to manage them will make the difference.

The Striver: Your Weaknesses

Most of your money problems are not hard to explain: They result from your tendency to *over*estimate your earnings and *under*estimate your spending. Perhaps you see something you want to buy. Instead of checking to see if you can afford it now, you decide that when you get your Christmas bonus or pay raise or realize a projected windfall, you'll easily pay the bill. So you go ahead and buy it. However, you usually come up short.

There's only just so much money coming in, and too many things have been bought and not paid for. This is tied to your second problem as a Striver: *a willingness to put yourself in financial jeopardy so you can have upscale possessions when you want them.* When such buying is out of control, especially for costly items, it can signal your financial downfall.

On occasion, you turn into a financial warrior and come out fighting for what you want to own. This would be admirable if your efforts were for a profit-making cause or a smart investment. Instead, when you don't have the money you need for a status item, such as a custom-tailored suit or a jewel-encrusted wristwatch or a sleekly remodeled kitchen, it's painful for you to accept the truth: You can't afford it. Not having the item makes you feel anxious. Your disappointment then escalates, and anxiety fuels your fighting spirit. You're determined to have what you want, and these are not your finest moments. You're not above deceiving others, finagling people, or riding roughshod over anyone to own what you want. The symbols of living rich are that important to you.

While being financially resourceful is normally a strength— that is, finding someone to fully or partially bankroll a project—here, it's to your detriment. In this case, you're driven by a sense of desperation to own something you cannot afford, and you're willing to be a little less than completely honest. Clients have confessed to making up stories that strain credibility to get a loan from a friend or relative. At the same time, they're calculating how to delay paying the money back before their benefactor sees where the money went: an upscale item. In times like these, I know that this side of being a Striver cannot feel good for you at all.

Any sort of unwise borrowing and spending leads you to live way beyond your means, thereby setting you up to fail. Strivers can leave a lot of wreckage—emotional and financial. By not staying conscious of your shortcomings, you can let lapses in good judgment based on hair-trigger responses and weaknesses get in the way of financial stability and professional success.

Ultimately, the little pieces of your Money Type puzzle can come together. This happens when you focus on the nature of the intimate relationship you have with money and figure out why, for you, spending money on appearances is more important than being financially stable.

Let's meet some Strivers. Even though the details of their experiences may be different from yours, it's likely that their financial and emotional predicaments will seem all too familiar.

You're Nobody Unless You're a Somebody

I received an e-mail from a Cleveland man (I'll call him Tim) who laid out the details of his finances, asking my advice on how he could find the money to keep his daughters in private school. The cost: $20,000 a year for each child. "They cannot go to public school," he wrote, and I could feel the emotion in his plea. "My daughters have to be somewhere better. They just do."

Tim's search for an extra $40,000 a year to pay for private school begins a Striver story full of emotionally loaded financial issues that have done him a lot of damage. You may understand his dilemma. After a number of conversations with him, I learned what went wrong. Tim dreams big, and he wants to feel important. That means having an important job title, clothes that tell others he has rank, a house that says he's "going places," children in private school, and an A-list social circle. As he summed it up, "being somebody." Unfortunately, he was willing to sacrifice too much for status, both emotionally and financially. He is a classic case of someone who *over*estimates his earnings and *under*estimates his spending.

Until two years ago, Tim and his wife, who also works, barely made ends meet to keep up the dream. However, Tim was downsized out of a large advertising agency after eighteen years with the firm and having been promoted to vice president. Tim was, he said, "chewed up and spit out by the company." His salary at the time was $120,000 a year. With a family to support, Tim found himself unemployed, in debt, and walking the streets in his new Ralph Lauren suits.

Even though they were living on his wife's salary as a teacher and had cashed in their stocks, CDs, and an insurance policy, Tim still believed in magic. He was sure that his image flashed "success" to others, and it would get him a big job at another company. Tim had come a long way, but he didn't see that he'd come to believe that he was his possessions—and that losing them would mean losing himself.

Tim's spending caused big fights with his wife. They had some savings but no money put aside for college for their twin daughters. His wife was often panicky about paying the steep private school tuition costs. But Tim could calm her down enough to sell her on his dreams. Eventually, Tim accepted a job at a level lower than the one from which he'd been down-sized. It was about this time that his Striver armor began to crack: "I discovered that appearances didn't really fool any-one." When his wife threatened to leave him unless he got his spending under control and had some therapy, he agreed. It was hard for him, however.

Talented, smart, and burning for success, Tim's problem at age forty-six is that he doesn't really function that well in a high-powered environment. He's great at midlevel jobs, but he can't accept it. He wants top spots and never gets them. He's just not a strong enough competitor. Unfortunately, Tim was buying a status suit he thought he'd pay for by earning a salary at a job he didn't have yet. By spending money in advance of making it, Tim wasn't activating his "somebody" dream. Instead, he was increasingly putting himself and his family in jeopardy. At this point, they're considering filing for bankruptcy.

The Somebody Factor:
Playing the Part to Get the Part

Tim's weakness in doggedly holding on to being a somebody underlines another Striver pitfall: getting into trouble by playing the part before you get it. Tim wore the clothes he thought made him corporate presidential material. But while others saw that his designer suit fit him, they knew the job would not.

Acting the part isn't the problem. Some behaviorists say that by auditioning a situation, you get a sense of how it feels and figure out how to fit into that world. You dress for the role and adopt the attitude you think will get you in. You make notes of how you interact with the group you want to impress. By playing a part, you can make others believe the part *is* you, and convince yourself at the same time. For example, if you park your VW at a lot and rent a Ferrari to look like an equal to the money guys you'll be meeting with, you're playing the part of a success. You present yourself as if you've already made it. Investors rarely, if ever, hand over money to people who say they *need* it and look as if they're struggling. Investors want to feel confident that you can manage their money, and you want to show that you justify that confidence.

This gambit is perfectly okay and is dangerous only when you can't deliver what you've promised. When playacting is really as far as you can go, you're bound to create a financial disaster not unlike Tim's.

However, another element of Tim's buying habits went beyond playing the part. He'd buy an expensive suit as a sort of talisman, as if the suit was endowed with powers that could make his wish come true. This is a belief shared by many people with Striver tendencies. Economist Robert Heilbroner wrote about this belief that "analysis finds that even after the child separates the world outside from the world within, he continues to endow outside things with the magical property of being part of himself. To put it differently, he sees his personality as contagious, shedding something of itself on objects of importance. His possessions are part of his self." For Tim, possessions *were* what made him feel like somebody. They were not inseparable from him. His raison d'être was wanting stuff, and his mantra was "I have this, therefore I am." The truth is that the feeling of success comes from the inside first, not from its outward symbols. Such thinking got Tim into debt, all for the sake of appearances.

Origins of the Somebody Factor

I've spoken to a number of therapists on the subject to ask why some Striver types, like Tim, are willing to hurt themselves and others. In general, the answer is that looking successful and owning status objects are proof that you have worth and importance. In other words, that you're somebody. This attitude boils down to wounded self-esteem, evident in every person who's a Striver and paying too high an emotional and financial cost. (I'll talk more about this later, in the Emotional Path. You'll learn how to start healing old wounds related to money and self-esteem.)

Certainly, some of the reasons for behaving as if life were a dream that is always about to come true can be found in one's history. Whether you grew up rich, middle-class, or working-class, maybe both your parents felt material possessions or money were acceptable substitutes for affection and attention—so you always felt neglected. Maybe your mother bribed you with food, gifts, or cash to win you over, or your father played money-love or money-power games of his own to confuse you.

The simple truth is that not everyone is able to have a brilliant business success, making and spending millions. Some people are go-getters who can go only so far. Tim is such a person, and he had difficulty accepting this about himself. But it didn't prevent him from dressing the part, even at his lowest points, or buying what he dreamed about: the symbols of being a somebody.

Some of the steps and exercises that Tim took to put his life back on track follow shortly.

And then there's Valerie, whose story has as deep an emotional component.

Entitlement: What Happened? I Was Meant to Be Rich!

While Tim dreams of impressing others by looking important, what fuels Valerie's Striver engine has more to do with deep ties to and identification with a mother for whom keeping up appearances is tantamount to lifeblood.

Raised to believe she deserved the finest things, Valerie was determined to marry a man wealthy enough to fulfill her dreams. Ironically, like her mother, she didn't find her millionaire. Instead, Valerie married a professional golfer who never quite made it and was now giving lessons part-time at a country club. Don was twenty years her senior. He thought his earnings and an annuity could support both of them comfortably enough, but Valerie wanted more. She kept her job as an executive of a sportswear company to assure herself extra income. "I didn't want to suffer the way my mother has," Valerie said. "She raised me to believe that whatever I wanted would be mine. I wanted to show her I had what it takes to get it all and that I could have what *she* always wanted—money without worry."

Valerie's parents had been rich as children until Valerie's grandparents on both sides of the family suffered reversals of fortune. The story goes that her father's family lost most of their money in bad investments in the late 1940s, and her mother's family fell on hard times at approximately the same time.

"My mother never quite recovered from watching some guy, sent by the bank, I think, getting into my grandfather's Cadillac and driving it off," Valerie told me. "She was maybe twelve years old at the time, and pampered. Her father was out of town. My grandmother was hysterical, shaken by seeing her car repossessed, and she was terrified that the house would be taken from them next—which it was. My mother was just a kid, but she felt humiliated, and she worried that her friends would know that her father couldn't pay their bills and shun her."

Valerie's mother could never shake her patrician tastes, and growing up, she dreamed of living rich again. She hoped to do so through a man who'd restore to her in marriage what she felt was unfairly taken from her in childhood: luxury. It didn't happen. Instead, she married Valeric's father, a man with a similar past of financial loss who would never earn enough to pay for the comforts she wanted. This didn't stop Valerie's mother from buying the best for Valerie and going into hock.

"I grew up in a house where money was scarce, but my mother never went out unless she was wearing a designer suit," Valerie said. "She'd find ways to wear the skirt or the jacket with some accessory so it would seem like four different outfits. The point was to look like she had something to show off. All we talked about was money. The tension was brutal. We lived in a small apartment, but that didn't matter to my mother. She rarely had people over to visit, preferring to spend the money on stuff for me. And she'd walk down the street in her outfits,

---

VALERIE'S FINANCIAL SNAPSHOT

Valerie doesn't want a life like her parents'. Years into her own marriage, she feels she and her husband are financially stable.

- Their combined income is $90,000.

- They own a few antiques bought at auction, but unlike Valerie's mother, they never went into debt to buy luxuries for which they couldn't manage the payments.

- Valerie and her husband, who's conservative with money, put most of their disposable income into bonds and some blue chip stocks.

- They both have life insurance policies.

- Valerie has a retirement plan at work that deducts $50 a month from her salary.

feeling like a million bucks, and she dressed me to do the same. My father was always depressed about money, so my mother went to work."

As she approached her fortieth birthday, Valerie gave in to her desire for a grand house and convinced her husband to take the leap. She invested most of their life savings in a huge three-bedroom house with a view. "I haven't slept well since we moved in," she told me. "Wasn't I meant to have it easier by now? Part of me is stunned that life didn't work out to my mother's grand design for me. Part of me is practical enough to know that I have to make my own way. I never thought I'd be this confused about getting the house I always felt I deserved." She loves the house, but now she can't figure out what to do next. Let go of the fantasy that she was always meant to live in

EXALTING STATUS: WHY WE DO IT

There are extreme and notorious Striver types for whom having money has become an exercise in arrogance and entitlement, and we hear stories about them every day. The E! Entertainment Television channel even documents how these people spend in such shows as *It's Good to Be . . .* They add up what athletes, recording stars, and celebrities who make astonishing paychecks spend for their entourages, financial management advisors, homes, and excessive lifestyles.

Status may have some magic about it, but sometimes it feels like a curse. Author and sociologist Alain de Botton wrote in his book *Status Anxiety*, "The hunger for status, like all appetites, can have its uses: spurring us to do justice to our talents, encouraging excellence, restraining us from harmful eccentricities, and cementing members of a society around a common value system. But like all appetites," de Botton concludes, "its excesses can do us damage."

such a grand place? Take out her frustration on her much older husband, who didn't want to move in the first place, thus ruining their relationship? "I'm carrying most of the financial burden. I knew Don wouldn't be financially helpful, so how can I be angry now?" she said.

Valerie's Striver image is particularly deep-rooted. She watched her mother spend money with a sense of entitlement, and although she's more practical than her mother, she identifies mightily with the woman's values. Tied to the past, Valerie believed her great house would provide her with a sense of well-being and prove to her mother, at last, that she was, she said, "entitled to the best and as good as everyone else."

The damage for Valerie is pegging the value of her self-worth to the value of bragging rights to a three-bedroom house in an upscale suburb. Putting yourself in potential financial jeopardy by wanting to satisfy a parent's dream is not unusual for a Striver. In buying a fabulous house, Valerie hoped to prove her love and loyalty to her mother.

Living Down Your Past by Pulling Yourself Up

While Valerie may want to fulfill a destiny her mother said she was entitled to, Mark is carving out a Striver future fueled by a drive to succeed in order to escape his past. Valerie and Mark both have mothers who were powerful influences on them while growing up. Valerie is still bound to hers, but Mark has cut himself off from his. Their once close relationship is now strained. In a way, for his mother, it's all about money. For Mark, it's all about class and what goes with it.

Mark's story is a classic tale of the shrewd kid who knows what he wants at a very young age—a lot of money—and works his way out of one kind of ghetto or another to get it. "The joke at the trailer park where I grew up was that the only way out was with a hit record," Mark tells me with a laugh. "Now it's hitting the lottery. But the point is the same—it's thinking that moving up is about bettering yourself through luck rather than anything else. I can't wait for luck. I want more, and I figured out that I'd find it through my own efforts. And I was right."

A recent transplant to Miami, Mark considers his $200,000 yearly salary—the most he's ever earned—barely sufficient to support his increasingly upscale Striver lifestyle. Having just bought a $1.2 million home, Mark is a very long way from the Arizona neighborhood of his childhood. Money is everything to Mark and Toni, his wife of ten years, who, he recently discovered, lies about her spending. Since he's just been transferred to Florida, this thirty-six-year-old is worried that any change in his company will put his job in jeopardy. He fears losing his job, his money, and his semi-socialite wife, and winding up back in a trailer park. "I'm not those people anymore," he says. Living rich is important to him.

Growing Up Wanting More

Mark's background is as full of conflicts about class as about what money can really do for you. Mark was born in Louisiana a few months after his parents, who weren't married, broke up. When Mark was four years old, his mother married. "She was in her 'we are the people' stage, and still a bit of a hippie, so she and my stepfather decided to move into a trailer park," Mark said. "Friends of my parents who grew up with real family money lived there, but those friends identified with the working class. They thought trailer park people were more real. I didn't like that reality at all. I saw it as cheap living, thrift shop clothes, periods on state rations. But I didn't hate how we lived until I got to junior high school. Even worse, I hate to say, I became ashamed of my parents. Then my mother had an awakening about money. Her thinking changed from avoid it, to get it!"

Bill Cosby once said the first rich kids he met were his own. Mark's mother was determined that her son would not make the same joke. When he was around thirteen years old, she started lecturing Mark about getting in with the money crowd at school, "insisting," Mark said, "that people with money were better than us—people without money. One big reason she changed was because my stepfather had no ambition beyond his paycheck, and she wanted me to be better than what I saw at home."

As far as his mother's ambitions for him went, geography was on Mark's side. The trailer park was still zoned from the days when it was part of a large farm and was at the outer fringes of the "better" school district. Thus, the trailer park kids went to a good school, populated with kids whose families had money. Mark said, "I started high school as a smart-ass redneck, then, by accident, I discovered tennis and became a

---

MARK'S FINANCIAL SNAPSHOT

Mark is stretched financially to the limit and was willing to reveal only this much about the state of his finances:

- His company takes care of his health plan and contributes to his 401(k) account, but as he approaches forty, he worries about the future.

- Because Mark is making up for how he didn't live while he was growing up, his cash flow reflects that he's still caught up in proving he's "better." In doing so, he lives from paycheck to paycheck.

- He owes the IRS back taxes and has had to pass up a number of good investment possibilities because he didn't have the capital.

- Above that, his wife, Toni, is high-maintenance, and she makes daily demands on him. He says he doesn't care how much it costs him to keep her happy.

preppie. I eventually got good enough to win some school competitions. It turned out to be my way into the top clique. I already had a paper route, but now I spent every cent of my month's pay on, say, a Lacoste shirt or shoes and shorts."

His mother was happy with the choices Mark was making and encouraged him to think of the future in terms of earning a lot. "Tennis made me more competitive and more determined to escape the trailer park," Mark added, "and from hanging around kids with money, I learned how to act, what to say. I even met the girl I'd marry eight years later."

Mark is proud of his Striver achievements, but he's haunted by how he treats his parents, who now live in a small house in the "wrong" part of town, in an area that "upsets" his wife to visit with their two boys. "Don't get me wrong," Mark says. "I appreciate what my mother did for me. But it's hard for my wife to be around her and my stepfather, who she says is 'too Archie Bunker.' I love my life in Miami and will do anything to keep it. Right now that means not visiting my parents and not having them visit us."

What's Class All About?

Mark has to work through a number of issues that clarify the meaning of money to him and further clarify the values of his semi-socialite wife. Mark's mother wanted him to better himself, but she didn't expect to be rejected into the bargain. What's happened to Mark is not uncommon. He's feeling what Alfred Lubrano talked about in his book, *Limbo: Blue-Collar Roots, White-Collar Dreams*, as being "status dissonance." Lubrano says that when people from a blue-collar background move up in the world, their core values and goals are challenged. The result is a deep emotional reaction that brings up conflicts and doubts. Striving doesn't erase these conflicts and doubts, unless you've made peace with your past. This is Mark to a tee.

Blue-collar values, as Lubrano describes them, are focused on loyalty to family, making money, marrying, and procreating, and if you move up, these values are supplanted, he writes, "by stuff you never talked about at home: personal fulfillment, societal obligations, the pursuit of knowledge for knowledge's sake." By moving up, questions arise, such as, are you deserting your past? Are you betraying your roots when you make a lot of money by accomplishing more with your life? Some people knock themselves out to succeed, then cannot endure what they achieve. I knew of a man who pulled himself out of near poverty to become a millionaire. Months before he died, he built a bonfire and burned all his stock certificates and nearly a million in cash. It was his way of saying he was sorry for having been ashamed of his parents and his early years, all his life. It doesn't have to work out that way.

"While race and gender have had their decades in the sun, class has been obscured and overlooked. It's the 'C' word—the troublesome component of 'the iron triad,'" Lubrano writes. "People would rather talk about sex than money and money before class." Class, he says, is a cultural network of shared values, meanings, and interactions . . . which creates a sense of belonging among its members. Class is script, map, and guide and tells us how to talk, how to dress, how to hold ourselves, where we live, the friends we choose, the jobs we hold, the vacations we take, how we decide to buy property, furniture, and cars, where our kids are educated, what we tell our children at the dinner table or whether we have a dinner table. Yet, Lubrano says, "class is an intangible metaphor that marks your place in the world . . . it's invisible and inexact, but it has resonance and deep meaning. When you're born blue-collar, it's different from growing up in a middle-class or upper-class home."

With all Mark's fears about losing status and returning unwillingly to his roots, it turns out that what people think constitutes class has changed over the last few years. Researchers whose work was reported in the *Proceedings of the Association of Financial Counseling and Planning Education* found that more than 85 percent of the study participants identified themselves as middle-class. This was based on variables ranging, the researchers wrote, from "income levels, material possessions, speech patterns and education levels, to spiritual and moral values." The conclusion? A lack of consistency in definition and widely divergent feelings and beliefs about one's own position in society provided significant evidence that these participants had no clear definition of the term *middle-class*.

Perhaps, as Lubrano says, for many people who grew up working-class like Mark, the emotional component of what class means goes deep. The issue is especially touchy when you feel you're not as good as other people because they have more money. It takes a while to figure this out for yourself. It also proves the theory that money is never just money, but that it is always about your emotions.

But that *can* be worked out.

MAKING CHANGES: THE EMOTIONAL PATH

If you're a Striver Money Type with experiences similar to those of Tim, Valerie, or Mark, this is your chance to learn how to rein in the status impulses that get you into financial trouble. To improve your situation, you'll need to rethink your values and examine what money means to you. I'll guide you through a number of important exercises so you can begin to make small but meaningful adjustments and develop a sense of proportion. Any small changes in your financial behavior will help you build a healthier relationship with money *and* with your partner or spouse. Remember: The goal is not to change you fundamentally. Instead, learn to make concessions to your Striver money habits so you can find security and still indulge yourself, but at a more reasonable level.

Instead of wanting to live up to a status image that may not be you, now's your chance to do damage control for your own ego and finances. If your Striver lifestyle is all-important to you, it's probably because your self-esteem hinges on what others think of you. Give yourself a break. You are not your possessions, but rather a complex person with more to offer the world than the objects you've paid for.

Start by asking yourself the following questions to clear up how you feel about what money means to you. In answering these questions, you want to figure out the origin of a troublesome money issue and make those important connections to how you think it's affecting you now. What do possessions and the need for status really give you? Where does the impulse come from? Sometimes people just want a big house. This is different from wanting a Porsche in order to feel better about yourself by impressing others, and not being able to afford it. This is where you get into trouble.

Ultimately, you want to identify at least one money issue tied to your past that could be throwing you off track now, such as living down a deprived childhood by overspending on clothes. The point is to identify the issue, separate it from the past, and accept that you didn't have nice clothes then, *period*. You can't change the past, but you can influence the future. Ask yourself, what can I have now that will be better without dragging the past into it? That's an essential distinction to make. Even if your home is a mansion, in your mind you're still living in a shabby little house unless you make peace with old issues. You don't get out of that house until you close the door psychologically.

- What do all your things mean to you?
- Do you feel you don't have to have the most, but at least be equal to?
- How would you describe your biggest problem with money?
- When you earn a lot of money or buy upscale items, do you feel that what you have is not enough a short time later?

I recently read an interview in the *New York Times* with Laura Nash, author of *Just Enough: Tools for Creating Success in Your Work and Your Life*. She tells of an entrepreneur who sold his business for $19 million and, astonishingly, "felt ashamed to tell his peers he hadn't made more." One reason for his feeling inadequate is big celebrity paychecks. Some of us tend to adopt celebrity standards, and the bar for "best" or "enough" is raised daily. This is financially self-sabotaging.

To begin resolving some of these emotional issues, try these exercises:

Are You Living Something Down from the Past?

In a way, all the people you've met in this chapter are living something down from the past, and striving was the pill to blocking out the pain. What about you? Maybe Dad drove a wreck of a car, which embarrassed the family, or you lived on the wrong side of the tracks or wore hand-me-downs or your parents had money but were begrudging tightwads. Where does your story about regrets, defining experiences, or influences from the past begin? How do you express them in your financial life?

If you're like Mark, who grew up in a trailer park, you could ask yourself, "Do I have to be super-upscale to prove I moved on to where I am now?" Can you say, "No, I don't have to be the absolute opposite of where I came from to know I'm somebody worthwhile"?

Even though he earns $200,000 a year, Mark doesn't ever want to do without, feel embarrassed about not measuring up, or look like the low man on the totem pole. He is influenced by upscale trends and how celebrities spend, but they are not his true models. It is his wife's upper-middle-class background and America's old-family moneyed class that most impress him. He wants to join them and to be them. This is fine, but not when you're still ashamed of your roots. Such striving has to cost you.

Mark said that his wife, Toni, is high-maintenance, but he thinks she's worth the trouble. He likes that she comes from a richer family than his and looks good on his arm. He desperately fears that she'll leave him if he doesn't keep earning more and more money to provide her with status. Toni clearly has her own definition of the word *value*, and Mark, unfortunately, is buying into it. What is value to Toni, really? What does value mean to Mark? Think about what value means to you.

Mark's version of having a life he can be proud of may never be enough. This is because he still hasn't resolved his feelings about being deprived or cheated in the past. What about you? If you feel psychologically cheated, spending more to appear as if you were to the manor born won't ease the pain for long. The moment of purchase gets you high, but it's almost always followed by a crash. Which is eased by another shopping high, and on and on. But resolving the issues and getting them out of your life for good will make the difference.

Try this shift in thinking:

As does Mark, you need to understand that you shouldn't run from your past but be proud of where you've arrived. If you spend all your time running, then your decisions are made out of fear of your real self coming through. You reckon, "If I don't do this, I'll end up back where I started." Money has become Mark's lifeline, and he thinks that if he loses it, he has no identity.

Second, if you, like Mark, have an impulse to buy something upscale that you think will better your image, stop. Where did you see the item and who had it? What were you thinking about when you saw the object? Were you replaying an episode from your past where you felt that you didn't belong because of how little money your father earned? Face the old issue and defuse its power over you. Make the choice to live in the present.

Is Not Feeling Like a Somebody Your Greatest Fear Related to Status?

If you're like Tim, you know that having had some success and losing it is a painful experience. For you, it's difficult not to look like a winner in the eyes of others. Tim's job gave him more than an income—the job title was as important as the money in affirming that he was somebody to be admired and respected. So until you've regained some success, you suffer a lot of emotional turmoil about mistakenly feeling insignificant.

Try this shift in thinking:

You're more than your job position, and you're more than your possessions. *Self-worth, your authentic value, is the gift you give yourself.* It's priceless. It makes you distinct, someone worthy of respect. If you hang on to an idealized image of yourself—your idea of a somebody—to give you value, then you lose yourself.

When I spoke to Tim, I realized that he was cheating himself by modeling himself on a preconceived image of success that had little to do with his real abilities. He was a skilled manager and a great team player, but he wasn't a leader. He wasn't good at future planning, but he could pull an immediate disaster out of the fire with a clever solution. And then there are his past emotional issues: A dreamer, he thought success assured him that he was better than his father. Getting sacked from his job was tantamount to being like the man he didn't want to be—a nobody. These attitudes continued to put him and his family in financial jeopardy.

Are you acting on similar attitudes and getting yourself deeper into financial trouble? If you've lost a great job and your income has gone down so that you feel toppled from a pedestal, stop here. Ask yourself: What was great about what I had? Make a list. Maybe one of your answers is like Tim's: "That job made me feel that I was in charge and that people liked me. I liked dressing for the job, looking like I had the corner office. I felt like a man who could take care of his family and that my wife respected and loved me. I want to get all that back."

If you want your old life back, acknowledge that it may never be the same, but that you can build another and make it better. You may not be able to duplicate your old success, but you can create a new one. In talking to Tim about this, I helped him figure out that he could pursue a more realistic career path, not at the top but starting in the middle, so to speak, where he'd find his niche—and become someone with a renewed sense of authentic accomplishment.

My hope for you is that you separate yourself from your idea of status and see yourself as a whole, capable, creative, compassionate person who is responsible and functions at optimal level.

Do You Ever Fear That You'll Lose Someone's Love and Respect If You Lose Your Money?

This is an emotionally loaded question and one that can be hard to deal with. None of us wants the answer to be yes, yet it's such a common concern. Even so, much of the time, our fears are greater than the reality. I've talked to so many people who are living in a way that pleases a parent or a spouse, but who are unhappy or frustrated. Valerie is a perfect example of this. "I often think we wish for things we believe we deserve, but we don't know what we really need," she told me. "My mother wanted so much for me, and I feel that unless I make it happen, she'll die feeling that I failed her."

If you're like Valerie and feel entitled to live rich but are afraid of how much it costs you, you might ask, "Can I be happy with what is right for me now, not my mother's wish for what I should have?" See if you can answer, "Yes, I can stop thinking that I deserved more and didn't get it. I have a good marriage, great kids, and a fairly secure life. I can separate from my mother's values by living my own."

Try this shift in thinking:

If the answer to this question for you is, "Yes, I *am* afraid to lose love and respect if I lose my money, and therefore, whatever status I have," what do you do? First, stop here and start being kinder to yourself! Remember that if you don't value yourself, no one else will. The bottom line is that when you respect what you accomplish and who you are, the chances of other people treating you respectfully increase.

Valerie, the woman who is living out her mother's entitlement fantasy, has to individuate from her mother and really become her own person. She's still too attached to her mother's value system and worried about pleasing her. Valerie spent her life believing she deserved more, yet when she got that grand house, she felt unworthy of it! Did her mother love her any more when she got the house? Did her mother love her any less before she got the house? No, to both questions.

What about you? Whom do you feel you are pleasing? Why do you fear you'll lose them? Do you feel you are sometimes buying someone's attention, affection, or interest? If so, who is that person, and what are you getting in return?

What Is the Effect of Your Striver Lifestyle on the People Who Matter Most to You?

One of the aspects of being a Striver that interests me is how they are partnered, both personally and professionally.

Your behavior affects others around you, and sometimes that behavior can be destructive. Tim undermined his family's welfare by spending money he didn't have on himself. Some Strivers may go so far as to undermine a business partner's livelihood. Let me tell you about Rick, whose Striver impulses got totally out of control by conniving and deceiving others.

Larry, a Chicago man, told me how his partner, Rick, walked away with the proceeds of a major deal. Rick turned into a financial warrior—riding roughshod over Larry and hurting the people who cared about him. Rick wouldn't apologize for taking all the money. Instead, he said he needed the money to pay his mortgage and his wife's charge account bills and that Larry would have to wait for his cut. Larry found out that Rick used the money as a down payment for a boat and bought an expensive status-brand watch.

Larry had to retain a lawyer to sue his partner. Larry wrote, "Rick couldn't believe I'd sue. He said I may have done the scut work to put the deal together, but he was the one who knew how to impress the buyers and sell the plan. He paid for the $500 dinner. I told him I was at those meetings and pulled him out of the fire more than once. He felt entitled to the money, though, and said he was running a business and he got the money first."

Yes, Rick is dishonest and makes excuses for his greed. But what is interesting is that he used the money for more and bigger symbols of success, not to pay outstanding bills—a Striver shortcoming. I don't know if Rick lives beyond his means, but his behavior with Larry is very much that of a person who does. You may not go so far as to undermine someone else's livelihood by walking off with the money, but if you are driven by a sense of desperation for something you cannot afford, you'll find a way to get it. You'll make up a story to get a loan from a friend or relative and hope you can pay it back before they see where the money went: for an upscale item.

Try this shift in thinking:

Think about which relationships are important to you, personally and professionally. Examine them in detail and figure out how your money habits are causing trouble. First, define those relationships. What do you get from those people? How does that person enrich your life in ways that have nothing to do with stuff? How do you think you enrich that person's life in ways that have nothing to do with material objects? Whom can you rely on to be there, no matter what your fortunes may be? Whom do you trust?

Once you're clear about how you feel about those closest to you, be willing to be brutally honest with yourself about the effects of your spending habits on others. Understand where you need to compromise. Figure out where you can cut back. Understand what others need in terms of security now and for the future. There's a huge gap between the yearning to live rich and doing so without you and others paying too high a price.

By staying conscious of your shortcomings, you can avoid lapses in good judgment based on hair-trigger responses and weaknesses that get in the way of financial stability and professional success.

MAKING CHANGES: THE FINANCIAL PATH

Because Strivers tend to have trouble matching their income with their expenses, there are a number of options that, if you follow them, can be truly life-changing.

My goal is to help you develop a sense of proportion so you can gain control of your money, accumulate capital, and feel good about yourself. By gaining control, you finally match your income with your expenses and avoid living on the financial edge—not unlike the people you've read about here. The good news is that I won't suggest that you give up buying the upscale items you want. Instead, you'll figure out how to afford some luxury items and, most important, learn how to put money aside for the future, too—thus vanquishing a shortcoming of your Money Type.

Of course, my goals for you can't be set in motion unless you determine what your financial goals are for yourself. You're the power behind your money. Gaining financial control means change. And the most important element in change is the one thing I can't do for you—take action. When it comes to money, nothing feels better than knowing your finances are under control and you're not a runaway train about to crash! I can keep you focused on the destination—security, prosperity, and understanding what you need to know about them—but it's you who are at the throttle.

Preparing Yourself for the Striver Financial Control Plan

Let me start out by asking you three important questions:

1. *Can you choose one area of your life where you'd be willing to make a small financial shift every day?* For example, this could mean cutting back on eating lunch or dinner out from five times to once or twice a week.

2. *Can you choose another area of your life where you'd be willing to make a small financial shift on a regular basis for at least six months?* For example, could you resist splurging on a luxury item that's on sale but is still significantly pricey? Or, could you reduce your summer clothing expenditure by $50 to $250?

3. *If you could make any small change that saves you money on a regular basis, would you feel a renewed sense of accomplishment in how you manage your money?* As someone who's helped thousands of people find their way financially, I feel confident enough to make you a promise: Yes, you will feel not only a sense of accomplishment but an even greater sense of peace.

For now, consider the following steps as you go through my upcoming financial help:

Begin where you are today. You're not limited by what happened in the past, nor must you correct every money mistake you've ever made to enjoy a successful future. You just have to take a step forward now. Your enthusiasm and the new awareness you've gained about the power of your Money Type should motivate you into action.

To feel at peace and reap the benefits of your hard work, you need to get your worst money impulses in check. One key to success is being willing to understand the kind of money problems you get into again and again. Have courage and face them. When you do, you can finally stop being a victim of your worst money habits.

Build a better relationship with a spouse or partner by understanding each other's financial needs. Let me start out by saying that marriage is a lot more complicated than marital

TRY THIS: EMBRACE A NEW MIND-SET THAT LETS YOU MAKE ADJUSTMENTS TO HOW YOU SPEND

Although living large sounds ideal, a *Money* magazine survey of affluent Americans revealed that the financial golden rule for 67 percent of people living the good life is to live within your means. These people believed that being in control of their money was a sign of being in control of their lives. This meant keeping debt low and planning for the future so they could maintain the affluent lifestyle during retirement and not worry about paying for their children's college education. Sounds good. Further investigation showed that a small proportion, *only 19 percent*, of affluent Americans said that one very important aspect of living the good life was buying the nice things they wanted. You may disagree with what's important when you have the income to spend, but it makes sense to live within your means so you can aim for those special items.

One way to get that control of your life is to suspend judgment about yourself and not pigeonhole your Money Type as good or bad. If your personality is drawn to living rich and you are attracted to status items, okay. Recognize your Money Type and accept it, but know, as the survey on affluence proves, that living within your means is the closest you can get to financial satisfaction. Status isn't everything. When you accept this, you *can* gain a sense of harmony and continuity with money. Ultimately, you become more successful by learning how to maximize your capabilities and keep your passion for extravagance in check. But remember, you want to reach a state of peace.

finances. If there's a bottom line, it's about honesty, and all the work that follows will encourage it. Honesty is critical.

SmartMoney Magazine did a survey and found that spouses

do lie about how much they spend. More than 70 percent of those questioned said they talked to their partner about money at least once a week. However, "not all of that talk was truthful. Roughly *40 percent* of both men and women admitted lying about how much something they bought had cost." Do your best to honor your partner and tell the truth.

Reap the benefits of learning to look ahead. It's never too early to think about the future. Find a few dollars to put in an interest-bearing account. I know from experience with clients that spending now to keep up with the Joneses means you may forget to plan for the future. I recently spoke to a woman whose Striver husband died at age fifty in a car crash. He'd apparently had nine or ten financial balls in the air, including borrowing to keep a business going. His widow was rightly upset as every ball dropped leadenly at her feet. Their accountant told her the bad news: Not only had the husband been overextended, he'd never put away money to finance their retirement as she'd trusted him to do. She was left with debts and an insurance policy that paid them off. At fifty, she had to start over. Be smarter!

Understand that the Striver guidelines can offer a life-changing framework for you. Not only do you get your money under control, you also get to decide what percentage of your income can be spent on indulging your Striver impulses. The remainder is used to cover your living necessities, planning for retirement, investments, and, if it's the case for you, paying high school and/or college tuition for your children.

You can learn to redefine your financial goals realistically within your income and determine what's most and least important to you. There is no right or wrong financial goal as long as you make a conscious decision to set limits so you can live within your means *and* be a Striver, but selectively.

The material that follows provides you with part of the story in getting your Money Type on track. I've guided you through the sensitive areas of your feelings about money and why you spend; now we move on to the practical side of how and where you spend. Most importantly, you'll begin at an authentic starting point—your financial goals and the shape of your financial life in vivid detail. Only you know these numbers. It is by facing those numbers and believing you can make a difference for yourself that you can break self-sabotaging money habits. I know you can do it. Keep following the exercises, and prosperity will follow.

Defining Your Financial Goals

Let's begin the work of putting your money into action.

Once you're willing to change your attitude just enough, you can define and examine all your financial goals realistically. Can you meet your monthly expenses for necessities—what I call the basic nut—such as housing, utilities, food, any insurance payments, and so on? Okay. What do you want to plan for with the remaining money? Do you want to buy a bigger house, send your children to better colleges, get the hottest car, buy shares of a recommended stock, rent a house in Saint-Tropez for the season, get a couture outfit you can wear for years?

No matter the goal, what's important is that your decision to spend the money is a rational one and not based on an emotional need to feel more successful by owning the object. What's important is that you can afford what you buy, and that you didn't buy a status item in a misguided effort to assuage a bruised ego.

There are two parts to defining a financial goal. The first is filling out a short-term goal-setting agenda, which asks basic questions about naming your goal and how much you need to achieve it. The second element is allocating the money and calculating the time needed to attain what you want. Both factors are determined by the amount of money you earn—and can spend. If you share finances with a spouse or partner, goal setting in terms of striving must be done mutually. This mutuality avoids friction when both of you agree on which goals get the highest priority.

I've provided a simple Short-Term Goal-Tracking Agenda below, which is meant to help you figure out how to allocate money for extras on a short-term basis of six months to one year. This agenda is important for you. It helps you focus on what you want and gives you the steps that tell you how much money you need to set aside each month to get it. The agenda lists the most relevant points to consider when working out any financial goal, short- or long-term. For example, suppose you want to take a luxury winter vacation next year, consisting of two weeks' skiing in Aspen, or you've targeted a new car. Hitting the slopes or sitting behind the wheel of a Lexus is the end result, but what are your means to get either one?

After answering the questions, you'll begin the process of setting your goals into motion. When you make small changes in your Striver lifestyle, you'll find more money working for you—*your* money.

What's Your Net Worth?

Do your assets and liabilities match or mismatch? To find out where you stand financially, add up the total value of what you already own, known as your assets, and subtract the amount of

---

YOUR SHORT-TERM GOAL-TRACKING AGENDA

1. My financial goal: _____

2. Date when I'll need the money for this goal: _____

3. How many months from now? _____

4. Amount of money needed to accomplish this goal: _____

5. Money already accumulated for this goal: _____

6. Money remaining to be accumulated for this goal: _____

7. Monthly amount to be saved (divide the amount on line 6 by the number on line 3): _____

debt you owe, known as your liabilities. This bottom line is your net worth. It is a snapshot in time, good only for the moment you calculate it. But it's a picture you can keep and use as a benchmark to compare yourself against as your net worth grows over the years. It's a good idea to check the figures at least once a year to track how you're doing, especially if there's been some sort of change in your financial situation.

I've provided two worksheets for you on the following pages: One focuses on your assets and the second one on your liabilities. When you complete the liabilities worksheet, read my directions for what to do next, coming up.

What is your net worth? This is the moment of truth: Take the final number from your assets worksheet and subtract the figure from your liabilities worksheet, thus:

Total assets: $_____

(Minus) Total liabilities: (_____)

Equals final positive (or negative) net worth: $_____

Is your final net worth positive or negative? If it's positive, you're doing a good job of building assets and keeping liabilities under control. You're in a fine position to see your net worth grow even more in the future. If your net worth is negative, don't despair. You've revealed an important state of your financial affairs, and the first step will be to get out of trouble. Clearly, you have too much debt for the amount of assets you've accumulated. But this is only a snapshot of your finances as they are now. As you go through this book, you'll find many solutions to increase your net worth—whether it's positive or negative now.

But first, let's continue looking at how you spend and save.

Figure Out Your Cash Flow

How much are you worth, and what are your financial goals? When you do a detailed cash flow analysis, you can trace your

YOUR ASSETS WORKSHEET

Assets	Date Purchased	Original $ Value	Current Date	Current $ Value
1. Current Assets				
Bonuses or Commissions (due you)	————	————	————	————
Certificates of Deposit	————	————	————	————
Checking Accounts	————	————	————	————
Credit Union Accounts	————	————	————	————
Money Market Accounts	————	————	————	————
Savings Accounts	————	————	————	————
Savings Bonds	————	————	————	————
Tax Refunds (due you)	————	————	————	————
Treasury Bills	————	————	————	————
		————	————	————
TOTAL CURRENT ASSETS		$ ————		$ ————
2. Securities				
Bonds (type of bond)				
————————	————	$ ————	————	$ ————
————————	————	————	————	————
————————	————	————	————	————
————————	————	————	————	————
Bond Mutual Funds				
————————	————	————	————	————
————————	————	————	————	————
Futures	————	————	————	————
Warrants and Options	————	————	————	————
Individual Stocks				
————————	————	————	————	————
————————	————	————	————	————
————————	————	————	————	————
————————	————	————	————	————
————————	————	————	————	————

YOUR ASSETS WORKSHEET (Continued)

Assets	Date Purchased	Original $ Value	Current Date	Current $ Value
Stock Mutual Funds				
_____	_____	$ _____	_____	$ _____
_____	_____	_____	_____	_____
_____	_____	_____	_____	_____
_____	_____	_____	_____	_____
TOTAL SECURITIES		$ _____		$ _____

3. Real Estate

Mortgage Receivable (due you)	_____	$ _____	_____	$ _____
Primary Residence	_____	_____	_____	_____
Rental Property	_____	_____	_____	_____
Real Estate Limited Partnerships	_____	_____	_____	_____
Second Home	_____	_____	_____	_____
TOTAL REAL ESTATE		$ _____		$ _____

4. Long-Term Assets

Annuities	_____	$ _____	_____	$ _____
IRAs	_____	_____	_____	_____
Keogh Accounts	_____	_____	_____	_____
Life Insurance Cash Values	_____	_____	_____	_____
Loans Receivable (due you)	_____	_____	_____	_____
Pensions	_____	_____	_____	_____
Private Business Interests	_____	_____	_____	_____
Profit-Sharing Plans	_____	_____	_____	_____
Royalties	_____	_____	_____	_____
Salary Reduction Plans (401(k), 403(b), 457 plans)	_____	_____	_____	_____
TOTAL LONG-TERM ASSETS		$ _____		$ _____

YOUR LIABILITIES WORKSHEET

Liabilities	To Whom	Interest Rate %	Due Date	Amount Due $

1. Current Liabilities

Liabilities	To Whom	Interest Rate %	Due Date	Amount Due $
Alimony	_____	_____ %	_____	$ _____
Bills				
Electric and Gas	_____	_____	_____	_____
Home Contractor	_____	_____	_____	_____
Oil Company	_____	_____	_____	_____
Physician and Dentist	_____	_____	_____	_____
Retail Stores	_____	_____	_____	_____
Telephone	_____	_____	_____	_____
Other	_____	_____	_____	_____
Child Support	_____	_____	_____	_____
Loans to Individuals	_____	_____	_____	_____

TOTAL CURRENT LIABILITIES $ _____

2. Unpaid Taxes

Liabilities	To Whom	Interest Rate %	Due Date	Amount Due $
Capital Gains Taxes				
Federal	_____	_____	_____	_____
State	_____	_____	_____	_____
Income Taxes				
Federal	_____	_____ %	_____	$ _____
State	_____	_____	_____	_____
Property Taxes	_____	_____	_____	_____
Sales Taxes				
Locality	_____	_____	_____	_____
Social Security Taxes				
(self-employed)	_____	_____	_____	_____

TOTAL UNPAID TAXES $ _____

3. Real Estate Liabilities

Liabilities	To Whom	Interest Rate %	Due Date	Amount Due $
Home #1				
First Mortgage	_____	_____ %	_____	$ _____
Home Equity Loan	_____	_____	_____	_____
Second Mortgage	_____	_____	_____	_____

YOUR LIABILITIES WORKSHEET (Continued)

Liabilities	To Whom	Interest Rate %	Due Date	Amount Due $
Home #2				
First Mortgage	_____	____ %	_____	$ _____
Home Equity Loan	_____	_____	_____	_____
Second Mortgage	_____	_____	_____	_____
Rental Property				
First Mortgage	_____	_____	_____	_____
Second Mortgage	_____	_____	_____	_____
TOTAL REAL ESTATE LIABILITIES				$ _____

4. Installment Liabilities

Liabilities	To Whom	Interest Rate %	Due Date	Amount Due $
Automobile Loans	_____	____ %	_____	$ _____
Bank Loans for Bill Consolidation	_____	_____	_____	_____
Credit Cards	_____	_____	_____	_____
Education Loans	_____	_____	_____	_____
Equipment and Appliance Loans	_____	_____	_____	_____
Furniture Loans	_____	_____	_____	_____
Home Improvement Loans	_____	_____	_____	_____
Liability Judgments	_____	_____	_____	_____
Life Insurance Loans	_____	_____	_____	_____
Margin Loans Against Securities	_____	_____	_____	_____
Overdraft Bank Loans	_____	_____	_____	_____
Pension Plan Loans	_____	_____	_____	_____
TOTAL INSTALLMENT LIABILITIES				$ _____
TOTAL LIABILITIES				$ _____

sources and uses of money to figure out where you can afford an indulgence—and when and where you need to cut back and be smarter about spending.

Even though it's a simple exercise, most people never get around to doing a cash flow analysis. Instead, they wait anxiously for their next paycheck to pay their bills. Yes, I know this exercise is tedious, but keep at it. Sharpen your pencils and turn off the TV. By doing an analysis, you will know exactly how much income you can expect to receive as well as nearly all the expenses you plan to cover with that income. Don't plan on any windfalls, such as an end-of-the-year bonus, winning the lottery, or an inheritance, but you should anticipate a few surprise expenses.

This cash flow analysis should be filled out yearly. Some income, such as bonuses or capital gains distributions made by mutual funds, is received only at certain times of the year, in December, for example. Similarly, many expenses, such as tuition payments, fuel oil bills, or quarterly tax bills, occur only during certain months. By totaling all your annual income and expenses, you will get a sense of how your cash flow looks for the year. With your bank, brokerage, insurance, and credit card statements, as well as last year's tax return, your final year-end paycheck, and other records you have accumulated for the past six months, fill in the real numbers on the worksheet. This is not an exercise in wishful thinking. This is a document that will show you, for better or for worse, how you actually are earning and spending your money now. It's no use inflating the income and lowballing the expenses because you're the only one who'll be hurt by not knowing the truth.

In the following worksheets, you'll see that I've broken the income side of the analysis into six categories: earned, self-employment, family, government, retirement, and investment income. For each of the subcategories, I've provided a line on the worksheet to subtotal the income, which will make it easier to add up your total income at the end.

CASH FLOW WORKSHEET

Annual Income	$ Amount	$ Total

1. Earned Income

Salary after deductions	_____	
Bonuses	_____	
Commissions	_____	
Deferred compensation	_____	
Overtime	_____	
Stock options	_____	
Tips	_____	
Other	_____	

TOTAL EARNED INCOME _____

2. Self-Employment Income

Freelance income	_____	
Income from partnerships	_____	
Income from running a small business	_____	
Rental income from real estate	_____	
Royalties	_____	
Other	_____	

TOTAL SELF-EMPLOYMENT INCOME _____

3. Family Income

Alimony income	_____	
Child support income	_____	
Family trust income	_____	
Gifts from family members	_____	
Inheritance income	_____	
Other	_____	

TOTAL FAMILY INCOME _____

4. Government Income

Aid to Families with Dependent Children income	_____	
Disability insurance income	_____	
Unemployment insurance income	_____	
Veterans benefits	_____	
Welfare income	_____	
Workers' compensation income	_____	
Other	_____	

TOTAL GOVERNMENT INCOME _____

CASH FLOW WORKSHEET (continued)

Annual Income	$ Amount	$ Total

5. Retirement Income

Annuity payments	_____	
Pension income	_____	
Income from IRAs	_____	
Income from Keogh accounts	_____	
Income from profit-sharing accounts	_____	
Income from salary reduction plans		
(401(k), 403(b), 457 plans)	_____	
Social Security income	_____	
Other	_____	

TOTAL RETIREMENT INCOME _____

6. Investment Income

Bank account interest:

CDs	_____	
Money market accounts	_____	
NOW accounts	_____	
Savings accounts	_____	

Bonds and bond funds:

Capital gains	_____	
Dividends	_____	
Interest	_____	
Other	_____	
Limited partnerships (real estate, oil, gas)	_____	

Money funds and Treasury bills:

Taxable funds	_____	
Tax-exempt funds	_____	
T bills	_____	

Stock and stock funds:

Capital gains	_____	
Dividends	_____	
Interest	_____	
Other	_____	

TOTAL INVESTMENT INCOME _____

7. Other income (specify)

_____ _____

TOTAL OTHER INCOME _____

TOTAL ANNUAL INCOME ═══════

CASH FLOW WORKSHEET (continued)

Annual Expenses	$ Amount	$ Total

1. Fixed Expenses

Automobile-related
    Car payment (loan or lease)   _____
    Gasoline or oil   _____
    Other   _____

TOTAL   _____

Family
    Alimony
    Child support payments   _____
    Food and beverage   _____
    School tuition   _____

TOTAL   _____

Home-related
    Cable or satellite television fees   _____
    Mortgage payments Home 1   _____
    Mortgage payments Home 2   _____
    Rent   _____

TOTAL   _____

Insurance
    Auto   _____
    Dental   _____
    Disability   _____
    Health   _____
    Homeowners   _____
    Life   _____
    Other   _____

TOTAL   _____

Savings and investments
    Bank loan repayment
    Contributions to 401(k), 403(b), etc.   _____
    Emergency fund contributions   _____
    Salary reduction plans   _____
    Other   _____

TOTAL   _____

CASH FLOW WORKSHEET (continued)

Annual Expenses	$ Amount	$ Total
Taxes		
Federal	_____	
Local	_____	
Property	_____	
Social Security (self-employed)	_____	
State	_____	
Other	_____	
TOTAL		_____
Utilities		
Electricity	_____	
Gas/Oil	_____	
Telephone	_____	
Water and sewage	_____	
Other	_____	
TOTAL		_____
Other (specify)		
_____	_____	
TOTAL		_____
TOTAL FIXED EXPENSES		=========

2. Flexible Expenses

	$ Amount	$ Total
Children		
Allowances	_____	
Baby-sitting	_____	
Books	_____	
Camp fees	_____	
Day care	_____	
Events (parties, class trips, etc.)	_____	
Toys	_____	
Other	_____	
TOTAL		_____
Clothing		
New purchases	_____	
Shoes	_____	
Upkeep (cleaning, tailoring,		
dry cleaning, etc.)	_____	
TOTAL		_____

CASH FLOW WORKSHEET (continued)

Annual Expenses	$ Amount	$ Total
Contributions and dues		
Charitable donations	_____	
Gifts (holidays, birthdays, etc.)	_____	
Political contributions	_____	
Religious contributions	_____	
Union dues	_____	
Other	_____	
TOTAL		_____
Equipment and vehicles		
Appliance purchase and maintenance	_____	
Car, boat, and other vehicle		
purchases and upkeep	_____	
Computer purchases	_____	
Consumer electronic purchases	_____	
Licenses and registration of		
cars, boats, etc.	_____	
Parking	_____	
Other	_____	
TOTAL		_____
Financial and professional services		
Banking fees	_____	
Brokerage commissions and fees	_____	
Financial advice	_____	
Legal advice	_____	
Tax preparation fees	_____	
Other	_____	
TOTAL		_____
Food		
Alcohol	_____	
Food and snacks away from home	_____	
Restaurant meals	_____	
Tobacco	_____	
Other	_____	
TOTAL		_____

CASH FLOW WORKSHEET (continued)

Annual Expenses	$ Amount	$ Total
Home maintenance		
Garbage removal	_____	
Garden supplies and maintenance	_____	
Home cleaning services	_____	
Home furnishings	_____	
Home office supplies	_____	
Home or apartment repairs and renovations	_____	
Home supplies	_____	
Lawn care or snow removal	_____	
Linens	_____	
Uninsured casualty or theft loss	_____	
Other	_____	
TOTAL		_____
Medical care		
Dentist bills	_____	
Drugs (over-the-counter)	_____	
Drugs (prescriptions)	_____	
Eyecare and eyeglasses	_____	
Hospital (uninsured portion)	_____	
Medical devices (wheelchairs, canes, etc.)	_____	
Medical expenses (parents, etc.)	_____	
Nursing home fees	_____	
Personal beauty care (hairstylist, manicurist, etc.)	_____	
Personal care (cosmetics, toiletries, etc.)	_____	
Physician bills	_____	
Unreimbursed medical expenses	_____	
Other	_____	
TOTAL		_____
Miscellaneous		
Mystery cash	_____	
Postage and stamps	_____	
Recurring/nonrecurring expenses	_____	
Unreimbursed business expenses	_____	
Other	_____	
TOTAL		_____

CASH FLOW WORKSHEET (continued)

Annual Expenses	$ Amount	$ Total
Recreation and entertainment		
Animal care	_____	
Books	_____	
Club dues	_____	
Cultural events	_____	
Health club memberships	_____	
Hobbies	_____	
Lottery tickets	_____	
Magazine and newspaper subscriptions	_____	
Movie tickets	_____	
Music events	_____	
Photography (camera, developing, film, etc.)	_____	
Play admissions	_____	
Recreational equipment	_____	
Sporting events admissions	_____	
Videotape/DVD rentals	_____	
Other	_____	
TOTAL		_____
Savings and investments		
Bank savings contributions	_____	
IRA contributions	_____	
Keogh account contributions	_____	
Stock, bond, and mutual fund contributions	_____	
Other	_____	
TOTAL		_____
Travel and vacations		
Bus fares	_____	
Subway costs	_____	
Tolls	_____	
Train fares	_____	
Travel expenses (other than vacations)	_____	
Unreimbursed business travel expenses	_____	
Vacations (airfare)	_____	
Vacations (car rental)	_____	
Vacations (food)	_____	
Vacations (hotel)	_____	

CASH FLOW WORKSHEET (continued)

Annual Expenses	$ Amount	$ Total
Vacations (others)	_____	
Other	_____	
TOTAL		_____
Other (specify)		
_____	_____	
TOTAL		_____
TOTAL FLEXIBLE EXPENSES		_____
TOTAL ANNUAL EXPENSES		_____
TOTAL ANNUAL INCOME (MINUS)		_____
TOTAL ANNUAL EXPENSES EQUALS		_____
TOTAL NET ANNUAL POSITIVE (OR NEGATIVE) CASH FLOW		=======

List Your Expenses

This next step lets you figure out where all that income disappears to every year—and when you add up all your receipts, it pinpoints exactly how much you're laying out for upscale items.

Expenses can be divided roughly into two categories:

1. What is fixed: This refers to anything that must be paid on a monthly, quarterly, or annual basis (home-related, family-related, insurance, taxes, utilities, car-related expenses, and savings and investments in an automatic saving plan such as a 401(k) and debt payments).

2. What is flexible: You have more control over these expenses, especially whether, where, and when you spend your money

(clothing, education, computers and other electronics, cars, professional services, food and eating out, medical care, travel and vacations, recreation and entertainment, savings and investments in such vehicles as tax-deferred IRAs or a Keogh). And if you're out shopping every weekend and at least one night a week after work, you'll get a chance to see what those trips are costing you.

Note: You'll find a category in the cash flow worksheet called "recurring/nonrecurring expenses," which is about *putting some money aside in a contingency fund targeted for emergencies.* Everyone understands these expenses, because they are unexpected and suddenly impact your finances. A *recurring* expense can pop up many times, but you don't know when. For example: maintaining your car. You get a flat tire and need to buy a spare, and a year later you need a new battery; six months later, following a fender-bender, you need to take your car in for body work. A *nonrecurring expense* is also unexpected, but it will usually occur one time and not again for decades. For example, the last snowstorm makes you decide to put on a new roof instead of just patching the damaged spots. Your ice maker breaks down and instead of buying a new one, you spring for the cost of the $40 part that will keep it operating for another twenty years.

By filling out the expense portion of the worksheet in these two categories, you will be able to see what percentage of your income is eaten up by fixed expenses. Since we want to allot 5, 10, or even 15 percent of your income for Striver indulgences, the final number will give you a clearer idea of how much money you have left over for any discretionary spending.

Skip any categories on the worksheet that don't apply to you now. Eventually, you'll get to the bottom line: After you've filled out both the income and expense sides of this worksheet, subtract your expenses from your income and you'll reach your annual cash flow. If you're taking in more than you're spending, congratulations on a positive cash flow. Your next job is to figure out the best uses for your extra cash, probably savings vehicles and investments, after you set aside an emergency reserve.

However, if your expenses total more than your income, not an unlikely situation with Striver types, you are in a negative cash flow, and it's time to really scrutinize your expenses. Just because you have negative cash flow does not mean you're in trouble. You still may be putting away money in your company savings plan, so you're investing more than you might realize. But if the reason you're spending more than you're taking in is excessive debt for high-ticket possessions or for daily spending habits that mount up, it's time to take notice and pull back.

Let me make a suggestion that sounds obvious but can save you approximately $100 or more a month on those daily costs. Here's what I mean, and the math is really simple, too. Let's go back to my earlier question: Could you choose one area of your life where you'd be willing to make a small financial shift every day? For example, this could be cutting back on eating lunch or dinner out from five times to once or twice a week.

If you work outside your home, add up what you spend on take-out coffee, lunch, and dinner (if that's the case) on a daily basis. A lowball estimate is $5 a day; in bigger cities, $10 a day. So over the course of the workweek, it's $25 over five days or $100 a month. That's $600 six months later or $1,200 in bigger cities. That's not insignificant! Instead of eating out, you could bring your lunch from home and put the targeted lunch money in an interest-bearing money market account. At the end of six months, you can use the money to pay credit card debt, put it into a retirement fund, or, yes, spend it on a special luxury item, which then has more meaning to you for the effort you put into getting the cash.

It's really simple and very satisfying when you see your shifts in spending and saving actually taking shape!

Creating a Personal Financial Control Plan That Works

It's easy to get carried away and buy the car or take the vacation that makes you think you're affirming a status image, but if you don't have the money, the bills come in fast and you have to deal with the problems caused by overreaching. The truth is: If you want to live rich and are struggling to keep ahead of the game, you need to consider a budget to ultimately get what you want. Although not a glamorous object, a budget can have more value to you in the long run than any possession: You're going to find that designated percentage of your income in it to indulge yourself.

If the word *budget* reminds you of something dreary, finicky, or limiting, then call it a Personal Financial Control Plan. Most of all, this is a chance to do what *Money* magazine says 67 percent of affluent people do—live the good life by living within their means.

Here's how: A budget is a friend who thinks of your best interests. It's a living, breathing document that expands or contracts as your circumstances and priorities change. A budget, in itself, will not increase your income or cut your spending, but it helps you see what's really going on with your money so you can improve your financial situation—and be able to afford that status item you covet. Your budget allows you to see the direction you want to go in, while giving you several options for how to get there. It is a support system that gives you control over your finances in a way that lets you decide what is most and least important to you. The ultimate test of a budget's worth to you is if you can set it up so that you do not feel deprived.

Thus, a budget is an intensely personal plan. Others may have a few of the same priorities as you but not the exact amount of money with which to attain them. If you find it important to include in your budget a lavish beach vacation every winter at an exclusive Caribbean resort, so be it—as long as the numbers tell you that you can afford it.

Where to begin? You know what your assets and debts are because you've just done a comprehensive net worth analysis. You've clearly prioritized your financial goals and analyzed how your income matches up with your expenses. Using this information as a base, the next step is to project these figures into the future to create a budget that works for you.

There are two kinds of budgets: annual and monthly. The annual plan takes more thought—you probably can't do a good job of forecasting all your income and expenses in an afternoon. Plan to do this budget in several sessions over about a week's time. Try several different scenarios, and do your first few rounds of budgeting in pencil, so you can erase freely until all the numbers add up. Some commonsense approaches can help ensure its success. Keep these points in mind when setting up your budget:

Be realistic and specific to your situation. Don't count on levels of spending or income that you wish you had because that will only frustrate the exercise.

Set priorities. Define your financial goals realistically within your income, and determine what's most and least important to you. There is no right or wrong financial goal as long as you make a conscious decision to live within your means.

Don't sweat the dollars-and-cents details. Use round numbers in your budget planning—the goal is to help control your spending and meet your financial goals so you can find that 5 or 10 or even 15 percent to spend on luxuries. The goal is not to drive yourself crazy by getting the numbers right to the last penny. There are monthly or yearly budgets, so choose what's best.

Involve everyone. Begin by discussing the budget with your spouse or partner, so you can figure out and explain your target goals—and your spouse can explain his or hers. When you engage your life partner, you have a much better chance of meeting your target goals than if he or she had no input. When I spoke to Mark—the man who fears losing it all and winding up back in a trailer park—he openly admitted that satisfying his wife's need for an upscale lifestyle was as motivating as his own need to earn as much as possible. So he's working hard not only for his own security and satisfaction but to maintain a social image that is important to his wife. (You'll find much more on marital money management in detail in later chapters.)

In addition to doing an annual budget, you should keep a running tab of how you are doing on a monthly basis in at least the major categories. I know this system works.

I recently spoke with a woman in Galveston, Texas, who originally e-mailed me about needing to get her finances on track after twenty years of spending to keep up appearances. Her story is an inspiring before-and-after Striver experience, with a surprise ending.

Six months ago, Donna wrote to ask my advice on how she and her husband could break their spending patterns and still enjoy the sense of prosperity they'd worked so hard to achieve. The problem: Their cash flow was all outgo. "So here I am at forty-eight years old," she wrote me. "My husband is fifty, and we've got virtually nothing in the bank. Neither of us has a retirement plan. Is there help for us?"

Interestingly, Donna's request for financial advice came on the heels of a big expenditure. She and her husband, Steve, had decided to install a bigger swimming pool since it would improve the value of their property. "But," she wrote, "if I thought about the cost, I'd be really panicked." Donna was having serious conflicts about wanting to spend for now and needing to stop the flow. I felt sure I could help her and her family rethink their priorities with a Financial Control Plan. First, I needed to know something about her history and thinking about money.

Donna grew up with social activist parents, both of whom spoke about money as a bad thing. For them, status symbols were superficial. Donna had other tastes and other values. She wanted more, and she wanted it all to be new and designer-made. She married a chef, and during the early years of building his reputation in his own small restaurant, they were always dipping into whatever savings they had. Steve wanted to join a country club to make contacts. Donna wanted a diamond ring. "I knew how much it cost," she wrote, "but I wanted something that said 'money.'"

Donna and Steve are classic Striver Money Types with fairly stable working careers. "I've been working for an oil company for about five months and make a fair salary," Donna wrote. "But the money comes in and goes right out for basics."

Donna's money trouble is a classic Striver's shortcoming: thinking about money for today, rather than putting aside money for tomorrow.

It's always a shock when you realize, as Donna has, how close retirement is. Then there will be the expense of putting their daughter through college—also part of their future financial outlay. The future not only comes upon all of us all too quickly, but the future is *now*. Donna and Steve need a management plan that makes sense for their combined income level of approximately $110,000 a year. They've got equity in their house and some debt, but they fall short on future-oriented investments and savings.

But fate stepped in. The effects of Donna's Striver lifestyle were suddenly made clear to her when a few months after she unveiled her new pool, her father died suddenly. Donna discovered that all his money had gone for medical bills, leaving her an estate of about $5,000 and a small house and property in East Texas that she didn't know he owned.

Donna wrote that she was stunned, not about the cash amount but that her father had bought a home he'd kept secret from her. At first she was angry with him; then she felt sorry that he hadn't felt able to share it with her family. Her father had always had a so-what attitude about her lifestyle and was always unimpressed with her latest status purchase. "It turns out that he was smarter about money than all of us," Donna said. "I want to keep my inheritance and not blow it. How do we cut back? Should we sell my father's house? How do we maximize that $5,000? Where do we begin?"

Donna's questions about putting her inheritance to work show that she's ready to make some real adjustments in her Striver lifestyle. Donna and her husband each filled out goal-setting worksheets and were united in their decision to capitalize on her inheritance. After doing the cash flow analysis, they added up their debts, projected their income to the end of the year, and figured out how to find additional cash to pay off the pool: Donna would work the dinner shift at Steve's restaurant on Friday and Saturday nights and put her tip money toward paying the bill.

And her inheritance? They chose to put the $5,000 in an individual retirement account, or IRA. Since Donna is not yet eligible for a retirement plan at her job (she's been there under six months) and Steve is self-employed, as a couple they can make a fully deductible IRA contribution because their adjusted gross income is under $150,000. This officially kicked off their retirement fund, a good place for Donna and Steve to start. There are a number of sources of income once you've retired, assuming you've built up assets. IRAs are a good bet, since you can take your money out when you're fifty-nine and a half years old without penalty or pay a 10 percent penalty if you withdraw the funds sooner. (More on traditional and Roth IRAs and how they work and pay out in a later chapter.) And instead of taking a vacation this year, Donna and her family decided to stay at her father's legacy house for a few weeks and then turn it over to an agent who can find them a paying tenant. Meanwhile, the house will appreciate in value and bring in rental income.

At first, Donna said, she thought that cutting back on a vacation to save money and putting in extra working hours was too hard, but it was worth the effort. "Within three months, we'd begun to make a dent in paying off the pool," she told me. She and Steve paid a contractor to make a few upgrades in her father's place, but the expense paid off. They rented it and have the extra income.

Donna added, "Maybe doing a budget has helped me grow up. At first, you want to fight and kick and keep your lifestyle going. Then you look at the control plan and reality really bites! I couldn't believe how much money goes into 'keeping up.' I still love looking good, but Steve and I feel like we've got a grip on spending. I know I've really done something important for myself and my family, and I can still dream."

I know you can be as successful as Donna has been. Here goes:

YOUR MONTHLY BUDGETING WORKSHEET

Month _____   Year _____

Income	Budget	Actual	YTD Budget	YTD Actual
Earned Income	$	$	$	$
Family Income				
Government Income				
Investment Income				
Retirement Income				
Self-employment Income				
Other Income				
TOTAL INCOME	$	$	$	$

Expenses

Fixed Expenses

	Budget	Actual	YTD Budget	YTD Actual
Automobile-Related	$	$	$	$
Family				
Home-Related				
Insurance				
Savings and Investments				
Taxes				
Utilities				
Other				
Total Fixed Expenses	$	$	$	$

Flexible Expenses

	Budget	Actual	YTD Budget	YTD Actual
Children	$	$	$	$
Clothing				
Contributions and Dues				
Education				
Equipment and Vehicles				
Financial and Professional Services				
Food				
Home Maintenance				
Medical Care				
Miscellaneous				
Recreation and Entertainment				
Savings and Investments				
Travel and Vacations				
Other				
Total Flexible Expenses	$	$	$	$
TOTAL EXPENSES	$	$	$	$
TOTAL INCOME LESS EXPENSES	$	$	$	$

YOUR YEARLY BUDGETING WORKSHEET

Year _____

Annual Expense	Actual Last Year	Budget This Year	Actual This Year	+/(-) Budget vs. Actual This Year
Earned Income	$ _____	$ _____	$ _____	$ _____
Family Income	_____	_____	_____	_____
Government Income	_____	_____	_____	_____
Investment Income	_____	_____	_____	_____
Retirement Income	_____	_____	_____	_____
Self-employment Income	_____	_____	_____	_____
Other Income	_____	_____	_____	_____
TOTAL ANNUAL INCOME	$ _____	$ _____	$ _____	$ _____

Expenses

Fixed Expenses

	Actual Last Year	Budget This Year	Actual This Year	+/(-) Budget vs. Actual This Year
Automobile-Related	$ _____	$ _____	$ _____	$ _____
Family	_____	_____	_____	_____
Home-Related	_____	_____	_____	_____
Insurance	_____	_____	_____	_____
Savings and Investments	_____	_____	_____	_____
Taxes	_____	_____	_____	_____
Utilities	_____	_____	_____	_____
Other	_____	_____	_____	_____
Total Fixed Expenses	$ _____	$ _____	$ _____	$ _____

Flexible Epenses

	Actual Last Year	Budget This Year	Actual This Year	+/(-) Budget vs. Actual This Year
Children	$ _____	$ _____	$ _____	$ _____
Clothing	_____	_____	_____	_____
Contributions and Dues	_____	_____	_____	_____
Education	_____	_____	_____	_____
Equipment and Vehicles	_____	_____	_____	_____
Financial and Professional Services	_____	_____	_____	_____
Food	_____	_____	_____	_____
Home Maintenance	_____	_____	_____	_____
Medical Care	_____	_____	_____	_____
Miscellaneous	_____	_____	_____	_____

YOUR YEARLY BUDGETING WORKSHEET (continued)

Annual Expenses	Actual Last Year	Budget This Year	Actual This Year	+/(-) Budget vs. Actual This Year
Recreation and Entertainment	_____	_____	_____	_____
Savings and Investments	_____	_____	_____	_____
Travel and Vacations	_____	_____	_____	_____
Other	_____	_____	_____	_____
Total Flexible Expenses	$ _____	$ _____	$ _____	$ _____
TOTAL EXPENSES	$ _____	$ _____	$ _____	$ _____
TOTAL INCOME LESS EXPENSES	$ _____	$ _____	$ _____	$ _____

FINALLY: POINTS TO REMEMBER FOR STRIVERS

Indulge yourself within reason and allow yourself the comfort of knowing that what you acquire is *enough*!

If there's a psychological trigger that impels you to buy status items to feel better about yourself, tap into its origins. Begin the process of defusing its power over you. Seek counseling if the spending urge is out of control.

Clarify your financial goals on a regular basis to figure out where those status items can fit in without causing you financial strain. There is no right or wrong financial goal as long as it is a conscious decision on your part.

Be honest about your income, expenses, and budgeting (your forecast of future income and expenses) because you're the only one who will benefit from or lament the truth.

Think of a budget as a road map that allows you to know the direction you want to go but gives you several options for how to get there. Involve everyone who is and will be affected by it.

RESOURCES FOR STRIVERS

Do you constantly find yourself living beyond your means? Do you go for risky investments but don't know where to begin with conservative ones? Do you have enough insurance? Do you have enough of a nest egg to fall back on once you retire? If you're a status seeker or an optimist, you might want to consider toning things down a bit and learn to be a bit more conservative. Give some of these books, Web sites, and other resources a try.

Books

The Budget Kit: The Common Cents Money Management Workbook, by Judy Lawrence (Dearborn Trade Publishing, 30 South Wacker Drive, Suite 2500, Chicago, IL 60606; 800-245-2665; www.dearborn.com/trade). This book and Lawrence's Web site, www.moneytracker.com, help you budget and manage your money better.

Investing Success: How to Conquer 30 Costly Mistakes and Multiply Your Wealth!, by Lynnette Khalfani, with a foreword by Charles Schwab (Advantage World Press, PO Box 452, South Orange, NJ 07079; 973-324-0034; www.advantage-worldpress.com). Explains how beginners and experienced investors can invest successfully, make fewer mistakes, and easily fix the ones they do.

The Pocket Idiot's Guide to Living on a Budget, by Peter J. Sander and Jennifer Sander (Alpha Books, 1633 Broadway, New York, NY 10019; 212-366-2000; http://us.penguingroup. com). Short and to the point, yet compelling.

Publications

Annuity Shopper (8 Talmadge Drive, Monroe Township, NJ 08831; 877-206-8141; www.annuityshopper.com). Provides updated performance on immediate, deferred, fixed, and variable annuities.

Organizations

Independent Insurance Agents and Brokers of America (127 South Peyton Street, Alexandria, VA 22314, 800-221-7917; www.iiaa.org). This association of agents not tied to selling any particular insurance company's products offers several free Consumer Education Guides on various insurance topics.

Life and Health Insurance Foundation for Education (2175 K Street, NW, Suite 250, Washington, DC 20037; 202-464-5000, ext. 106; www.life-line.org). This group is a resource for educational information about life, health, disability, and long-term-care insurance.

Web Sites

AARP.org/money. AARP, the nonprofit organization that caters to people fifty and older, has an online calculator to check whether you're saving enough for retirement. The site also has sections on credit and debt, reverse mortgages, tax aid, and legal issues, to name a few.

Banx.com. BanxQuote provides yields on savings deposits, money market accounts, and CDs bought throughout the country.

Imoneynet.com. The company provides Money Fund Report Averages and lists of the top-yielding money funds that are printed in newspapers and magazines and on databases across the United States.

Insure.com. Basic information on auto, home insurance, health, and life insurance. Consumers can also obtain instant quotes from more than two hundred insurers.

Insweb.com. Site allows you to compare quotes from a variety of insurance companies. Quotes available for auto, life, home-owners, health, term life, and more.

Mfea.com. In the retirement section you can calculate how much you'll need for retirement, and it's chock-full of advice and suggestions of other places to go for help.

CHAPTER 4

The Ostriches

Do you ever feel incapacitated by confusion, anxiety, or guilt about money, and ignore a money problem at hand, rather than deal with it?

Are you afraid to assert yourself with a financial "authority" or anyone who is handling your money, such as a spouse, parent, or broker?

Do you fear financial disaster but hand over your money to someone whom deep down you're not sure you can trust?

Dorothy Parker, renowned writer and wit, said that she thought "the most beautiful words were 'check enclosed.'" Yet when she died, her executors were shocked to find uncashed checks all over her apartment—many of them still in unopened envelopes—in dresser and desk drawers, some used as bookmarks, or tossed on a stack of magazines. Parker frequently complained about not having enough money. Although she was in control of her career and selling her work, she was out of control when it came to handling her money.

When you hear about such careless money habits, you may think, "She was foolish with money." While that may be true, the total picture is much more complicated. As you'll see, the financial personality types I'm calling Ostriches are clearly conflicted about handling their own finances but actually have excellent untapped potential to do so. As it turned out, in the midst of her financial chaos, Parker was able to get herself to a lawyer to make out a will, eventually leaving millions to her chosen heir—a favorite charity.

You may know someone who appears careless with money, or maybe you are an Ostrich who's ready to pick envelopes off the piles and finally turn your attention to putting your finances in order. I'm determined to encourage every Ostrich to focus on developing confidence to tackle money issues of any sort. You may start out feeling uncomfortable, but the only way to deal with money is to start counting it to see where you are. If you're not happy with your money situation or are afraid even to look at where you are, you will find many answers to your financial questions as you read on.

THE OSTRICH REVEALED

I read an interesting study following the events of 9/11. It reported that many survivors of the 9/11 victims discovered that their loved ones had not made adequate financial arrangements, that insurance was insufficient, that beneficiaries were not designated, and that contingency plans for spouses and children were incomplete or nonexistent. So, beyond the catastrophe of the events, there was a real financial shake-up for those survivors.

If ever I worried that we were a nation of Ostriches, it was then. I wondered how many people holding down jobs had not completed some basic steps to ensure their own and their families' financial futures.

As a financial consultant I know there are no benefits to avoiding money issues, because they don't go away, they just grow! Understanding the Ostrich provides some answers for change.

What makes an Ostrich avoid basic money issues? Many reasons. You tend to be confused, intimidated, or even embarrassed by money. If you're a classic Ostrich, you don't budget, you don't know how much you owe or how much you spend or how to keep financial records. Oddly enough, most of you are not in debt, usually pay your bills, and have a partner or relative who tends to be your financial backup. You may be an Ostrich who is embarrassed by how little you know about money and always changes the subject when it comes up. The idea of working with a financial planner is as onerous as if you'd been asked to push a boulder up Mount Fuji.

And then there are Ostriches who are proud of their indifference to money. You're likely to talk about how money bores you or how your career or family life takes too much of your time and you just can't be bothered reading stock charts. *Whenever I talk to such an Ostrich*—and there are many of you in every profession, including law, teaching, medicine, and the arts—*I'm struck with your deeply held belief that you will always survive, even though it's hard for you to deal with money on a day-to-day basis*. But I mostly get calls and e-mails from Ostriches like you, who finally realize that they've ignored their finances too long and are worried, frustrated, and ready to take action.

I've also encountered a more extreme variation of this type, who are waiting to be rescued from their money troubles. These are the White Knighters, people who not only avoid money matters as long as they can, but whose beliefs about money are out of touch with reality. The wished-for white knight can be a winning lottery number, an inheritance arriving just when it's needed most, marrying rich, or finding money in some miraculous manner.

The result of too much dreaming and too little taking care of business can be imminent financial disaster. As their finances slowly worsen, White Knighters wish someone will relieve them of their burdens, instead of acting immediately themselves to rectify the situation. Both types of Ostriches are stuck with the thorny misguided belief that they can't learn about money basics. I'm here to prove you can, finally, master money issues.

The Ostrich: Your Strengths

You're usually not consumed or driven by money. Your Money Type often includes artists, intellectuals, or people more interested in accomplishment and/or spiritual matters. As an Ostrich, *you don't keep score with money—the way a Striver or High Roller type might—but focus first on creativity, productivity, responsibility to others, and in developing good relationships.* Some Ostriches are doctors or other prosperous professionals who are so involved in their work that they resent the time they must devote to money matters.

Because you're essentially smart, when you put your mind to changing how you manage money, you will persist until you reach your goal.

The Ostrich: Your Weaknesses

As an Ostrich, you're true to your animal mascot—keeping your head in the sand while all hell breaks loose around you. What's broken loose are mounting problems you haven't taken care of—taxes or back taxes, applications for loans, figuring out how to pay for the first year of your child's college education due in six months, setting up a budget so you can find extra cash to invest. And more. All put to the side. The reasons you ignore money problems may vary, but the results are the same: Ignoring money problems doesn't make them disappear, and they don't solve themselves without your intervention. You may even put off preparing for the future because you feel you don't know how. While you worry about what's ahead, you're still stuck in the present, unable to act, not knowing what to do first and embarrassed to ask someone who does.

I get many e-mails from Ostriches who are too trusting and have handed over control of their finances to someone who's "good with money"—who may also be good at cheating you. Instead of monitoring such people, you're passive and accepting of what they say about what they've done with your money. This easy trust is based on a belief that you can't understand a financial or legal document but others can. Some Ostriches are simply overwhelmed by what they feel they cannot do and don't check out what they've been told about where their money is and how much they have. When you perceive yourself as being inadequate with money, the smallest decision triggers those feelings of doubt in you. You have to trust others because money doesn't take care of itself.

Also believing themselves inadequate with money, White Knighters not only want others to manage their money, but seek out rescuers to produce it for them. White Knighters can grow old wondering why others have all the luck and feel as if they are never singled out for good fortune. This need for the impossible dream is similar to a childlike belief in miracles. Ironically, even when a real white knight comes along, the Ostrich can be left with nothing after a few years. *Money* magazine did a story on lottery winners, checking out their financial pictures three years after their wins, and the majority of them had gone through most of their cash.

If you think of yourself as inadequate, you have a lot of Ostrich company. According to a study in 2002, "Americans in virtually every category have demonstrated their lack of financial expertise," while another study reported, "Financial literacy is the key to a fundamental personal value: achieving life goals and dreams."

I advise Ostriches all the time—people who tend to let issues about money become far more troublesome than they should be. Let me share two stories that typify how that can happen for this Money Type and show you how to embark on an effective emotional and financial turnaround.

"Life Would Be Perfect if Only Money Took Care of Itself"

Julia and Pete are in their mid-thirties and live in a comfortable Pittsburgh neighborhood with Eric, their seven-year-old son. Julia recently closed her catering business, which she ran from home for about a year after opting out of the corporate world. Not getting any new clients was more intentional than a comment on her talents. The truth is, Julia was tired of working, and she wanted a few years off to be a stay-at-home mom. But she was also uncomfortable with her growing success, especially in relation to Pete's. Pete is a full-time freelance media specialist whose work now accounts for all of their income. Most of his business, however, comes from one client, and he hasn't taken the initiative to find new ones. He makes a good living, but he finds his work unfulfilling.

For a couple who are managing, you might think they have no real problems. The irony is that both Pete and Julia are at a turning point of their own where their fears about finances could get them into trouble. As with most Ostriches, they've hit an *emotional* wall, but neither one of them can see why that is or how to change their attitudes.

After talking at length with Julia, I discovered some important information about both her and Pete. Julia is very much a modern thinker, but in many ways she has made herself into a traditional 1950s married woman who confuses being a stay-at-home mom with being passive and incompetent about money. Julia's happy to manage the household expenses, but, she said, she can't assert herself with any "financial authority" and has stopped trying.

Julia never has been motivated about making money, but she loved being creative and taking care of children. "I never had to pay for a thing until after college," she says. "My parents were secretive about money, which was something adults took care of. It didn't occur to me to think any different." But she did, and it panicked her. When Julia went into business for herself,

JULIA AND PETE'S FINANCIAL SNAPSHOT

As with most Ostriches, Julia and her husband are good at maintaining the status quo, which looks like this:

- Their annual income from Pete's business is $75,000.

- They have a mortgage. A year ago they took out a $200,000 home equity line of credit to build an addition onto their home, which they've owned since 1993, and they don't have any difficulty repaying it.

- Debt is minimal. Their credit cards are paid in full every month.

- Julia has a pension from her corporate job, and her 401(k) was rolled over into an IRA when she left to open her own business. Pete has an IRA.

- They have a 529 college plan for their son's education, and Pete's father set up an additional fund for Eric.

she was able to manage the business profitably and hired a part-time accountant to handle the details. Instead of feeling successful, she gave up her business because she was sure she'd "screw it up and lose too much." Even though she was succeeding, she was stuck with an old image of herself as "not good with money." The fearful side of her wished, "If only money could take care of itself," while the reasoning businesswoman decided to close up shop and quit while she was ahead.

To make sure I understood how "bad" she was with money, Julia gave me further examples of what she's done: Details of the home equity loan confused her to the point where she lost her ability to focus on it; she kept having to ask Pete to explain it to her. She receives an electronic financial newsletter, but she has never read it. "I deleted it the first time by accident, and now I just delete it," she said with an embarrassed laugh. She's learned the money basics, but she gets to a point where she feels "overwhelmed by the practical stuff."

Julia chooses to live uneasily with her head-in-the-sand reaction to money, while Pete is a highly functioning Ostrich who lives in his own state of denial. He earns a good living, has kept himself and Julia out of debt and is proud of it, and has financial goals, but he tends to get stuck making progress beyond basic money management, like paying bills. And then there is the issue of confronting his true feelings about money.

Pete wants to give up freelancing to go into business with a friend. So far, the career move is only talk, since Pete has yet to contact his friend for the details of what it would cost to buy into the business. Julia is worried that a change of careers would put the family in jeopardy, especially since Pete, she wrote, "would rather have $3,000 in twenties under the mattress than invest it. Life would be perfect," she said again, "if I could get Pete to cope with his fears about money and let a professional help us figure out a money plan for the future."

The more I read her note, the more I realized how much of Pete's story revolved around Julia's own relationship with money—and vice versa. Truly, theirs is a not uncommon marriage of two Ostriches stuck in two nonproductive points of view about money and deep in a financial dilemma. For Julia, it is about playing dumb, and for her husband, Pete, it is about running scared.

Pete's Ostrich tendencies are reflected in Julia's sense of urgency. "If Pete goes into business with his friend," she said, "he'll drive himself and me crazy. He has a dream about making a lot of money, which is nice, but I worry that he doesn't have the ability to run a business, which is something entirely different." She hesitated a moment and then added, "The thing is, Pete wants me to get a part-time job so he'd feel less worried about money if he changes jobs. He's been at me. But he knows I don't want to do it. I think he's using my not wanting to work as an excuse for why he hasn't done more with his friend's business. If he prefers cash under a mattress to investing it, I'm pretty sure that's not exactly the mark of a smart businessman."

Ultimately, Julia thinks a financial planner would give them the structure they need to cope better with their financial fears and would provide them with a better plan for the future. But it's a tough hurdle to clear, given Pete's attitudes now.

Stuck in the Middle

Pete is stuck. He's passionate about wanting to change his line of work, but his fear that he can't learn about money is holding him back. "I don't think at this point I could convince Pete to go to a financial planner, even to get advice about going into his own business," Julia says. "He's not trusting. It would take a lot of convincing for him to see the benefit, and I'm not sure I could convince him." Then she asked me, "How do you get a man like Pete to wake up and take charge?"

This Ostrich couple is managing so far on a day-to-day basis, but they have financial aspirations that only they can take charge of. Julia is more practical about money and more assertive than she gives herself credit for. Pete wants to go into business with a friend, and he needs both Julia's emotional and financial support—he wants her to get a part-time job to supplement their income. She worries that a man who has only rudimentary skills with money, such as paying bills, can't partner successfully in a business.

We'll see shortly how Pete and Julia can make much needed changes, but first let's take a look at Ken, whose case illustrates another typical Ostrich issue.

"I Want to Change, but Is It Too Late?"

Ken wrote to me about another problem Ostriches talk about: *being shaken awake in their forties, fifties, and sixties from a sort of financial slumber and worrying that it is too late to build up greater assets for the future.* The good news is that you can catch up, depending on when you start, how much money you want, and the amount of effort you're willing to put into making up for lost time.

This is what Ken went through. Ken was raised in a middle-class family, the child of late–Depression Era parents who were rigid about money. Everything was centered on money, mostly in a negative way. Money always was an elusive concept—the idea of investing it and growing it. Ken worked from a young age and spent all his earnings, never able to make money work for him. "My parents never helped me to understand what to

---

KEN'S FINANCIAL SNAPSHOT

Ken lists these features in his snapshot:

- His debts are manageable. The family's two credit cards have balances of $4,000 and $2,000, and the cards are used only for vacations, emergencies, and the like. "We did without them for a long time," Ken says, adding that the family always pays cash.

- Ken and Janet are paying off an $80,000 mortgage, and they have monthly car payments of $300.

- Ken has $20,000 in student loans that have been put into deferment more times than he'd like. "But then, with the girls' needs, sometimes that's all I can do," he notes.

- He and Janet both contribute to 401(k)s at work, but those retirement plans are the family's only investments.

- Janet handles the family's bills. She grew up in a home where money was always an issue, and she "learned how to juggle. She makes it work," Ken told me.

do with money to make more. They gave me a lecture and wrote out a check. They never gave me any lessons. They would point me in the direction they wanted me to use it for, which left me resentful," he says. "I was always interested in starting some sort of business, like my grandfather had, but my parents wouldn't lend me the money to start up. I wanted to be like my grandfather and get the kind of respect he got from others."

Ken never started his own business, but he is finally stabilizing his career. After job hopping through a string of building trade jobs, he went back to school to get a degree in engineering. He has been married for fifteen years, and he and his wife, Janet, have two girls.

Now that Ken is in his late forties, his financial future seems to be on the rise. Ken is looking at a promotion—he's the only one in his field at his company, and plans to increase staffing are pointing to a supervisory position for him. For the first time in his life, he feels as if he is getting somewhere, but he's afraid it's too late to learn the financial skills he needs to build for the future. "I need to learn how to invest. Master the basics of real estate. I've always been a late starter. Late finding a career. Late getting married. I'm about bad timing! There's always a gap between now and then. I can always see five years down the road, but not about tomorrow," he said. "What do I do about making more money now?"

Ken has taken the Ostrich's point of view that he's hopeless in some way about money. The evidence as it is stacked up shows that he's doing all right, that he's providing for his family, and that with a supervisory job on the horizon, he will continue to do well. Yet, Ken is still setting up boundaries and living within limitations about what he can learn and when he can learn it. This is Ostrich thinking beating up on him!

And then there's June, a White Knighter with a different story to tell.

"Who Will Rescue Me and Make My Money Dreams Come True?"

Determined from childhood to have a career, Ken is finally seeing the possibility of achieving his dream of greater financial success. June's connection to making dreams come true is different. Twenty-eight years old and married, June wrote to me at a point when she was feeling desperate about getting her finances in order. A substitute teacher who was adopted as an infant, she was thinking about whether to continue subbing or move on to a permanent job with benefits.

June's inability to decide what to do in life was reflected in a belief about herself that had been getting her into money trouble for years. It is this: "I have a strong story repeating in my head that tells me I don't have what it takes to make money," she wrote me. Rather than deal with the realities of her situation, June avoids them. She doesn't pay her bills until the warning notices arrive or collection agencies start calling. "I'd say to myself, 'We don't have the money for this,' and toss the bill in a shopping bag," she told me. "Ed, my husband, tried getting me on a disciplined payment plan, but I had a challenging time sticking to it. I kept making mistakes with my checking account and felt lost. I wish I could find a simple way out of this. My mother never went through stuff like this. She had it all done for her. I often think about that."

June told me of other wishes, too. She wishes she could win the lottery, or meet someone who would give her a lot of money, or go onstage and be discovered. She even dreams of encountering her birth mother, who, June fantasizes, will turn out to be rich and will embrace her and bail her out of her financial mess.

June later told me about a few experiences from her past that formed her belief system about herself and where money would come from. June's adoptive mother, who came from a fairly well-off family, was generally cheerful and always encouraged June to "live on the edge, be full of life" and to "not get

JUNE'S FINANCIAL SNAPSHOT

June may have taken the idea of not caring about money too seriously, and it may eventually sink her finances. Here's how:

- She has about $10,000 in unpaid medical bills, the result of an auto accident and inadequate coverage on her husband's family health care insurance.

- In addition to this debt, June owes $2,500 on a bank loan and $750 on her credit cards.

- Her husband, Ed, carries about $15,000 in debt, including delinquent taxes.

- Neither of them has savings or investment plans.

dragged down by a conventional existence, or you'll regret it." June often took care of her younger brother, who was also adopted, while her mother went off to her social engagements.

Her father's influence was the opposite. The manager of a chain supermarket, June's father was as tightfisted with money as her mother was a free spirit. The family always lived comfortably, but anything to do with money provoked an argument. Her father always fought about spending money, usually giving in to her mother's requests eventually. However, he was stingy with June. If she asked him for a bigger allowance or for spending money, he'd refuse. Her mother usually went to bat for her, and sometimes that would start an argument between her parents.

June then summed up her youth: "I was responsible for so much of my brother's care, while my mother went off, having fun," June said. "And then I saw how well my mother was taken care of, and I guess that was what I wanted, too. When I got older, I didn't want to be responsible for anything or anyone else."

As June said in true Ostrich form, "We've got dreams. The bills can wait." The other half of the "we" she refers to is Ed, her husband of four years, a man ten years her senior. Ed is a sound engineer at a recording studio and is trying to put together a production company. He's having trouble finding start-up funding. June substitute-teaches at local schools one to three days a week, while dreaming of being a singer and working on one of Ed's projects.

At a friend's urging, June applied for a sales and distribution job that she clinched. She's excited about it because it will double her present income and provide some stability. Her friend at the company told June that June's supervisor earns at least $100,000 a year. "This number seems far out of reach to me," June says, "but it's time for me to work with someone who actually earns that much. Maybe I can learn something and be like her. Maybe it'll get us out of this money pit."

Giving Up on Yourself and Giving Up on Money

When June thinks about money and growing up, her memories focus on how little she felt she got in return for being a good daughter. Her mother may have told her to grab life, but June was unable to do that. Instead, she seems to stroll through life, letting things happen to her, while dreaming for more. June essentially describes herself as a Cinderella, deprived and denied love, and still waiting to be rescued by her prince, the white knight. Her husband, Ed, with his Ostrich tendencies, is so far not the redeemer she seeks. Ed hasn't been able to do what June's father did for her mother, that is, take care of her and relieve her of all financial obligations. Instead, Ed's own self-destructive tendencies with finances affect June and add to her burden and her lack of confidence with money.

Let's go back and see how Julia, Pete, Ken, and June can shift their thinking to improve their relationships with money.

MAKING CHANGES: THE EMOTIONAL PATH

Because Julia and Pete demonstrate two different Ostrich tendencies, I'll take them one at a time. Money issues confuse and overwhelm Julia, and sending me an e-mail is the closest she has gotten to making an effort to understand what she and Pete are going through. She knows Pete needs her emotional and financial support, and she's conflicted in a number of ways that she hasn't yet resolved. I've advised so many Ostriches like Julia, and I know that it's possible to pull out of that dreamlike state of wishing "if only . . ." and face reality with real optimism.

Julia's chief objections about dealing with money are that "there's too much to know and too many variables about money to digest." "Frankly," she said, "I'd rather not deal with them." Not surprisingly, she's insecure about what the future holds, which only creates more stress about financial issues. She's right: There *is* a lot to know, and everyone gets baffled or stymied by some aspect of the financial world, from tax laws to balancing a checkbook. Yet what many Ostriches forget—Julia included—is how they have been successful, and they don't give themselves credit for what they *do* know. Being an Ostrich and dismissing the entire subject doesn't help you learn, though. Nor does playing dumb. This, psychologists tell me, is Julia's real stumbling block. What is it all about?

Playing Dumb: Never a Smart Money Strategy

Although men play dumb on occasion, many more women have been raised to believe that they should, could, or will be incompetent or less competent than men about money. Some women are still taught that if they are smart about money, men will be intimidated by them, and that will threaten any intimate relationship. So it is with Julia. Julia is worried that her success with her own business might show up her husband, who is now considering being an entrepreneur. She may be surrendering her success so that her husband, she believes, will appear stronger and more capable. It's an old-fashioned notion, and in this case it's undermining Julia and Pete's financial future. But something else is going on.

Julia has been infantilized for most of her whole life, first by her parents and then by herself. She talks about how she deals with money in a childish way that belies her real abilities. If she plays the dumb little girl, not ready for the grown-up world of responsibility, she knows someone will be there to take care of her. In typical Ostrich style, she's in the habit of laughing at herself with embarrassment about "accidentally" deleting financial information or glazing over when she needs to know some point about the mortgage, and turning her actions into a joke. This is how she presents herself to Pete, but he's had enough: He doesn't think she's funny anymore. He wants her to grow up, and he'll still love her, but she's not sure of it.

Try this shift in thinking:

The fact is, playing dumb is a defense. Julia would probably rather cry because she fears not understanding finances and losing her husband if she does. If you catch yourself playing dumb when you're not, my suggestion for you, as it is for Julia, is to step out of the past and into the future you truly long for. You shouldn't be afraid to face what you know and put what you know about money into action. It can only help you financially, not hurt you. Playing dumb might have been more acceptable at some other point in your life, but not now. And not at any critical juncture in your life.

Understand that you're a grown-up, that you're not a baby anymore, and that it's not cute to play dumb and hide behind the pose. You *can* learn, and it's all right to do so at a pace with which you are comfortable. You don't have to learn everything overnight or even in six months. No one does, not even the great wizards of finance that you read about all the time. The point is that you can change! Take it one step at a time, one item at a time.

As I advised Julia to keep the newsletters she gets and read half one day, the other half the next day, so would I advise you to pick a subject about money that you know will help you right now—for example, how to construct a budget. Check the Strivers chapter to see what actually goes into making a budget work for you. Make a list of questions that occur to you about the information, and be willing to ask someone for the answers or look them up. Little by little, you will free yourself of an outmoded and totally self-sabotaging perception of yourself as "not someone who is on top of money" and finally grow. The evidence in Julia's life, for example, tells her that she can manage a household and she has managed a small but profitable business. These are positive truths about her competence. Once she begins telling herself she's able to deal with money and accepts it, she'll be fully on the road to change. The same is true for you. Believe in your ability to deal with money and you will.

Pete's Emotional Path issue is different.

Revealing Your Money Secrets to Each Other: Freeing Yourself to Go On!

Pete's core emotional problem is his inability to confront or admit his money secrets. One secret is that he fears failing or looking like a failure, and the other is that he wants more from his wife, who, he feels, is failing him. This may be an issue that is getting you stuck, too.

Are you at a point in your life where a career opportunity has presented itself, but you worry about making it real? Do you, like Pete, have a friend or associate who has had a meteoric success in this business, and you'd like to duplicate it? But are you afraid to make the move? Pete has frozen, and delays and avoids learning the details of the deal because he's afraid to try anything experimental—although he'd like to, "if only. . . ." As Julia told me, "Pete will take a lot of risks, but he's not willing to take the risk of making a huge deal with his friend." She called it "an ego thing." Meanwhile, he blames Julia for not getting a job in advance of his calling his friend. Pete needs every bit of Julia's assurance, but not this way. Is this situation too familiar to you?

Try this shift in thinking:

Are you, like Pete and Julia, not only hiding from your money, but hiding from each other? You need to sit down with your partner in life and talk out what you're going through, no holds barred. When you're frightened about change, you don't want to admit what you don't know about money—whether it's in relation to a potential business deal with a friend or discussing matters with a financial advisor. This is common with Ostriches and something that can be understood and managed. It means that you and your spouse or partner must face your expectations of each other! It means that you need to reveal your secret and accept that it isn't weak to ask a spouse to help out financially—either so that you can pursue an opportunity or to ease your financial burdens.

First, let's look at career change and how it will affect your finances: If you're over thirty, you really must make informed decisions about any serious career change. If you're married, the decision must be unanimous—you and your spouse must agree that you will make this change and be able to prepare for financial changes. If you are on your own, obviously, you have no one to answer to but yourself. Next, you must decide whether you want to take on a career opportunity that excites or interests you. If, like Pete, the deal involves a friend, you must know if you feel too competitive with your friend to work with him and make the business flourish. If personality and competition are not the issues, you need to check how much and what is expected of you. Either seize the opportunity or walk away and stop blaming your spouse or partner for your not taking the risk. And if you're the one seeking a career change, know what you need in the way of financial and emotional support from a spouse or partner. Pete, for example, feels that Julia doesn't have the right to criticize his lack of risk taking because she's unemployed. Doesn't he have a family to support? If he wants the career opportunity, he must let Julia know how important it is for her to contribute some income to the household while he gets his bearings in a new business.

Next, go deeper into your relationship with your spouse or partner. If you want your spouse to get a job or a better-paying job, is this desire hiding another secret: a wish that your spouse would grow up. You are two adults, possibly with a family and big financial responsibilities. Would you like your spouse to jump in more willingly and get a job, to ease the way for you? In Pete's case, if he doesn't go into business with his friend, at least he feels Julia's really on his side and finally no longer babied. No matter where your aversion to risk comes from, it's certainly made worse by a spouse dumping all the financial responsibilities on you and then expressing concern about your future.

Both of you may be scared to take a good long look at the future, but you'll never get out of your rut when one of you can't look seriously at the present and the other is too afraid of what's to come. Once you confront your spouse about your secret money issues, you will feel as if you have a real partner. And you need a real partner to make your next move. It can only help strengthen the marriage when both of you know the financial facts of life and you both accept them!

Are You Asking for Bad Directions and Taking Them?

Ken's fate was growing up with parents whose own early years were affected by a global financial crisis and a serious daily struggle to survive. That they eventually had money during their adult years and begrudged Ken money and support is his misfortune. Many Ostriches are children of parents who denied them money and dangled in front of them what they "one day might have." Along the way, such Ostriches have suffered from real doubt about ever having and deserving money or making smart money decisions. They become used to asking for advice from people who will keep them down or control them—and tell them why they shouldn't have money. Ken was a bit tougher than that, but he wasn't quite sure that he was. He worries that it's too late.

Try this shift in thinking:

Just because others once held you down financially and you continued the behavior by holding yourself back doesn't mean you have to carry on depriving or cheating yourself. Even if your parents withheld money from you at one time, understand you don't have to be that passive child anymore. You can get into gear to get what you want—and catch up financially in some measure.

Ken, for example, really internalized his parents' negativity, not only about money in general, but in the belief that if he had money, he'd mishandle it. When he asked for their help in business, they turned him down and refused to release the accounts kept for him. As a result, Ken put off his decisions, but each one has paid off for him. He may have jumped from job to job because of the nature of the construction business, but he was always employed. He went back to school, financed the loans, and married a woman who is emotionally supportive and handles the bills competently, and now he seeks a more solid financial future.

Yes, Ken and you can do some financial catching up, but you have an emotional task to fulfill first. You need to forgive yourself for not being more assertive about doing what you wanted to do and thinking of your parents as the only source of money with which you could have done it. Think about how you speak about your parents and what they did or didn't give you. Do you talk about them in a way that shows how passive you were, such as by thinking, "They didn't give me lessons" about handling money? Have you given your parents a lot of power for leading you down a path with too many dead ends? Or have you, like Ken, found your way out, better later than not?

Here's another factor to consider. Let's go back to Ken's case again to help you find the points of similarity for you. He's been on the slow track because he had problems deciding what to do with his life. He was in his late thirties before he got his engineering degree. He just didn't think about a career before that, he said. He worried now and then about his future, and hoped it would all be okay. He's not in serious debt and has barely planned for retirement, and now that he's almost fifty, he's pulled his head out of the sand. If this sounds like your situation emotionally, you need to understand why you allowed yourself to stay on the slow track and forgive yourself for this seeming weakness.

Right decisions find their time. When people reach their forties and fifties and look back, they can get depressed about where they've been and say, "This is what I should have done," or "What have I done!" Let the past go!

When you accept who you are, you'll give yourself some real psychological strength by acknowledging everything you've accomplished. You need to stop beating yourself up for decisions made later rather than sooner. Put down the whip, and use the energy to pat yourself on the back for your accomplishments.

And what you've accomplished is probably a lot. It's a sad waste of a good life to walk around feeling as if you've done nothing, dragging along your parents' warning that you can't have the money. By forgiving yourself, you can fully believe in a more positive picture of yourself and then turn to the problem at hand: making more money for the future.

Ken awakened later in the game, but he's still got a good chance. And so do you!

Are You Giving Yourself a Chance to Rescue Yourself?

If any trait marks the White Knighter, it is that childlike attachment to rescue fantasies. Who does not want to be handed a life of ease and feel rewarded just for being who they are and just for being alive? How many of us get this? Very few. And being handed a gift of money, splendor, and access to whatever and whomever you wish does not always bode well. Consider the life of the late Princess Diana.

Many people who have had childhoods full of problems or hardship fight their way out and learn to build lives that leave deprivation behind. They've rescued themselves, and it is never easy. You give yourself a chance to rescue yourself, though, when you give up the image that you are living as a victim, not a victor. When you think like a victim, you become indecisive, careless, and immature about handling the most basic obligations—paying the utility bill before threats of the power being turned off, for example. Tossing unopened bills in a shopping bag is just not cute. Such behavior keeps you stuck in the past, feeling put upon. Do you do the same thing?

Furthermore, an unrealistic approach to handling money will always put a dent in your relationship with a spouse or partner. In June's case, she feels guilty that they're so far behind, partially because of her debts, her erratic earnings, and her attitude about money. However, she told me, she knows both she and Ed with their Ostrich tendencies are responsible for their financial plight.

This is the time to start acting like a victor. Take action that shows you're allowing yourself to grow up. This is personal rescue at its best. You need to learn how to believe in yourself as worthy of having more, and not destroy your chances for achieving your dreams and your goals—for real. How do you begin?

Try this shift in thinking:

White Knighters are emotional types and still believe in magic and depending on others or on fate. When magic rules your life a little too much, you're in trouble, unless you're Harry Potter. Instead, make your own magic by understanding the difference between goals and dreams.

Wishing for money usually gets you nothing but more frustration. What can help you is knowing the difference between having a dream and making a goal come true. When you change from wishing to acting, you really make miracles happen by your own efforts. Every small success in making a goal come true will build a sense of self-determination and competence.

My sense of June is that she knows more about managing money than she wants to admit. What about you? June keeps creating situations where she will force her husband, Ed, to take care of her. Yet he's too much of an Ostrich to give her what she needs. Are you acting in a similar way with a spouse or partner? Is this person unable to fulfill your dreams? If so, this could truly be your lucky break. In June's case, Ed's money issues have forced her to take action and take a potentially better-paying job.

Next, keep dreaming, but distinguish between a dream and a goal. A *dream* is a picture of something you want. This can be something that's possible, requiring a leap of faith. A dream is raw and emotion-based. You have a dream to be an entrepreneur and become successful. Or your dream is impossible, such as wanting to go into partnership with Warren Buffett. Then there is a *goal*: an objective that you can make real by constructing a plan, giving it a timeline, and following through to make it happen. The satisfaction you get from accomplishing a goal further inspires you to keep going. How much do you want to fulfill that goal? This is your trigger to get you into action.

When you begin relinquishing a dependency on others and begin taking action on your goals, you will become more self-sufficient and smarter about mastering money.

MAKING CHANGES: THE FINANCIAL PATH

As an Ostrich, you've underestimated your money management skills for too long! Until now, you ducked from full financial responsibility, and if you've learned any lesson, it is that money issues don't disappear or solve themselves. Many of you entrusted your finances to someone who was "good with money" and, rather than being protected, perhaps found yourself either controlled or even taken advantage of. I know you've had enough of either situation.

How can you change? Start fighting the inertia and apathy syndrome that your type suffers from. Nothing transforms your financial picture more than when you energize, take action, and face the light! I want to assure you that you can take charge of your finances, do it easily, and begin to gain real confidence in managing money!

My goal is to inspire you to set up effective money management plans, which I've tailored to complement your Ostrich personality. Getting these plans working for you is easier than you imagine. I know your Money Type has a great ability to turn your money picture around once you commit to taking the first step to help yourself. Taking this first step out of the dark is the key to your success.

Preparing Yourself for Painless and Surefire Financial Changes

Let me begin by asking you a few questions:

1. *Can you shake up the status quo?* Look at your life right now and see how much better it could be if you were managing your financial problems. The status quo is telling you that doing nothing returns nothing on your investment of time and effort, and simply delays the day of reckoning.

2. *Can the status quo shake you out of your reverie?* I know it can. Let me tell you about a formerly confirmed Ostrich type who swore she'd never figure out how to deal with money and who inadvertently proved herself wrong. Hers is a life-changing true story.

Kitty first contacted me a few months after her husband's premature death, seeking advice on what to do first. She told me that Todd had always taken care of their money "for most of the big stuff" for the twenty years of their marriage. That is, Todd handled the mortgage, investments, insurance, and so forth, and Kitty paid for utilities and food, and had her own checking account. She worked as a paralegal for a large law firm, and her husband had his own small business, which had always done well enough for them. Although he was a Squirrel Money Type—tending more to being frugal and preferring saving over spending—Todd had a weakness: the stock market. He spent at least an hour a day following the trends and talking to his broker.

Four years before Todd died, Kitty met an investment counselor at her company's Christmas party and, acting against type, decided to hire her. "Fran was highly recommended, and even though I barely understood what she did, I trusted her. She said the minimum she'd start with was five thousand dollars," Kitty said. "I knew Todd would hit the roof, but I thought, maybe I'll double my investment and surprise him." Kitty never told Todd about the money and, true to her Ostrich personality, tossed the monthly statements from the counselor, *unopened*, into a box on the top shelf of her closet. She soon after changed jobs and rarely spoke to Fran, except to lie and say she was "okay with the investments." Kitty was still afraid to see where her $5,000 had gone.

When Todd died, Kitty had months of bills and other documents to sort out. "I was overwhelmed," she said. "I didn't know where to begin. What needed to be transferred to me. What could be cashed in. How to find all of Todd's assets. And I was terrified to open the forty-seven statements from Fran." When Kitty contacted me for the second time, she'd just gotten the latest one. After carrying the statement around in her handbag all day and looking at it with dread, Kitty finally tore it open. The balance on her original $5,000 account was now $29,000!

"I had an instinct that Fran knew her stuff," Kitty wrote me. "I was just hoping my investment wouldn't be a total loss. I know I didn't do anything to make the money grow and that it was completely passive on my part. But strangely enough, this success made me feel as if I could deal with money better than I had been. I made a list of everything I had to sort through from Todd—the house, my son's tuition at college, taxes—and started on them alphabetically. I don't like doing the math, but I sit at my desk with a calculator at least an hour a day and do it. I realized it was scarier to put myself in jeopardy with a son to raise than to deal with money and just face it!"

You may not have a stash of unopened envelopes yielding good news, but you can take Kitty's true story as a cautionary tale: When you shake up the status quo by taking action, even an hour at a time, you will always come out ahead!

3. *If you could handle money in a way that gives you a new sense of freedom and accomplishment, would you do it?* Believe me when I say there's no downside to getting a grip on your finances and finally feeling a sense of peace about managing money. I've helped thousands of Ostriches awaken from their financial slumber and become believers in their own ability to manage money with a super-simple turnaround plan, which follows shortly.

My extensive experience with Ostriches is that you don't or, more likely, won't go to a financial advisor on a regular basis. One visit is pointless—an ongoing relationship to discuss your finances is essential and probably not something you would be willing to do. (Julia and Pete's story is a perfect example of this.) A good alternative is to set yourself up on a number of automatic systems, where you don't have to make any effort beyond signing up. You automatically do the right thing for yourself, as opposed to automatically doing nothing and getting more and more into serious trouble.

I'll list a number of solutions for you shortly, but first you need to know what you may not know about your money now.

What to Do First: Get Your Big Financial Picture and Then Focus In

Okay, let's say it right here: Yes, it may be a little unsettling to finally deal with the many aspects of your financial life that you've been putting off, but you can do it. The trick is to figure out what you need to know about your money in a number of key categories and not worry about how you *feel* about sorting out the solutions. For now, put any doubts aside ("I'll never be able to do this!"), and jump in.

As many psychologists would advise: Do what is in your best interest and not what your feelings tell you. It's in your best interest to get your money in order, so do not surrender to thoughts such as, "I'm not in the mood to think about how we'll pay for our son's college tuition—that's eight years away" or, "It's too depressing to make out a will." My suggestion for you is to make a list of where your money is right now and what you most have to address. Investing? Insurance? Wills? Paying your bills? Setting up a retirement fund? Paying for future college tuitions? Pulling money together for a down payment on a house?

I just got an e-mail from an Ostrich couple who were married for three years and decided they wanted to buy a house and start a family. They'd spent all their money on a high-rent apartment and had nothing in the bank for a down payment. This is a double Ostrich dilemma where both people avoided future planning and thought there was "always time enough to save for that." Your interests, needs, and financial situation can change all of a sudden. Instead of allowing a financial crisis to erupt, be prepared. And do it automatically.

Doing What Comes Automatically—Setting Up Easy Services and Plans That Do the Work for You

The best financial plan for you Ostriches is to get the money out of your hands and save it, invest it, or use it toward paying your bills. Once you know what your short- and long-range goals are and you have income coming in, you can sign up for many automatic plans that will, as Kitty, the secret investor, would say, "do the math" for you. There are a number of automatic plans, and they are:

Automatic Investment Plans

Automatic savings plans, or what I call AIPs, are great to sign up for. All mutual funds will allow AIPs to take money automatically out of your checking or savings account every month and deposit it into the mutual fund of your choice. For example, TIAA-CREF (800-223-1200 or www.tiaa-cref.org) will allow you to deposit as little as $50 a month into their mutual funds. This allows you to track the stock, bond, real estate, or international markets with minimal fund expenses and no commission. This is a classic winning strategy for an Ostrich. You tend to think you need to accumulate large amounts of money, perhaps several thousands of dollars, before you can even start investing. Therefore, you let even small amounts of money pile up uninvested.

Savings Bonds and Annuities

You can sign up for U.S. savings bonds through payroll deduction plans or, if your employer doesn't offer such a plan, you can go directly to the U.S. Treasury (Web site http://treasurydirect.gov) and arrange for $25 or $50 or whatever you wish to be automatically deducted from a checking account into a savings bond. Again you're saving money. Here's more good news for Ostriches regarding automatic investments—you only have to sign up once, and then the account is handled for you.

Another step you can take to have money automatically invested for you is in the form of an annuity, which is an insurance wrapper around an investment. In addition to term and cash value life insurance policies, insurance companies sell annuities. Although they are issued by life insurance companies, annuities work differently from cash value or term insurance policies. Annuities pay a regular stream of income while you live, usually after you retire, in contrast to life insurance, which pays your beneficiaries a lump sum when you die. Annuities also provide the advantage of tax-deferred compounding on the investment portion of the account.

So, a fixed annuity is kind of like a CD (certificate of deposit, purchased through a bank), and a variable annuity is like a mutual fund where you can pick stocks or bonds or cash or what you like. And your principal is growing tax-deferred because it's in this insurance wrapper, all administered by an insurance company.

I'm not an Ostrich type, but I do take advantage of automatic annuities that make sense to me to add to my holdings. For example, every month I put in a certain amount of money into an American Express annuity, held by an American Express insurance company. The plan is conservative and pays a fixed 4 percent interest, which compounds tax-deferred. American Express invests the money in, say, bonds that yield 6 percent interest, pay me and other annuity holders 4 percent interest, and keep the difference.

I charge the amount to my credit card and get frequent flyer miles for the charge, another bonus. The money adds up. American Express will actually project how much I'll earn at this rate of savings and at this rate of interest in ten, fifteen, or twenty years or by the time I reach retirement age. In fact, by the time I retire, this account will yield several hundred thousand dollars that I wouldn't otherwise have had. Pretty good.

Dividend Reinvestment Plans

These plans are highly recommended for any Ostrich who wants to own stock and make the process as painless as possible. It's very simple: You buy stocks, the plan then reinvests your dividends automatically, and you profit. This is how it could add up for you, with very little effort after signing up and making out your first check. If you start with two shares of, for example, ExxonMobil, which today is about $40 a share, you've made an $80 investment. When the stock pays dividends, they add up and automatically buy more shares for you. Then, on top of that, you can agree to an optional cash purchase, which is a way to increase your investment automatically above your initial $80. This plan takes a set amount, say, another $25 a month, out of your checking account. Now, without any effort on your part, you're buying more shares of ExxonMobil, which pump more dividends, which compound as the stock grows.

My caveat here is to choose *conservative high-quality stocks for this plan.*

There are two Web sites where you can sign up for this plan. One is called DirectInvesting.com. Another source is Money paper.com, where you can sign up for 1,300 different investment plans—with no commissions. In the meantime, during your working or even retirement years, you're building up a nest egg and overcoming your investment inertia. (Check the Appendix for details.)

Sign Up for Account Aggregation

If you ever wished you could monitor all your accounts and financial activity from *one* central Web site, instead of going from one account to another, account aggregation makes your wish come true. Ostriches will appreciate this no-fee service, which is offered by banks or brokerage firms. Sign up, and you get one online access point on the Web, where you track where your money is going and how it's accumulating. You can monitor, for example, your bank accounts, brokerage accounts, credit card activity and payments, and frequent flyer programs. Another simple, automatic solution for you!

College Funds

Ostriches write to me all the time about the upcoming "college tuition payment crisis." The problem is usually occasioned by having a sixteen-year-old planning for college, while you have not yet begun to put money into a fund to pay for it. Ideally, a college fund where you'd contribute $50 or $100 a month should be opened when your child is three years of age and no older than six. One such fund is a 529 College Savings Plan, named after the section of the Internal Revenue Service code that authorized it, and operative in all fifty states. There are two varieties: The older is called a prepaid tuition plan, through which participating state residents contribute a fixed amount of money for tuition to a state school, guaranteeing that the full tuition will be saved by the time a child enters college. The newer version is an investment program, similar to a 40l(k) retirement plan.

Here are a few encouraging notes on the 529 plan. Unlike other college savings vehicles, you can contribute a lot of money to it, to a maximum of as much as $269,000 in some states. Also, in some states, the plan matches part of your contribution. Some states require a minimum amount of time before you can make a withdrawal, while others offer accounts that invest only in certificates of deposit. Fees and expenses vary, too. Check with your state for rules and regulations about this fund and how to report the contributions to the IRS. And check with savingsforcollege.com, an award-winning Web site that has all the information you need on the 529 plan as well as other plans to compare it with.

The Coverdell Education Savings Account is a newer type of account that was created as part of the Taxpayer Relief Act of

1997. It used to be called the Education IRA, but the name was changed. This account allows you to save up to $2,000 a year per child under the age of eighteen to help pay educational expenses, such as tuition, fees, books, and room and board, and applies to both private and religious secondary schools and colleges and for tuition for about 771 foreign schools. So, for example, if you invest $2,000 a year and earn 8 percent interest, in fifteen years you'll end up with about $58,000 tax-free dollars.

COLLEGE COSTS AND SAVINGS NEEDS WORKSHEET

Step 1: Estimate Your Child's College Costs

Enter the Following Information	Example	Your Child
1. Your Child's Age	2	
2. Years Until College	16	
3. Current Annual College Cost of Preferred School	$22,533	
4. Inflation Factor (see Table A)	2.18	
5. Anticipated Annual College Cost (Multiply line 3 by line 4)	$ 49,121.00	
6. Total Cost of College (Multiply line 5 by the number of college years planned)	$196,487.00	
7. Estimated Amount of Future Income, Loans, Work-Study Income, and Other Sources of College Financing	$ 50,000	
8. Net Cost of College (Subtract line 7 from line 6)	$ 146,487	

Table A: College Inflation Factor

Years to College	1	2	3	4	5	6	7	8	9
Inflation Factor	1.05	1.1	1.16	1.22	1.28	1.34	1.41	1.48	1.55
Years to College	10	11	12	13	14	15	16	17	18
Inflation Factor	1.63	1.71	1.8	1.89	1.98	2.08	2.18	2.29	2.41

COLLEGE COSTS AND SAVINGS
NEEDS WORKSHEET (continued)

	Example	Your Child

Step 2: Calculate Your Regular Investment Amount

9. Investment Factor — 29.18 — ___
   (Enter the appropriate factor from Table B)

10. Annual Investment Amount — $5,020 — ___
    (Divide line 8 by line 9)

11. Monthly Investment Account — $418 — ___
    (Divide line 10 by 12)

12. Quarterly Investment Amount — $1,255 — ___
    (Divide line 10 by 4)

Years to College	Inflation Factor
1	1.07
2	2.21
3	3.42
4	4.72
5	6.11
6	7.59
7	9.17
8	10.86
9	12.66
10	14.58
11	16.64
12	18.83
13	21.17
14	23.67
15	26.34
16	29.18
17	32.23
18	35.47

But if it's years later and you haven't put aside enough money, don't give up. A small college fund you start now may not pay for all four years of college, but it could go a long way toward preventing panic. Chances are, you won't be rescued from the funding problem by your child getting a full scholarship—it could happen, but we need to get real and begin solving the problem for you in some practical way.

Putting yourself on automatic pilot again can deflect some of the expenses.

Before you become discouraged and convinced you could never amass a large enough sum, realize that you can take many steps today to make college education a reality for your children tomorrow. Despite the obstacles, millions of people finance their children's college education, and I want to make sure you're one of them!

Let's begin by "microinvesting," which lets you put aside very small amounts of money over a long period to reach a goal. Here, your two automatic microinvestment funds are in the area of college savings. I recommend you investigate BabyMint and Upromise, which are newer innovations in the area of college savings. These two vehicles can change your mind about easy financial investing.

Both BabyMint.com and Upromise.com are easy sites to use and benefit from. You register with their services for free, and when you purchase items from participating retailers and manufacturers, you get *up to a 20 percent rebate* on everyday purchases made through such retailers as Wal-Mart, Toys "R" Us, the Sharper Image, Crate & Barrel, Pizza Hut, Macy's, McDonald's, and the Gap, or you get a rebate when you buy products from popular brands like Huggies, Kellogg's, and Keebler. The results are like getting free air miles when you use a credit card. But in this case, actual dollars are going into a savings plan for a college fund. For example, if you bought a gift at the Sharper Image for $100, they'll contribute 8 percent of the sale or $8 into your college savings plan—and it costs you nothing. There are thousands of companies participating in these plans, and you can find stores and products that fit your lifestyle and shop and save for the future at the same time!

You can also save with Upromise points when you buy or refinance your home. These rebates can be automatically tracked and deposited in your 529 plan or Coverdell account. Upromise savings can be deposited in plans sponsored by Fidelity and Smith Barney, while BabyMint rebates can be deposited in any 529 plan or Coverdell account.

Automatic Retirement Funds

If you don't have kids to send to college, but you are thinking about retirement funds and you like the idea of automatic rebates, then NestEggz.com is tailored for you. It operates exactly like BabyMint and Upromise, but your rebate money is routed into a retirement savings account of your choice, or you can arrange to get the money rebated in a lump sum. For Ostriches like you who may leave additional retirement funding sources until too late, I encourage you to sign up now. It couldn't be easier. There are no fees, and every time you shop, money is automatically put into an account you will be glad you opened one day. This plan can help divert disaster down the road.

With NestEggz, you can direct your rebates into an IRA, mutual fund account, money market account, or virtually any other retirement savings plan except a 401(k), which can receive contributions only through your employer.

While you shop, retailers will contribute rebates in a range between 2 and 20 percent of your total purchase. Your earnings are collected and stored in your account until you accrue what NestEggz calls Bucks, or specifically, a $25 Bucks minimum in your account. At the end of the month, they convert these earnings into dollars and deposit them into your retirement savings plan. Or you can choose to receive rebates on a monthly basis when your balance reaches a minimum of $25.

Making Up for Lost Time

Some Ostriches are part of "the Catch-Up Generation," often looking back at what they didn't do to make their financial life easier for themselves and unsettled by fears of money troubles in the future. Of all the questions I get from Ostriches, the ones that I hear most frequently are reflections of these fears, which are variations of "How do I make up for twenty or thirty or even forty years of not investing . . . of not saving?" Or, "I'm fifty-five, and I have no retirement plan. When I think about the next ten years, I panic!" My answer is that it's possible to make up for *some* of that lost time. This depends on how much you need, how much you have to invest, and when you need the money.

As an Ostrich, nothing mobilizes you to action faster than an imminent disaster or a looming financial goal, such as college tuition or retirement. I've seen Ostriches wake up in time to pull themselves out of a crisis and shine in an area where they mistakenly believe they are least competent: managing money. Most of all, however, making up for some of that lost time requires real risk taking and being attentive to your investments. Any action you take will make a huge difference—and keep your head out of the sand. If the idea of high-risk investing makes you queasy, seek the assistance of a financial counselor who can help you work through your emotional concerns. You'll simply have to make a choice: take action by taking more risks or do nothing and watch the sands shift around you.

Here's my suggestion to start making up for lost time: *Be more aggressive in your investing.* The further away you are from when you need the money for the goal, the more aggressive you should be. Give yourself time for the investment to pay off. If you have to pay a hefty tuition bill next month, you have no time for a high-risk investment to work out. But with five years of investment time, you have a reasonable horizon.

What to invest in? Junk bonds have been doing well recently, getting yields of 8 or 9 percent. Junk bonds, remember, are high-yield bonds that are issued by corporations with less than investment-grade ratings, and are either on their way up or on their way down—on their way far up, you hope. Junk bonds are more volatile moment to moment, but you have a much better chance to realize a big gain. High-yield bonds come with higher risk. You don't have to buy individual junk bonds, but you can invest in junk bond mutual funds. Since the U.S. economy is doing well with relatively few companies defaulting, you have a fighting chance to profit.

Other higher-risk stocks are in biotechnology, technology, and Internet stocks. In 2004, Google went public and soared from $85 to $200 a share. It was a risky stock and not guaranteed to soar, but it did.

IT'S NEVER TOO LATE TO PLAN FOR INVESTING!

If you're an Ostrich of fifty-five or older and a "last chance" retirement planner, think either ultra-aggressive or ultra–financial reorganization.

On the aggressive side: There's some good news, since the IRS now has a "catch-up" contribution plan to compensate for missed savings opportunities, and you can still take advantage of the new maximums. Since 2002, the maximum you could contribute for 401(k)s, 403(b)s, and 457 plans was $22,000, seen as $11,000 for a regular contribution and $11,000 for the catch-up. The amount has risen in $2,000 increments until maxing out at $30,000 in 2006. If you don't have any of these plans, open an IRA (individual retirement account) or Keogh plan and contribute as much as you can.

On the ultra–financial reorganization side: Save and invest more aggressively. Do this by slashing expenses to free up cash to invest so you can meet your financial goal. Start moonlighting. Delay retirement by a few years to build up your funds.

Getting on Track from Your Twenties to Your Sixties and Up

To help you stay on your toes so you can deal with immediate money issues as well as more specific needs as you get older, I've created a breakdown of financial highlights and sorted them by twenty-year periods. I know Ostriches tend to malinger, so I want to prevent your saying at fifty or sixty years old, "I wish I'd put money away for a retirement fund when I started working," or, "I wish I'd started investing sooner," or, "Who knew I'd ever worry about making out a will?" I've chosen three of many possible financial areas for you to focus on per twenty years—areas where Ostriches get into most trouble. Of course, you should also set up regular savings plans, be sure you have the right insurance coverage, and set up college funds for your kids at every age.

These are both reminders and guidelines so that you can begin to catch up on what you've been avoiding or unsure of, and prepare properly for the future.

For Ostriches of Any Age

Recent statistics show that the personal savings rate for Americans is at its lowest since the Great Depression of the 1930s, and I'm sure that Ostriches are prominent among the types not saving. Reasons vary as to why you don't save regularly—for example, living paycheck to paycheck and not having a surplus to save, or not knowing which savings plan is best and discarding savings as an option.

Start saving: Savings accounts may not yield the highest interest, but they do something more important: *Savings can quickly provide a reserve in case of a crisis or when you're in need of a temporary cushion, or to fund a future financial goal.* Investigate interest rates of savings plans and start small. "Find" the cash every week to bank. For example, if you've paid off a loan, pay the same amount (or not less than half) to yourself instead. As an Ostrich, you've probably gotten used to the rhythm of paying this bill, so continue paying it, but benefit by saving the cash. And do what 56 percent of Americans do as a habit: Toss spare change into a jar every night, count it up, and bank it at the end of every few months. Dollars add up.

Get financial advice: Your financial knowledge begins now. Give yourself a chance to learn, and do it slowly, step by step. No one learns everything about finances in a glance! It takes me a lot of time and effort to read and digest material, too.

Sit down with a spouse or partner, broker, or financial advisor, start at the top of your list, and say, "I'd like to review my finances. I don't understand what's going on, and I want to start learning what I need to know." Or, if this applies to you, as it does to many couples sharing financial responsibilities, "You keep telling me not to worry about what we've got, but it's important for me to know *this*." You don't have to get all the information in one sitting. Depending on whom you are talking to and what your priorities are, your questions could be framed like these or contain these ideas:

- What are our largest investments, and how much are they worth?
- If you own your home: What is it worth in this market?
- If anything happened to your spouse or partner, could you stay in that house, or would you have to sell and move to a smaller place?
- What's in your spouse's or partner's will? Do you know the provisions and understand them? In fact, does your spouse or partner have a will? Do *you*?

Take in the information, and research the details you don't understand. If your spouse or advisor says, "One thousand dollars went to capital gains tax," and you don't know what that means, ask for an explanation or look it up. (Check the chapter on Squirrels for more information on planners and the Resources section for whom to contact.)

Your Twenties and Thirties—Establishing Your Financial Foundation

These decades are a great time to establish solid financial habits. For example, set up an efficient record-keeping system, track your cash flow carefully, and create a budget you can follow. Even if you still rely on your parents for financial help, balance your income and expenses without regard to parental support. You do best by prioritizing short-, medium-, and long-term goals. You have most of your life ahead of you, and the sooner you determine what you want to accomplish first, the greater the chance you have of realizing your dreams.

Don't expect to meet all your goals at once. Saving for a down payment on a home, for example, may be a higher priority than buying a car or having a child.

In assessing your risk tolerance, realize that while you may not yet have a great deal of money, you do have a great deal of time for your investments to grow. At this age, you have a lifetime to bounce back if a risky investment fails. In addition, if you can tolerate more risk, your investments will have longer to appreciate significantly. Most people in their twenties and thirties are apt to be too conservative with their money. Instead, take more risk in hopes of higher long-term returns. A few tips for your age to avert ongoing Ostrich traits:

Investing: Start to assemble a portfolio of stocks, bonds, and mutual funds as early as you can afford to save. Aim to set aside as much as 10 percent of your after-tax income. If you don't have much capital, mutual funds probably make more sense than individual stocks or bonds.

Credit: Get off to a good start by establishing credit with several lenders—merchants or credit card companies—and pay punctually. Remember, credit-reporting agencies track how well or poorly you repay your debts. And if you have a mortgage, be sure to make every payment on time.

Employee benefits: By participating in all your employer's benefits programs as soon as you start your job or qualify for the programs, you can get off to a solid start laying your financial foundation. Enroll in every available retirement savings program, such as profit-sharing and salary-reduction plans. The earlier you begin participating, the more the company's matching contributions will total, and the larger your retirement nest egg will grow.

Your Forties and Fifties—The Peak Earning Years

By the time you reach your forties and fifties, your income should be substantially higher than it was in your twenties and thirties, and you should have accumulated a considerable pool of assets. All this should be reflected in a sizable net worth. You probably have accomplished many of the short- and medium-term goals you set when you were younger, though you have new goals to meet. Some of your long-term goals, such as saving for retirement, traveling extensively, or starting a business, may still be ahead of you. Many Ostriches slow down their saving activities in these years, but don't give in to your Ostrich tendencies to spend rather than save, give up on a goal for lack of energy, or even hope someone will rescue you and take charge of your money.

In these years, you should have more sources of income, as well as more expenses. When you assess your risk tolerance, you may find that you have mellowed a bit since your youth. If you have built up a substantial portfolio of assets, you may be more interested in preserving it than making it grow. On the other hand, if you have not invested much, you will have to become even more of a risk-taker to earn the high returns you need to finance a comfortable retirement. By the way, be sure you have a valid will, and update it regularly to account for changes in your family situation.

Credit: Establish a solid credit record that allows you to borrow as much as you need. Do what you can to pay off debts now. Borrow less than you did in your twenties and thirties. Your biggest loans, other than a mortgage, will probably be to finance your children's college education. Instead of taking out a loan to buy a new car, consider leasing.

Financing education: Your children will probably enter college while you're in your forties and fifties, so if you haven't been saving, you'll have to borrow a large sum from many sources and go through the difficult process of applying for financial aid and grants. If you have a few years before your oldest child's freshman year, save as much as you can, as soon as you can! The more you reduce the amount of money you borrow when your children enter school, the more capital you will accumulate for your own goals, including retirement. (See the chapter on Coasters for more hints on financing college.)

Retirement: You still have time to plan for and fund your retirement, but that time is getting short! If you have short-changed your retirement fund for seemingly more urgent needs, such as a child's education or medical expenses, start to set aside money for yourself and increase that amount as much as possible over the years. (See the chapter on Coasters for more information on retirement planning.)

The Sixties and up—The Retirement Years

Hopefully, you have amassed a significant amount of assets and paid off most, if not all, of your debts. You should be operating with much positive cash flow because many of the expenses of your earlier years, such as college tuition and buying everything from baby clothes to furniture, no longer apply. Meanwhile, once you retire, you should receive income from Social Security, your company's defined benefit and/or defined contribution pension plan, your investments, and your annuities. Your living expenses should not exceed your income, and if they do, use the budgeting exercise in Chapter 3 to help reduce them.

Investing: Once you stop bringing home income, as an Ostrich you might be tempted to convert your investment portfolio from a broad mix of stocks, bonds, and cash instruments to solely income-oriented bonds. That would be the worst investment move you could ever make. If you live for another twenty or thirty years, not only will your portfolio have to provide you with current income, it will also have to protect you against inflation. If you lock yourself into current yields by buying only bonds, your capital will not grow as it most likely will if you own stocks. The best investing strategy in retirement is to assemble a conservative mix of stocks, bonds, and cash vehicles that produces enough income to live on but also grows in value over time. This might mean keeping about 80 percent of your assets in cash instruments, like money market funds, and in fixed-income assets such as municipal, junk, Treasury, and high-quality corporate bonds, mortgage-backed securities, and the mutual funds that hold these assets.

Taxes: You want to minimize your tax bite and receive your retirement income in a way that will stretch out your tax liability for as many years as possible. For example, unless you absolutely need the capital to live on, do not take distributions from your IRA or Keogh until you reach age seventy and a half. This strategy allows the maximum amount of time for your assets to accumulate tax-deferred. Also, if you live in a high-tax state, buy bonds issued by the state to sidestep both federal and state taxes. Be sure to take full advantage of the many provisions in the tax code aimed at senior citizens. Your accountant will know exactly what they are and how they apply to you.

Estate planning: You need a will to instruct a probate court how to distribute your assets, no matter what they may be. To avoid probate, look into establishing a living trust, which you control while you are alive but that can curb estate taxes and complications to your heirs when you die.

To guard against ramifications should you become mentally or physically incapacitated, execute a living will, durable power of attorney, or health care power of attorney, which allows your spouse, children, doctor, or a close friend to make vital medical decisions for you.

There's such a tremendous gain to be had by paying attention to all these aspects of your finances! Give yourself those gains. Don't forget to secure the right insurance coverage. Keep good records and withhold correctly, so your tax affairs are in order. Follow a livable budget so you know where your money is going. These ideas of basic financial management are like low-hanging fruit—easy to grab and they sweeten your life! Take the first step, and reach out for them.

FINALLY: POINTS TO REMEMBER FOR OSTRICHES

Give yourself a chance to see the light. Stop seeing yourself as inadequate with money, and believe you can figure out what to do.

When you learn more about your own money, you don't have to trust others. Your money doesn't take care of itself—you do.

Understand how much better life could be if you were managing your financial problems. The status quo tells you that doing nothing returns nothing on your investment of time and effort. Shake things up!

Get the money out of your hands, and save it, invest it, or use it toward paying your bills. Make things as easy for yourself as possible, such as by signing up for many automatic plans.

RESOURCES FOR OSTRICHES

Books

I've Been Rich. I've Been Poor. Rich Is Better: How Every Woman Can Find Economic Security and Personal Freedom, by Judy Resnick with Gene W. Stone (St. Martin's Press, 175 Fifth

Avenue, New York, NY 10010; 212-674-5151; www.stmartins. com). Guides women step by step through the financial concerns that come up during each stage of their lives.

The Road to Wealth: A Comprehensive Guide to Your Money, by Suze Orman (Riverhead Books, 1633 Broadway, New York, NY 10019; 212-366-2000; http://us.penguingroup.com). Written in a question-and-answer format with lots of practical advice.

The Wall Street Journal Guide to Understanding Money and Investing, by Kenneth M. Morris and Virginia B. Morris (Lightbulb Press, 112 Madison Avenue, New York, NY 10016; 212-485-8800; www.lightbulbpress.com). User-friendly guide explains how financial products and markets work.

The Wall Street Journal Guide to Understanding Personal Finance (Simon & Schuster, 1230 Avenue of the Americas, New York, NY 10020; 212-698-7000; www.simonsays.com). Easy-to-read guide that covers topics such as banking, credit, home finances, planning, investing, and dealing with taxes.

Your 401(k) Handbook: 2004 Employees Guide to Investments and Decisions, by Mark L. Schwanbeck (Your Money Press, PO Box 10153, Arlington, VA 22210; 703-243-6139; www.yourmoneypress.com). Will help you determine how much to save, teach you about stocks and bonds and how to allocate your money based on your age and other factors, and avoid costly financial mistakes.

Publications

Moneypaper (555 Theodore Fremd Avenue, Suite B-103, Rye, NY 10580; 800-388-9993; www.moneypaper.com). This monthly newsletter covers a range of investment strategies designed to put individuals on more equal footing with wealthy investors and institutions. It is credited with popularizing direct investing, or investing without a broker, and offers a stock-giving service that helps investors buy the first share and register with the dividend reinvestment plan (DRIP). For those who need to brush up on what DRIP plans are and how they work, the Web site (www.moneypaper.com) has a plethora of information.

Organizations

Women's Institute for Financial Education (PO Box 910014, San Diego, CA 92191, 760-736-1660; www.wife.org). Non-profit group dedicated to providing financial education to women. You'll find articles on planning for retirement, budgeting, investing, family matters, and much more.

Web Sites

CheckFree.com. Site makes it possible to receive and pay bills online at one location and at no charge. You select the companies whose bills you want to receive and view online, and you schedule the date to make payments.

401k.org. This site is maintained by the Profit Sharing/401(k) Council of America. It has a 401(k) calculator, a retirement checkup, and numerous articles about retirement savings.

LowerMyBills.com. Pay your bills online and also receive customized reports that tell you, for example, when you are within $100 of your credit card spending limit and when you are within fifty minutes of your cell phone plan limit.

MsMoney.com. A women's financial services site, full of helpful information about personal finances, investment, banking and credit, and buying a house or car.

Pathtoinvesting.org. Site sponsored by the Foundation for Investor Education provides information on numerous topics including basics of investing, choosing investments, managing a portfolio, and how markets work. The site offers tips for beginners and an online dictionary of terms.

Sec.gov/answers/drip.htm. This link contains basic information about direct stock plans (DSPs) and DRIPs.

Sec.gov/investor/pubs/perpayplans.htm. This link explains periodic payment plans and the differences between them and automatic investment plans. Ostriches may find automatic investment plans particularly useful since funds are automatically deducted from their checking/savings account or their paycheck and invested in a retirement account or mutual fund.

Womens-finance.com. Offers calculators, worksheets, and a plethora of information on health care, taxes, retirement, mutual funds, and more.

www.wfn.com. Women's Financial Network. Online financial source for women. Offers financial advice targeted to women; gives them access to the financial information they need. Also offers brokerage services.

CHAPTER 5

The Debt Desperadoes

*Do you have more than six credit cards? If so, how
many of them are maxed out?*

*Do you feel that your debts are out of control—but
that you're ready to get a grip on your finances
and aren't sure where to begin?*

*Do you increase your debt by borrowing more money
in an effort to pay off what you already owe?*

You may call it crashing, going into hock, bottoming out, or
maxing out, but no matter how you describe it, you're talking
about debt. Of all the many life situations you can find yourself
in, owing a lot of money is near the last place you'd want to be.
Yet you may be teetering on a financial edge. Some financial
experts say that being broke in America is considered normal.
I'm not one of them.

There is nothing so inextricably tied to a sense of well-being
and security as money. Not having enough or owing too much
not only limits your choices, it affects how you feel about yourself and how you shape your future. Yet being in debt has
become an American epidemic, so if you answered yes to two
of the three questions listed above, you're not alone. You may
feel as if you're a Debt Desperado, on the run from creditors,
while seeking a way to get your finances under control. Don't

despair—help is here. With information, planning, and lots of effort, you can turn your financial life around by taking charge of how you deal with money. I'll show you how!

I'm on a crusade to help curtail, and even end, the staggering debt too many of you find yourselves in. My message is both practical and radical: practical, because I'll offer ideas on how to rethink debt and suggest effective ways for you to pay off what you owe so you can begin to build a better, even prosperous life; and radical, because I want to motivate you to face the self-destructive money habits that keep you in the red. When you understand *why* you wind up in money trouble, you're one step closer to making real changes in your bank balance. Breaking negative habits is never easy, but you can do it, one small step at a time. Both the practical and radical recommendations will take time, but any effort that gets you closer to solvency is time well spent. It's your money—take charge of it and enjoy it!

Debts accumulate in as many ways as there are to overspend, and you may be saying to yourself, "How did this happen to me? I work hard! Where did the money go?" Take the quiz below, and you'll have a pretty good idea if overspending is likely to get you into trouble.

Are You an Overspender? A Quiz*

Following are statements pertaining to your spending techniques. Circle one of the five responses after each statement.

SCORING:

Totally me:	1 point
A lot like me:	2 points
Equally like and unlike me:	3 points
A little like me:	4 points
Not like me at all:	5 points

*This quiz was created by Paul Richard, RFC, executive director of the Institute of Consumer Financial Education (ICFE), www/icfe.ino, and is reproduced by permission.

1. I always live within my income range.

   Totally me   A lot like me   Equally like and unlike me
   A little like me   Not like me at all

2. Each income period, I set aside at least 10 percent for savings.

   Totally me   A lot like me   Equally like and unlike me
   A little like me   Not like me at all

3. My finances are managed according to a written spending plan.

   Totally me   A lot like me   Equally like and unlike me
   A little like me   Not like me at all

4. All household and grocery spending is planned in advance and done with a list.

   Totally me   A lot like me   Equally like and unlike me
   A little like me   Not like me at all

5. I rarely make more than one trip a week to the grocery store.

   Totally me   A lot like me   Equally like and unlike me
   A little like me   Not like me at all

6. Grocery and other coupons and rebate offers are utilized whenever possible.

   Totally me   A lot like me   Equally like and unlike me
   A little like me   Not like me at all

7. Comparison shopping for quality, value, price, etc. is something I/we do for practically every purchase, large or small.

   Totally me   A lot like me   Equally like and unlike me
   A little like me   Not like me at all

8. I have no revolving debt carried on credit or charge cards.

   Totally me   A lot like me   Equally like and unlike me
   A little like me   Not like me at all

9. I have not had an overdraft of my checking account nor paid late fees on a credit card.

   Totally me   A lot like me   Equally like and unlike me
   A little like me   Not like me at all

10. I regularly contribute to an employer-sponsored retirement plan, IRA, or a 401(k) plan.

    Totally me   A lot like me   Equally like and unlike me
    A little like me   Not like me at all

How did you do?

10–15 Doing Great. Time to teach others how you do it.

16–20 Doing Good. Concentrate on improving a few of the weaker areas.

21–35 Doing okay. An hour a week devoted to improving spending habits will equal greater savings.

36–40 Needs help. Immediate changes required, now, to avoid a financial disaster.

41–50 Needs professional help. Time to contact a credit and debt counselor.

The Debt Cycle: How We Live and How We Pay for It

The studies about debt and who owes what change every day. What changes most rapidly is the number of people who are putting their financial lives in jeopardy. Personal debt is in the trillions of dollars! And the story isn't a new one. Owing money was once considered a serious character flaw, implying—if harshly—that you were a poor earner, a poor money manager, or a laggard. You just didn't owe money and not pay it back within the time given you. Debtors' prisons confirmed the thinking that defaulting on a loan was a crime. Times changed, and along came store charge cards, credit cards, and ways of doing business that factored debt into the profit equation. Lenders make it easy and convenient for you to borrow and buy. This encouraged consumer spending—and more spending, so that more people than ever before are maxed out on their credit cards or are going bankrupt. Not good. Let's stop it now!

Americans are experiencing record levels of foreclosures, of not paying their property taxes, of crippling medical bills, all because of the rising tide of indebtedness. Many people who are unemployed use credit cards to live on. Others finance small businesses—stores and franchises—on credit cards. I hear tales like this all the time. It's an enterprising but risky way of getting off the ground and a good idea if the business flies. But if the business fails, you're paying 19 percent or more on a credit card for a business that will never show a profit and will still cost you money.

If the problem can be blamed on a single phenomenon, it would have to be credit card debt. The amount we owe on cards is a staggering $800-plus billion. How did we get here? Surveys reveal that the average American household owes close to $10,000, while the number of people who pay off their cards each month has dropped to 39 percent, according to the Cambridge Consumer Credit Index. Over the course of a generation, families have gone from having 11 percent of their income in savings while carrying 3 percent in consumer debt to having 1 percent (or less) in savings and being 14 percent in debt. Definitely not good! You can see the makings of a Debt Desperado.

The details about debt can leave you breathless as shown in the box below.

WHY PEOPLE ARE IN DEBT—THE SURPRISING ANSWERS

The National Endowment for Financial Education did a study on financial literacy in America and found that while the largest single source of indebtedness is represented by home mortgages, *the misuse of credit cards is actually the primary cause of the rising rate of bankruptcies* (about 1.6 million a year) and increased frustration voiced by people in debt. In fact, 20 percent of families with an annual income below $50,000 spend close to *half* of their net income on debt payments. More than three-fourths of college students have multiple credit cards with an average total balance of $2,748. In the last few years, there has been a 51 percent increase in annual bankruptcy filings among people twenty-five years old and younger.

If you are ready to clean up the mess and the stress that living in debt has made, I know I can show you how to get in control of your money. There's help for every Debt Desperado as long as you're willing to understand how you got into debt and sincerely want to climb out—and then learn how to rebuild financially. You will have to start by learning to separate your "wants" from your "needs"—and make paying for your needs the priority. Put your wants to the side until you can really afford them.

THE DEBT DESPERADO REVEALED

If you're a Debt Desperado, your life has changed in some significant way that indicates financial loss—a plight you feel stuck with. The reason you fall into debt can be the result of a number of events and/or choices. Sometimes debt is a consequence of losing your source of income. Maybe you've been downsized, or you've lost your own business, or you live in an area where the bigger companies have closed down and there are fewer jobs. The loss of jobs and/or the cutback in the ability to work over-time makes a huge difference. Reductions in bonuses and smaller pay raises also may be factors. Overtime pay was the extra fluff that consumers used to pay their bills, but now many companies have eliminated this option. Instead of cutting back, people use credit cards and hope for better times. When credit cards become temporary lifesavers, debt is racked up.

And then there are the Debt Desperadoes who are carried away by instant gratification or feel compelled to spend and charge it all, knowing they can't pay for most of their pur-chases. For them, it's not just about the false sense of buying something they can always pay for later—the act of shopping compulsively also factors in prominently. Some people have a lower threshold of endurable debt, so they don't max out and can stop their spending sooner rather than later. Others cannot stop until collection agencies come after them.

Generally, though, certain behaviors are typical of your Money Type, and they are:

- You juggle your bills, paying one company one month and another company the next.
- You frequently receive overdue notices from lenders.
- You make only minimum payments on your debt, and you never pay off the principal owed.
- You've reached your limit on most or all of your credit cards and credit lines.
- You pay credit card bills with other credit sources, bor-rowing from Peter to pay Paul.

The Debt Desperado: Your Strengths

Many Desperadoes need to max out or bottom out before they can start turning themselves around financially. If you have any strengths, it is that ability to rally after the humbling experience of dealing with what has become a painful relationship with money. Being in debt doesn't feel good, but finally learning how to practice more responsible ways of handling money feels great. Use your ability to bounce back to bring you a renewed sense of financial security.

The Debt Desperado: Your Weaknesses

Chris Viale, CEO and president of Cambridge Consumer Credit Counseling, a super-effective source for helping people get out of debt and stay on stable financial ground, says that one of the primary reasons people get into trouble is because "they *deny* how they're dealing with money." What this means, simply, is that reality tells you that you're lacking or losing money, but it's too painful for you to accept. Instead, you let bills mount and, too often, fuel the need to feel okay by adding on even more debt.

Sometimes, people overspend as a way to feel better about themselves. Shopping, for example, becomes a form of temporary self-medication, and in some cases, an expensive addiction. Often, shopaholics delude themselves as to why they've made yet another purchase. Psychologists say that such individuals feel as if they don't have what they need to make them happy and one more purchase will do the trick. Alas, nothing makes them happy, and they end up feeling worse about themselves and deeper in debt.

Overspending is not the only reason for debt. Many people suffer because of job loss and not having a cushion to keep them afloat until they get work; underpar earnings that don't keep up with the costs of housing, food, or caring for a family; or huge medical bills that were not covered by insurance. What happens when your circumstances change drastically? Many people rack up personal debts with family and friends, and typically fall back on credit cards to pay bills or use them to maintain their accustomed lifestyle. Chris Viale added, "So many clients with money trouble tell me, 'But I'll be working again or making more money in six months, and everything will be great, so I'll coast along until then.' And then they get trapped."

This is also why a lot of Debt Desperadoes reach retirement age and have no money or very little put away for a comfortable and secure old age. Your weakness is to take on more debt, while the interest increases and compounds against you.

I'm the financial analyst for the Cambridge Consumer Credit Index (www.cambridgeconsumerindex.com), which reports on Americans' debt behavior every month. Since we're interested in why people get into debt, we ask callers who contact us to tell us why they need help with their finances. Cambridge Credit Counseling's Index Client Survey finds that the top reasons people cite for calling are:

- Frustration with high bank rates and fees.
- Reduction in income as a result of job loss or reduction in hours worked.
- A lack of financial education that results in getting into debt.
- Inability to pull out of a hole and move toward a major financial goal, such as saving for a house down payment, college, or retirement.
- Divorce, widowhood, and large uninsured medical bills.

While I can encourage you to take *any* employment for the short run rather than suffer even more by not having an income, I can't help you get a job. But I can make a difference in the one area that causes a Desperado effect: lack of knowledge about how to manage your money. *Financial literacy is only rarely taught in schools anywhere in a mandatory program,* and many people like you are intimidated by the idea of balance sheets and adding numbers. I'm here to say it's easier than you think. You can give yourself hope by rebuilding your assets: Open some sort of investment plan, a surefire psychological booster. Instead of feeling down on yourself about being in debt, start your money growing, even if you invest only $50 a month. You'll be motivated to get out of debt faster.

I've spoken to a number of people about how and why they got into debt. Each story can give you insights into how you got into financial hot water and how you can begin to solve your own issues with money. Let's start with a man who always believed he'd have a job and a stable life, and how debt took him by surprise.

"Am I Still a Somebody When I Don't Have a Job?"

Unlike other Debt Desperadoes who may suffer the consequences of credit card abuse and irresponsible spending habits, Bob and his wife, Jane, were plunged into debt when Bob lost his job. Life feels brutal when you're unemployed and can't seem to catch a break—Bob would be the first person to agree, as would Jane. It's difficult to maintain a fighting spirit and keep debt to a minimum when your livelihood is yanked from you. But there are ways to get through these hard times.

Here's what happened. The company Bob worked for merged with a larger corporation, and his job was redundant. At age forty, he began feeling defeated when job offers didn't roll in. Severance pay for his nine years of service and unemployment insurance wasn't comfort enough. Bob wanted a job to go to every day—a job where he could feel secure again. His nearly half-year-long unemployment started a cycle of his feeling inadequate as a provider and frustration in trying to stay afloat financially.

Bob and Jane's money problems really started nine years earlier, however, when their first daughter was born. At this point, they were a two-income family with Jane earning more than Bob. Jane had worked in the corporate accounting office of a national retail chain for ten years, but the company did not have a policy of paid maternity leave, and she lost twelve weeks in income. Bob was a trainee at his company at the time and not earning much. Without any available disposable income, they cashed in their life insurance policies to buy groceries. When Jane went back to work, the company took a hard line, reducing her hours to part-time and cutting her salary.

Jane was still working at the same company when their second child was born, three years later. Bob's job was secure then, and he was earning nearly a third more than what he did as a trainee. But for Jane, the lost-income cycle from unpaid maternity leave repeated itself, as did the reduced hours she was obliged to maintain.

Bob said they still hadn't recovered from the loss of Jane being out of work those three months when their second daughter was born and all those years of Jane working part-time. "We

BOB AND JANE'S FINANCIAL SNAPSHOT

When Bob still had his job, he and Jane always managed to pay their bills on time and didn't use credit recklessly. With a combined income of $81,000 and two children, however, they were barely getting by since Jane was still working part-time. Here's where they were financially:

- They paid $920 a month on their $120,000 mortgage.

- They paid minimum monthly payments on their five credit cards, which carried a total debt of $65,000.

- Bob had a 401(k), while Jane had a pension and two Roth IRAs. But other than the initial payments, neither one has been able to contribute any more money to them. In fact, Bob took out a loan on his 401(k) to put a new roof on the house.

- Savings are nil.

both had good credit, but we couldn't get ahead," Bob told me, acknowledging their debt-to-income ratio was high. "Every single cent we made went back out. We were making decent money. If we didn't have the debt, we could actually *live*. We haven't had a vacation with the kids, ever."

When their younger daughter was three years old and in nursery school, Jane quit her job. She took a full-time government position where she was able to use her accounting and business skills, a much better-paying job. She also took a second job as a caregiver to an elderly woman, with whom she stays on weekends for the extra cash.

Then, after nine years with the company he thought he'd have a long and secure future with, Bob was let go. When he lost his job, the house of cards tumbled. Bob told me, "For the first time in my adult life, I felt like a failure. I know it's not my fault, being out of work, but I'm ashamed of it."

Bob was haunted by his inability to resolve the family's money issues as the months rolled by, and he was still unemployed. He told me that he tried his best to assure Jane that things would turn out fine, but he himself wasn't sure. He was embarrassed and ashamed—feeling as if he wasn't taking care of his family properly. The situation was creating a hardship in the marriage to the point where Jane didn't want to talk about money. For Bob, the lack of income and their mounting debt seemed ominous, and he tried to solve it, despite Jane's resistance to talking about the problem.

Bob did some reading about credit counseling and found a company that checked out with the local Better Business Bureau. This company acts on the debtor's behalf for unsecured debt, paying it off in three years. With a debt management program (DMP) offered by a top-quality credit counseling firm, Bob and Jane's monthly payment would be $700. The DMP would reduce their credit card payments by between 40 and 60 percent. Bob called it "a last-ditch thing," and he was afraid it would be a blot on their credit rating.

Bob was wary of *all* debt-relief programs, fearing—

incorrectly—that signing up for one would forever have a negative impact on their personal credit ratings. Nor was he thrilled about having to turn over power of attorney to the counseling firm, which would further wound his fragile ego. Furthermore, the representative could not guarantee that the credit card companies wouldn't call at Jane's workplace, another red flag. (Usually, such bill collector harassment ceases after the creditors become aware that you are enrolled in a DMP program.) In the counseling firm's view, bankruptcy wasn't an option because Bob and Jane paid their bills on time. Bob decided not to sign up with such an agency and kept looking for work.

After six months of pounding the pavement, Bob took a job that pays a few thousand dollars less than what he earned previously. "The lower salary makes me feel bad," he said, "but at the same time, I'm working and bringing in money. At least it takes some of the pressure off Jane. Now we're at a place where we can resume life if we can get out of debt. There has to be something for people like us, who aren't negligent or charging up a storm, besides bankruptcy. We're stuck."

Keeping the Faith Until You Find Work

Feeling ashamed about being downsized doesn't rectify the situation or get you rehired. It is only beating yourself up for no good reason. Although he did not find his ideal job, Bob was smart: He took what he could, while still looking for the right position. Income equals debt reduction.

That Bob is feeling defeated and deflated is not uncommon among men (and more recently, increasing numbers of women) who lose their jobs. Men in our culture are socialized to equate self-worth with, if not success or power, then certainly gainful employment. But Bob took a job—and I've been in contact with many Debt Desperadoes who do not or cannot—which proves he's capable of meeting his obligations. He needs to get over the shock of loss and give himself a break—he lost his job through no fault of his own. He's too hard on himself, looking

IT'S NOT ALL BAD—A FEW WORDS ON "GOOD" DEBT

Did you know that having some manageable debt is actually okay? This is what's generally called "good" debt and what you might ultimately aim for. Let me explain:

Many financial advisors, some with large public followings, think that all debt is bad, but I don't—and to a real and practical degree. There is a difference between "good" debt and "bad" debt, even if you're at a stage where you've gone beyond your usual limit.

Financial advisors who place "bad" debt in some sort of hell, making debtors the "sinners," are making a moral judgment about you because of what you owe. This is an extreme opinion, and one I don't hold. I make a distinction between the sin and the sinner and the debt and the debtor. If the "sin" is overspending, I don't believe you're a bad person (a "sinner"), but misguided or careless or uneducated about finances, or if you're suddenly in colossal debt to pay for, say, a child's surgery, unlucky and unprepared.

Living completely debt-free is neither practical nor desirable. You have to have some *temporary* but manageable debt. Try renting a car, checking into a hotel, or buying an airline ticket with cash. You need a credit card! Accrued wisely, reasonable debt is good debt you can handle.

Furthermore, when you pay bills on time, you not only avoid paying high interest rates, but you build up a good credit report that's useful when you need a big loan. Good debt can be a wealth-building tool for you, once you pay off what you owe and get your finances in check. Not only can you use debt as leverage to purchase an asset that stands to appreciate, such as a home or a college education, but a stellar record of debt repayment also enables you to borrow on the best terms, if you have to. This is a goal you promise yourself!

down on himself as a provider, not as someone who can keep the fight going.

If you're like Bob, the Emotional Path exercise, which is coming up, can help you understand how to accept a temporary downtrend. Being in debt does not make you unworthy or worthless! Don't let such negative thinking crush your spirit.

The "Shopping Cure"—And the Sickening Unpaid Bills!

Bob may be operating out of an ingrained pattern of equating his work with his self-esteem, but Margie is a different case. A twenty-eight-year-old woman who's an account supervisor at a technology company, Margie survived a childhood of hardship and hard times. Bob may have learned about how to endure need or even financial insecurity when he was forty, but for Margie, such disasters formed the pattern of her life. What those disasters did was shape her into a shopaholic. For Margie, shopping was an opiate.

To speak to her, you wouldn't detect in her positive tone that Margie had been psychologically abused by her mother and sexually abused by her stepfather. Her cheerfulness belies a sad string of events that she speaks about so candidly. "My mother was cold, begrudging with food, she hated buying me a pair of shoes when I needed them and made me feel like a horrible burden. All we did was scream at each other," Margie said. As a result of Margie's defiance, her mother gave up on her and delivered her to the foster care system at the age of eight, where she remained for most of her childhood. When she was thirteen, she was finally placed with kindhearted foster parents, who were determined to repair some of the emotional damage Margie had endured. They gave her hope for her future but not enough to keep her from eventual financial peril.

By the time Margie met Ted, the man she'd soon marry, she had worked her way through three years of college but had quit when a summer job turned into a career choice at an advertising firm. She loved being on her own, living with a roommate and earning her own money. "Compared to me," Margie said, "Ted lived the good life. He wanted to take care of me as no one else had. He got more than he bargained for." By the time she was twenty-four years old, and right before their marriage, Margie owed $22,000, most of it to credit card companies. Her salary was $30,000 a year.

Margie needed to be good to herself and bought more clothes than she could wear, and she leased a car for $379 a month. She loved nice things and saw no reason not to treat herself to them. "Something would come over me and set me off, and I'd shop," she told me. What "came over" Margie was to buy clothes that made her feel she was everything she wanted to be.

"Ted kind of married into debt," Margie told me. "I swore to stop the crazy spending. I agreed to live on a budget. I was even fine for a while. I buckled." Meanwhile, Ted had started a small auto repair business with an army buddy, and the shop was growing slowly over the years. Margie, who was still at the advertising agency, now earning $32,500 a year, was devastated when she didn't get the promotion she'd hoped for. She began shopping again, knowing Ted would be furious, but she couldn't stop herself.

Margie was right: Ted *was* furious. He'd just figured out how they could pay off her debts together, and she'd racked up another few thousand. "I started crying, feeling guilty about the spending," she said. "Ted wanted to be understanding, but he was running out of steam. He demanded that I return the stuff, or he'd haul it all back." Margie wound up bringing about half her purchases back to the stores.

"What we really need is a budget and to learn how to stick with it," she said. "In one month earlier this year, I spent $600 eating out, treating friends and co-workers . . . one month! We need to save our money, get a life insurance plan, put money into a 401(k). I want to have children and don't want to work full-time. But we need a fund with money to fall back on."

Ted now manages their money. After Margie racked up $120 in returned check fees, her husband took charge of her checkbook. She has a separate account with less than $200 for gas, food, and minor purchases. "If he had a choice, he wouldn't give me any spending money," she said. Ted's restrictions brought back Margie's childhood fears that by behaving in a way that was unacceptable, she would be tossed out by the person she loved. There were times when Ted wanted to leave Margie, but he would give her one more chance.

"A few months ago, I'd have said, I want to shop, threats won't stop me, and Ted will have to deal with the bills," Margie said. "Now at least I can say to myself, this is a real sickness. I don't want to destroy a marriage over a bunch of new sweaters and what they cost. Ted promises me he's here for the long run and believes I can change. I can't let him down. I can't let myself down. I need someone to take me by the hand and show me, item by item, how to stop."

Debt is life-draining, not love-enhancing.

The Buzz from a Spending High

Neuroscientists are studying the shopping syndrome and examining the possibilities of medical treatment, the way they'd treat anxiety or depression with medication. The reason: There is actually a chemical high that accompanies the purchase, and a definite low, or withdrawal effect, that follows. The cure? More shopping. It's probably an easier habit to break than smoking, drinking, or drugs, although Debt Desperadoes who shop would argue with me.

Some experts see compulsive shopping as the "ordinary pleasures of living getting out of hand." I agree. Shopping addicts like Margie start out as occasional or recreational shoppers—mall cruising is what to do on a rainy day with friends, for example. The problem becomes grave when what was a simple pleasure turns into an irrational compulsion. Hard-core shoppers find it difficult to think about anything else and are known to rack up bills through catalogue purchases or television shopping network shows, or on the Internet.

As the urge to spend builds, so does debt. Out-of-control spending is a dangerous habit, and you need to find a counselor to get your shopaholism in check. You can also try a local chapter of Debtors Anonymous, where you can find a support group to help you talk out your issues with money.

MAKING CHANGES: THE EMOTIONAL PATH

Where does real help begin? When you're in debt, you need the courage to face your demons *and* your creditors. Change really begins with you, though. You want to stop living way above your means, whatever that is for you, by overestimating your income and underestimating your spending. To stop being a Debt Desperado, you must be able to *separate your wants from your needs, and pay for your needs but not your wants.* This is your chance to make those key connections to old behaviors that are not operating to your benefit. When you pinpoint them, give yourself a break. Remember, there's a difference between a debt and a debtor. The debt may not be a good thing, *but you are a good person.* Believe in yourself and feel hopeful. Don't let the burden of debt keep you down.

I spoke to Washington, D.C., psychotherapist, money coach, and author Olivia Mellan about one of the critical factors in understanding why people get into debt: self-esteem issues. "The first thing you have to say is, I am okay, and I deserve better," she said. "And follow by asking yourself what you need to do to nurture your spirit. What will also help you, on a practical level, take care of yourself." How do you start believing in what you deserve and break out of this destructive pattern? One answer is awareness of your history, but, Mellan said, "Awareness can, but does not always, lead to change. So it's partly about keeping your goals front and center."

Let's look at that:

Accept Reality, and Then Take Action

As a financial consultant, I see many men who, like Bob in the first example, go through deep emotional turmoil when they lose a job. Who can't understand the shock of loss and the fear of what will happen next? Feeling stunned or humiliated and having it affect your recovery into the workplace can only hurt you. Even more destructive: denying that you're affected by the job loss and still spending as if you had money coming in, which only adds to your Debt Desperado status.

Try this shift in thinking:

Psychologists call the state of denial an inability to accept and deal with reality. It's almost like an emotional shock that cannot be processed, or a shock you *refuse* to process. Wishful thinking often accompanies denial. In combination, it's not so different from thinking, "If I don't go to a doctor, I don't have a disease." A man like Bob who's unemployed may think, "If I don't talk about how inadequate I feel as a man, I'm still a good provider."

If you're hard on yourself in hard times, you're not being as productive as you can be. If, like Bob and Jane, you need help to get out of debt, that is no shame. It is only a shame that you've added another day of debt to your load. Backing away from assistance because you're embarrassed to ask for it only hurts you. Check out some of the people I suggest you could talk to about your money problems in the Resources section.

Don't Fight a Sense of Emotional Deprivation by Getting Deeper into Financial Debt

If anyone has a money-love issue, it is Margie, the shopaholic I talked about in the second case. Her childhood was full of peril, and she's continued the pattern of threat to her survival by putting herself, and her husband, in financial jeopardy. What is a Debt Desperado thinking when he or she is also sinking a spouse into debt by compulsive spending?

Many people who grow up feeling helpless, vulnerable, doubtful of love, or hopeless about deserving anything material tend to spend. Some people spend continuously on small, compensatory items that make them feel better. Even a trip to the 99-cent store to buy a comb makes them feel better.

Something deeper is happening with Margie. Psychologist Olivia Mellan told me, "I talk about childhood messages and childhood vows. The problem arises when the model you saw of one or both parents is sufficiently upsetting in some way. Then you make a vow never to be like that parent, and you get locked in the opposite mode. In neither case are you expressing your own integrity or your own values. Instead, you're just *reacting* to the past." Margie's mother was essentially ungiving, and it's easy to see why Margie feels her mother didn't protect her—or want her to have anything much, including the basics of survival.

In reaction, Margie is going excessively in the other direction: indulging herself, while causing herself problems by getting into debt and passing it on to her husband, who, in his way, has vowed to rescue her from her past. Perhaps Margie still fears that she doesn't deserve financial security. Although her husband, Ted, loves her, he's made it possible for her to put them into hock. At least Ted doesn't want to hurt her. Margie's mother was unable to function as a parent to her, and although that early part of her life is damaging and painful, it is over. Unfortunately, Margie's childhood defenses are still operating, even though she finally can feel safe and know security with Ted. Her subconscious isn't convinced yet. Thus she rewards herself with stuff, telling herself she's worthy of it. She needs a financial planner most of all and, if she can't control her spending, a couples therapist.

What goes on in a shopaholic's mind? It goes back to distinguishing wants from needs, and not turning a want into a need. Whenever I ask people who come to me for guidance regarding why they got into so much debt, many respond, "I like nice things." This is a heck of an answer! In this case, it's about a want as a need, or really confusing the two.

Try this shift in thinking:

How do you defuse that old feeling of being deprived when it is turned around into a shopping addiction? Olivia Mellan suggested that "you have to work on yourself and know what you're all about. You have to learn how to nurture your core and not to indulge yourself on the surface. Surface indulgence is mutually exclusive from nurturing your core, which has nothing to do with material things. It has to do with self-esteem, self-love, creativity, self-respect, and the things that make you feel more connected to your world in a good way."

Why shop? Experts say that buying stuff is a way to fill an emotional void. The purchases are supposed to make you feel that at least you are being good to yourself. That may happen a lot for shoppers, but it's dangerous when shopping turns into a nightmare of debt. All kinds of deprivation is concealed by overspending, but remember, compulsive overspending is like a chemical addiction. There's a high. There's also a trigger to shop: When she felt unsure of herself or unsure of Ted, it made sense to Margie to spend money on herself. The need to buy takes over like a tidal wave, like an addiction.

If you're a shopaholic who has graduated to Debt Desperado, you need to take drastic action. *Cut up your credit cards and mourn them for a day or two, then pat yourself on the back for freeing yourself from mall and credit card fever.* Toss mail-order catalogues on the fire, change the TV channel when you hear a sales pitch, and stay off of Internet shopping sites. Get a friend to help you stay out of shopping zones, unless what you need are real provisions. Give yourself three months to break the shopping habit, taking a tiny step every day to not shop.

If you're a Debt Desperado, you need help getting through the numbers crunch to figure out how to really make a dent in what you owe. I hope to take you from "When do these bills stop coming?" to "What better use can I make of all or most of the money?" The object is to build up your capital, not add to your expenses by exhausting your capital. So, here goes.

MAKING CHANGES: THE FINANCIAL PATH

Radio talk show host Dave Ramsey, an aggressive crusader against debt, asks his callers to change their spending habits by first yelling out loud, "I'm free of debt, and it's not going to happen to me anymore!" Good idea! Even if you haven't met your goal of being debt-free, believing that you *can* be adds emotional power. I know that nothing feels as good as emerging from a whirlpool of back bills and being in control of your money again. A little financial evangelism can fire you up, but to be free, you have to make it happen *systematically*. That is, you must set up a system that takes work, a little sacrifice, a real commitment to following a financial plan, and, even when it hurts, saying no to unnecessary spending. It's your money, and you deserve to have it work for you.

I know it's easier to get into debt than to get out of it, so this is your chance to prove to yourself that you can finally manage your money. When you learn how to live within your means, your values change. Eventually, it will become easier to save and invest, rather than shop and spend. When you finally see the end of your debts, I hope you'll be disciplined and emotionally ready to say, "I'm never going through that again!"

I've seen people in debt turn their lives around thousands of times, and although the circumstances may be different, what gives all the stories a common thread is the powerful drive to feel at peace by being financially secure. Denise and Rick were such a story. They were living a comfortable life when Rick got a promotion that required moving five hundred miles from their suburban Boston home. Neither of them was prepared for what would soon happen: big losses beyond their expectations or experience. "Our lives changed so suddenly that we didn't know who we were or what to do," Denise told me. "Debt was that shocking to us." Here's what happened:

When the Big Job Falls Through and Turns into Big Debt

Denise and Rick were both raised in middle-class families, were well educated, and together built a life that continued to be worry-free. No shocks. No sudden reversals of fortune for either of their sets of parents or for them. There was never a suggestion of money problems—that was for other people, they thought. Their two salaries more than allowed for extras, even including lavish vacations for the family and private school for their sons. Rick was a successful executive at a multinational company, and Denise was a manager at an accounting firm. "We thought we had it all," Denise told me. "We could turn the corner on our block, pull into our driveway, and feel we've got as good as the people next door. We were safe. We had money."

Then Rick got the promotion. It meant uprooting their children and Denise's taking a similar position—but not a cut in salary—at a smaller branch office of her accounting firm. They agreed that the benefits of moving outweighed the disadvantages. Things were looking up, as they always had.

Instead of selling their home—"our nest egg"—they decided to rent it out. And because property costs were high in the city they were moving to, they rented a place temporarily. The idea was to get established, sell their old house, and buy their dream home in their new town. It made sense. The boys attended private school, and life continued to be good and stable. A year later, Denise quit the accounting firm because the job change didn't work out for her. She took her accrued benefits as a seventeen-year employee and then found a job as an executive assistant to a corporate VP. Things were still looking up.

Then Rick lost his job to downsizing, and shortly thereafter he was mugged. "Both experiences were brutal for Rick," Denise said. "They took a huge psychological toll on him and on me and the boys, too. He was suffering, and only a great job would pull him out of his misery." While Rick continued searching for a job, he eased into the role of house husband, doing the shopping, errands, and making dinner. To his surprise, Rick was comfortable enough at home, relying on Denise as the breadwinner. Except he wasn't really looking for a job. Instead, he was growing increasingly depressed, drinking a little, spending money, and brooding about their ever diminishing finances.

Rick had taken over the exclusive responsibility of paying the bills, telling Denise that he wanted to relieve her of any extra household burdens—especially since she was working long hours at her new job. When their mortgage company called her at work to say they were foreclosing on their nest egg home, the news was as catastrophic as any she could have gotten about someone she held dear. She bolted from the office at her lunch hour, drove home, and confronted Rick. "He hadn't been making the mortgage payments, even though we were collecting rent from the tenants," Denise related. "He was spending and juggling money. Our finances were so out of control that Rick was scrambling every day to pay household expenses, including double tuitions and car insurance. He never told me that we were in way over our heads. Drowning. It bothered me tremendously that Rick wasn't working. I felt all the responsibility was mine, and I struggled with the stress of making the money and dealing with a husband who'd more or less crashed."

Denise and Rick lost their house, and then, unable to afford the rental home they were living in, they traded down. Within a month, they moved to another nearby rental. "It's still slightly more than we can afford," Denise says. "But we want it to be safe enough for our kids and stayed in a middle-class neighborhood." Finally, Rick found a job, but the debt and money crisis took a toll on their marriage. Divorce or separation was never an option, and Denise's stress level was over-the-top. Once slim and athletic, she gained more than thirty pounds and was very unhappy. When the downward cycle started up again, Denise felt panicky. "Rick lost his job over a dispute with his boss. He loved the work, though," she added, "and it gave him the push to make another big change. Instead of looking for another job, he decided to start up his own competing company."

Denise insisted that she and Rick see a financial planner, since neither one of them knew what to do first. Budgeting was their Achilles' heel, and she knew if they mastered a plan, their financial lives would change radically. The planner helped them calm down and figure out where the money would come from to pay off their debts. They started by cutting up their credit cards, sparing one low-limit major card reserved for emergencies. Denise has one department store charge card, and they shop with debit cards exclusively. "If we don't have the cash, we don't buy it," she said. Denise has a 401(k) they decided not to touch, but there was a mutual fund account for the children and a small family inheritance, which in combination with their incomes enabled them to pay off some debts "to get some breathing room." Private school was out. In fact, the children themselves chose to switch to public school, a move that saved $30,000 a year.

As a family, they couldn't take expensive vacations the way they had in the past, but opted for road trips where they'd enjoy the outdoors and, Denise added, "stay in cheap motels and have a good time." Eventually, they paid off an old car loan and found the money to get Rick's business started. Their priority now is recovering their financial security and eventually buying that dream house.

At fifty, Denise feels the catastrophic changes have shown both her and Rick where the true value in life lies: relationships, trust, and living with some sort of financial balance. She added, "I worry more about our future as a couple as we get older. We're not quite secure now, having had the roof crash in on us not once but several times." Denise and Rick both feel they've come to terms with what they've lost and are thankful for what they have. "We talk to the kids about the realities of life and that money doesn't grow on trees. After two years, we're debt-free. We're going to stay that way."

Denise and Rick did something smart in the middle of chaos: They sought help and were not overwhelmed by their creditors.

This is my first piece of advice for taking that first step to be debt free:

Don't Be Overwhelmed by Your Creditors: Face Facts but Put Survival First

Anyone who is overwhelmed by debt is also overwhelmed by debt collectors. You may think you have no control over the demands for money, but you do. Take a breath. Cool down. Mobilize. Get stronger! Here's what to do.

First and foremost: *Don't ignore your debts*. Face them! Sit down and create a good strong household budget to figure out where your money's going. Get intimate with how you're spending your money, and understand why you're spending—do you *need* the stuff or *want* the stuff? These are two different reasons, and one of them—wanting—gets you into trouble. If you start a journal of your spending and put in every entry, every day for at least two months, you'll see what your money patterns are and what you're doing with your money. Then you can figure out ways to cut $100 to $200 just from routine spending. That extra money goes a long way to pay down debt.

The bad news: Whether the call comes from a credit card company's collection agent or an account manager at an outside collection agency, the effect on you is the same: You're reminded that you've got money problems and can't do much about them now. It can be gut-wrenching. There's nothing feel-good about this experience unless you can finally say, "I'll pay off the whole amount today. Take the money out of my checking account." Until then, there are the calls—lots of them. Not answering the calls doesn't help because you're just delaying the inevitable. You'll have to pay out either the full amount or an agreed-upon settlement sum.

Now the good news: If you feel your creditors are completely in control, understand that you still have some rights. The primary one is to *protect yourself and use what assets you have to take care of your needs.*

Deborah McNaughton, an expert on debt who runs a debt counseling company in California and the author of a number of books on dealing with debt, emphasizes self-protection. She told me, "Put your survival first. I've worked with clients who were bullied into paying their creditors first. They can't bear being yelled at or intimidated, and give in. This is not a good thing to do. It means they delay paying their utility bills or a rent or mortgage payment, and the worst happens. Their creditors have their payments, but they're sitting in the dark because the utility company has turned off the lights, or they're opening their mail to find eviction or foreclosure notices. Don't give in. You still have rights."

Collection agents at store or credit card companies want their money. They're tough on you, and they have no shame about calling you as often as possible to make demands. Your lenders usually resort to a collection agency when you've been unresponsive to their inquiries, and they think they have no alternative. Even fewer want to send an outside collection agency after you.

Most collection warriors of every ilk know you're feeling vulnerable, and they go for the jugular. They're not trained to be sympathetic—although they may suggest they understand—but they want those payments and usually won't get them by being your pal. It's nothing personal, although a call from them can feel like an assault. Instead of avoiding the calls or letting them get to you, it's to your benefit to learn to deal with both your creditors' collection department representatives or collection agencies. I've found that most lenders would rather help you work out a debt repayment schedule than seize your property or put you in some survival jeopardy. If you get to the point where a collection agency is on your case, you still have options, which follow.

Figure Out Where You Are Financially with a Debt-to-Income Worksheet

There are many ways to assess whether you are carrying too much debt. Completing a few simple financial planning exercises can help you get control of your finances by breaking them down in three different ways, that is, the debt-to-income ratio, which can help you figure out whether your debt is too hefty in proportion to what you make. There's a current ratio, which shows your assets and liabilities in absolute terms, and a cash flow analysis, which helps you assess how your debt-to-income ratio and current ratio got the way they are in the first place. The worksheet below will help you figure out your current debt-to-income ratio. You should also make use of the Cash Flow Worksheet on p. 72, in the Strivers chapter. If you would like to work out a more in-depth financial plan for yourself, check the Squirrels chapter, which guides you through the process.

Let's start with your debt-to-income ratio and see what it means to you. Lenders have long used the debt-to-income ratio in deciding whether to grant credit. You can complete this worksheet on a monthly or yearly basis, and I recommend doing both. In the short term, a monthly ratio will show how strong your financial situation is so that you can begin working on it right away.

To start, you may use a regular piece of lined paper that you divide into three columns. The first column has the lender's name, the second column is Monthly Bills and Payments, and the third column is Total Owed. After you complete your list, draw a horizontal line across the paper, right under your last listing, leaving enough space to list your income, investments, child support payments, and so on. Label this Monthly Income, which will become column four. Put together it looks like this:

DEBT-TO-INCOME WORKSHEET

MONTHLY BILLS

Creditors	Monthly Payment		Total Owed:	
Car loan	$345	_____	$ 7,800	_____
King Credit Visa	60	_____	2,100	_____
XYZ MasterCard	20	_____	800	_____
Mr. Green Lawn Care	20	_____	175	_____
ZCMI Dept. Store	15	_____	225	_____
Totals:	$460	_____	$ 11,100	_____

MONTHLY INCOME

Annual gross income	$ 45,000	_____
Alimony or child support	900	_____
Social Security or government pay		
Interest/investment income		
Regular overtime		
Total annual income	$ 45,900	_____
Divided by 12	$ 3,825	_____

Monthly Debt-to-Income Ratio

$460 ÷ $3,825 = .12 or 12%

Monthly Debt Payments ÷ Monthly Income = Debt-Income Ratio

Here's how to get your debt-to-income ratio:

Column one: List your creditors, let's say, car loan, Visa credit card, etc.

Column two: This covers monthly amounts owed to your creditors. Gather your most recent credit statements. Call lenders to learn what your current balance is if you do not receive your balance on a monthly basis. Some revolving debt, like credit card debt, does not have fixed monthly amounts (unless you are paying the minimum payments). You can call your lender and ask how the payments are calculated, or you can estimate that they are around 4 or 5 percent of the total amount you owe at one time. If it is a 5 percent payment, take the total amount you owe and multiply it by .05 to get your monthly payment amount. Alternately, you can look at several old statements to figure out how the monthly payments were calculated.

Column three: List the entire amount outstanding on each type of debt.

Column four: Income: Here, start with your annual gross income. This is income before deductions—federal, state, and local taxes; Social Security; retirement plan reductions; and child support. Add additional income such as alimony, investment income, and Social Security benefits. Do not include year-end bonuses unless they are guaranteed. To figure out your monthly gross income, do the following calculations:

If you're paid weekly, multiply your weekly income by 52 and divide by 12.

If you're paid every two weeks, multiply your income by 26 and divide by 12.

If you're paid twice a month, multiply your gross income by 2.

If you're paid irregularly, divide your annual gross income by 12.

Next, divide column two, your monthly debt payments, by column four, your total monthly income. The result, in fraction form, is your monthly debt-to-income ratio. Convert the number into a percentage, and that is the percentage of debt you hold to your income.

Analyze your tally. Ideally, experts say, your total monthly debt payments, including your mortgage and credit card payments, should not exceed 36 percent of your gross monthly income. That's one factor mortgage lenders consider when assessing your credit-worthiness. But you can break down your score further.

If your ratio is 15 percent or under, you are in good shape. In fact, you could probably afford to assume some "good" debt. Check the debt you do carry to make sure it has low or reasonable interest rates. If not, search for cheaper credit cards using the resources in the Appendix.

If your debt is between 15 and 20 percent of your gross income, you are still likely to get the loans you apply for, providing you have a good credit record. You might want to examine the rate at which you've incurred new debts: For instance, if you went quickly from a 10 percent to a 20 percent debt-to-income ratio, this may be an indication to lenders that your debt could rise just as quickly above 20 percent.

Carrying a debt percentage of between 20 to 35 percent is still acceptable to many lenders' standards, though most consider it high. On the basis of your debt alone, you are unlikely to be turned down for a loan. On the other hand, an unexpected financial emergency may throw your budget into a tailspin. Start chopping away at your debt now so that it doesn't exceed the 36 percent mark.

As mentioned, mortgage lenders and financial planners consider a debt-to-income ratio of 36 percent and higher too high. Although you still may qualify for new credit cards, mortgage lenders and other big-ticket lenders will probably not accept you for loans. Carrying a debt level that is this high is much more expensive because a higher proportion of your income will automatically be sucked into interest payments.

Design a Budget and Figure Out How to Cut Back

The debt-to-income worksheet will have given you a pretty accurate picture of where you stand financially. You know what your assets and liabilities are, and you have analyzed how your income matches up with your debt. Now that you've charted where your money is disappearing to each month, you will have an accurate picture of whether you are spending beyond your means. Using this information as a base, you now must project into the future to create a budget that works for you.

See a budget as your friend

A budget is a document that gives you control over your finances in a way that lets you decide what is most and least important to you. A budget is an intensely personal plan; probably no one you know has exactly the same priorities you have. When you've executed a budget, you will be able to answer those questions you have asked yourself in the past but were never able to resolve conclusively, such as:

- How much money am I paying out to cover debt (interest and principal)?
- Do I have enough money to cover the payments on more debt?
- What is my biggest debt?
- What debt can I pay off first?
- How long will it take me to pay off my debts at the rate I'm paying them now?

Creating a written budget accomplishes several tasks for you. It communicates your priorities in black-and-white. The process of doing a budget will, in itself, motivate you to take charge of your financial life. As the year goes on, you will feel in control of your money because you will know whether you are spending more or less than you expected. At the end of the month, you can evaluate how you did based on accurate information, making the next month's budget even better.

While I know your situation is about debt in the many thousands, not many hundreds of dollars, still, every penny counts until you're free of your financial liabilities. People always tell me they've cut back as much as possible, and often forget about small but significant money savers that add up:

- Join a food co-op or wholesale food club.
- Trim back on buying many new pieces for your wardrobe each season. Fill in last year's clothes by adding small pieces

(like a new shirt at a reasonable price), but do not buy any additional coats, suits, or outfits.

- If you commute, share a trip with a buddy and split the cost. You'll cut back on filling your tank as well as wear and tear on your car.
- Cut back on meals at work by bringing your own lunch or most of it. Pay for one beverage, but skip desserts, muffins, snacks from vending machines or office building coffee shops, and elaborate coffee drinks that cost four times the amount of a cup of tea. You should be able to save upward of $5 a day. That's $25 a week to put toward paying off a bill.
- Eliminate unreimbursed job expenses. Cut back on books or magazine subscriptions related to your job, and don't resubscribe. Don't buy any supplies, tools, desk calendars, software programs, or desk decoration paraphernalia for your workstation unless you know you will be paid back. You can save a few hundred dollars a year by eliminating these nonessential expenses.

Help Yourself by Leaping over the Biggest Debt Trap: Always Pay *More* Than the Minimum Amount on Your Credit Cards

Suppose you saw a big-screen TV on sale for $1,000 and put the purchase on a credit card. Every month you decide to pay the minimum amount, but four months down the line you see that the balance has barely been lowered by the sum of your payments. What if I told you that by paying the minimum amount, a $1,000 TV will eventually cost you $3,500! That's three and a half times what it would cost someone who paid in cash or with a charge card, like American Express, where you are obliged to pay the full amount every month.

Minimum payments are one of the debt creators of enormous proportion and can be the ruination of many people. Late fees, which can be from about $29 to $49, and overlimit fees, which are about the same, can cancel out your minimum payment and also keep your account over the limit. This is a cycle of debt that the credit card companies help create. It's up to you to break the cycle for yourself.

To give you a better idea of what the numbers look like for other charges, check out the following chart. It shows what it will cost you if you pay only the minimum amount. This is usually *3 percent* of the balance each month on different principal amounts over different periods of time at interest rates of 12 percent, 18 percent, and 21 percent. Some lenders even have interest rates that go as high as 24 to 30 percent, making the amount you'd owe much higher. Keep in mind that no additional fees or charges are factored into the amounts on the chart.

The minimum amount that a card issuer requires you to pay each month is based on a percentage of the total balance you are carrying. Some credit card issuers have lowered minimum payments in recent years to encourage cardholders to pay on time and to lengthen the period of time in which the issuer can collect interest payments. But many cardholders don't realize the actual financial consequences of paying only the minimum amount.

At least one U.S. politician, Connecticut senator Christopher Dodd, has the consumer in mind. He's trying to reform how charges are noted on your bills, by making it a law for credit card companies to disclose *how long it would take to pay off the balance of your debt* by paying just the minimum. Remember, the higher the balance, the longer it will take to pay it off. Some very high balances could take twenty or thirty years at ever-increasing, unregulated interest rates. So far, Senator Dodd's bill has never gotten very far in the Senate and is unlikely ever to become law because of opposition from credit card companies.

You must understand the life-draining effects of negative compounding. Make a minimum payment on a credit card, and you're just treading water, not paying off your debt. With negative compounding, you're paying the minimum due, but when

COST OF MAKING ONLY MINIMUM PAYMENTS

Principal Amount	12%	18%	21%
$ 1,000	$ 1,357.48 (6 years 3 months)	$ 1,683.52 (7 years 8 months)	$ 1,928.26 (8 years 8 months)
2,000	$ 2,850.13 (9 years 1 month)	$ 3,654.47 (11 years 4 months)	$ 4,271.89 (13 years 1 month)
3,000	$ 4,342.70 (10 years 9 months)	$ 5,625.32 (13 years 6 months)	$ 6,615.46 (15 years 8 months)
4,000	$ 5,835.30 (11 years 11 months)	$ 7,596.17 (15 years 1 month)	$ 8,959.10 (17 years 6 months)
5,000	$ 7,327.95 (12 years 10 months)	$ 9,567.05 (16 years 3 months)	$11,302.64 (18 years 11 months)
6,000	$ 8,820.53 (13 years 6 months)	$11,537.95 (17 years 3 months)	$13,646.05 (13 years 0 months)
7,000	$10,313.18 (14 years 2 months)	$13,508.75 (18 years 1 month)	$15,989.73 (21 years 0 months)
8,000	$11,805.75 (14 years 8 months)	$15,479.68 (18 years 9 months)	$18,333.35 (21 years 10 months)
9,000	$13,298.38 (15 years 2 months)	$17,450.53 (19 years 5 months)	$20,676.85 (22 years 7 months)
10,000	$14,790.95 (15 years 7 months)	$19,421.51 (19 years 11 months)	$23,020.47 (23 years 3 months)
11,000	$16,283.56 (16 years 0 months)	$21,392.29 (20 years 6 months)	$25,363.94 (23 years 11 months)
12,000	$17,776.22 (16 years 4 months)	$23,363.20 (20 years 11 months)	$27,707.62 (24 years 5 months)
13,000	$19,268.82 (16 years 8 months)	$25,334.04 (21 years 4 months)	$30,051.18 (24 years 11 months)
14,000	$20,761.43 (17 years 0 months)	$27,304.94 (21 years 9 months)	$32,394.68 (25 years 5 months)
15,000	$22,254.05 (17 years 3 months)	$29,275.75 (22 years 1 month)	$34,738.36 (25 years 10 months)
16,000	$23,746.66 (17 years 6 months)	$31,246.70 (22 years 6 months)	$37,081.89 (26 years 3 months)
17,000	$25,239.22 (17 years 9 months)	$33,217.46 (22 years 9 months)	$39,425.56 (26 years 8 months)
18,000	$26,731.87 (18 years 0 months)	$35,188.47 (23 years 1 month)	$41,768.85 (27 years 0 months)
19,000	$28,224.44 (18 years 3 months)	$37,159.24 (23 years 5 months)	$44,112.53 (27 years 4 months)

the interest is so high, the minimum payment barely touches your principal. Remember: Making just minimum payments can more than triple your original cost because of interest paid over time. But with every $100 you can pay down of your credit card balance, you're saving yourself $150 in interest cost. It's the best investment out there—a guaranteed, risk-free, tax-free return of 18 percent if you are paying 18 percent on a credit card. Paying as much beyond the minimum payment as you can will help move you out of debt faster than you imagine.

Survival Tip: If You Have to Deal with Debt Collectors

I met a man at a seminar who told me that he'd lost his job and was living on a $900-a-month pension. He'd moved to a trailer and had to repair the roof because of a fire, followed by storm damage. He charged $1,500 in supplies on a store credit card and did the repairs himself. He'd fallen behind on the store's payments by a few months and was looking for a part-time job to make up the slack. The crisis for him came during a Thanksgiving celebration at his trailer for his son's family: Dinner was interrupted by the store's collection department team, which called him a total of ten times. "I felt humiliated," he told me. "What could I say to my family, who didn't know things were this bad for me? What could I say to the guy calling me? I just didn't have the money?"

If creditors assign collection agencies to your case, you still have certain rights under the federal Fair Debt Collection Practices Act, governed by the FTC. Here are some of the points you should know. (You can get more information on your rights by contacting the Federal Trade Commission or National Consumer Law Center and asking for a guide called *Fair Debt Collection*. See Resources at the end of this chapter for contact details.) Here are just a few of your rights:

- Debt collectors cannot be abusive, deceptive, or unfair, threaten you with violence, curse at you, force you to accept collect phone calls from them, or advertise your debt to try to humiliate you into paying.
- Debt collectors cannot collect any amount greater than your debt, unless allowed to do so by law; may not deposit a postdated check prematurely; or make you pay for telegrams.
- Collection agencies must send a written notice telling you how much you owe, to whom, and what to do if you dispute the debt.

- Debt collectors cannot falsely imply that they are attorneys or government representatives, imply that you have committed a crime, or misrepresent the amount you owe.
- Debt collectors may not give false information about you to anyone, may not send you anything that looks like an official document from a court or government agency when it is not, or use a false name.
- If you send the agency a letter within thirty days saying that you do not owe the debt in question, the agency cannot contact you again unless it mails you proof of the debt, such as a copy of the bill that remains unpaid.

While this act protects you from insistent agencies in theory, it doesn't absolve your debts. My recommendation is to seek help with experts. Being bullied by creditors doesn't help you, but neither does avoiding the issue. Seek out a reputable debt relief organization (described below) if you cannot figure out how to pay off your creditors on your own. Once you have dug yourself out of debt, with or without the help of a credit counselor, you can finally feel peace and happily live your life. And when this happens, be even kinder to yourself: Make sure you change your spending and credit habits so you live within your means.

Get Help! Check In with a Debt Relief Counselor

With over three million consumers on debt management plans—and experts predicting that the figure will balloon to eight to ten million—you're not alone. Yet some people worry as much about debt relief counseling as the debt itself.

I told you the story earlier about Bob and Jane, who feared going to a credit counselor to sort out their debts. Bob's primary concern was that such a step would be a negative mark on their credit record. This is not always the case. Fair Isaac Corporation, the company that compiles the FICO credit score, officially says that signing up for a debt management program (DMP) with a credit counseling agency is a neutral event—and neither helps nor hurts your credit in itself. (The "FICO" score, an acronym for the Fair Isaac Corporation that developed it, sets the criteria for what goes into your credit rating.) Some creditors may see your using the DMP as a positive step to get out of debt, while other creditors may view it as your last resort before declaring bankruptcy, thereby harming your chances of getting a loan.

The Consumer Credit Counseling Services (CCCS) is a national group with about two hundred local chapters, where some debtors can go first for help. They ask you to fill out a form describing your financial situation, which you mail or e-mail in. After they refer you to a local chapter, you call for an appointment. At that appointment, your debt counselor evaluates your financial situation to determine if it would be best for you to enroll in a debt management program to help you pay off your debts.

If you decide this is the best route to go, the CCCS agency will submit a proposal to your creditors asking them to grant you lower interest rates if you enroll in the DMP. In most cases, you will be accepted. You will then make your payments to the credit counseling agency instead of the creditors, since the counseling agency will make the payments for you. The counseling is confidential, and the fact that you're seeking counseling will not show up in your credit file unless you enroll in its debt management program.

Instead of going to a local CCCS agency, you might find it more convenient and easier to deal with a high-quality national credit counseling agency, such as Debt Relief Solutions (800-4DEBTHELP; www.debtreliefsolutions.com). The clearinghouse refers you to the agency best able to solve your debt problems. They can help you with both unsecured debts like credit cards, student loans, and medical bills, as well as help prevent home foreclosures and settle back tax debts with the IRS.

The clearinghouse handles between ten thousand and twenty

thousand calls a month from people facing one sort of financial watershed or another. Generally, after doing a full budget and income evaluation with them, about 10 to 15 percent of people require a debt management plan. This plan allows them to pay down their debt over a more reasonable time. The credit counseling agency closes accounts, gets lower interest rates than the debtor could get on his or her own (down to between 3 and 10 percent), and the debtor makes one payment a month to the agency. As a fee, they take whatever each state allows in the first month, typically $50 to $75, plus a small percentage of each month's payment thereafter to service your account. Unlike most CCCS agencies, those of Debt Relief Solutions offer a full ninety-day guarantee if you have any problems with how your account has been handled.

Most of the other 85 percent who contact Debt Relief Solutions can manage a plan on their own once they figure out what spending needs to be cut out. Generally, about 3 to 5 percent of people who contact the organization are too far gone to be helped or for them to help themselves. For them, bankruptcy is the only option. But that's fine, too. It's the right tool to give people a fresh start, if necessary.

After working successfully with millions of clients who have gotten out of debt, I asked Chris Viale about the benefits of seeking help through a debt relief program. He said, "Many of the people who we help out of debt are then able to stay on course and not fall back into debt. Also, the myth is that credit counseling is a strike against you, like bankruptcy, so you fear you're going to be tagged a deadbeat for the rest of your life. This is not the case. If you make one year's worth of payments on time, you're considered rehabilitated and back in the eyes of the financial world—who are ready to lend money to you again. I think the biggest story line is home ownership. Sixty percent of the people who come to us have the aspiration of someday owning a home. We get them out of debt, make them understand how to start saving and making a plan to own a home."

This is good news: If you can keep your payments going for a year, you can turn your credit around. The two largest governing bodies over home mortgage lending say that if you're on a debt management plan for at least twelve months, lenders can't hold it against you. (See Resources at the end of this chapter for more information on contacting these agencies.)

Hitting an Extreme: When Your Next Option Is to Declare Bankruptcy

When you've accumulated a lot of debt, have too many creditors hounding you for money, and you see no escape, you might have to consider bankruptcy—a decision not to be taken lightly. It will remain on your credit record for seven to ten years and impair your ability to obtain credit in the future. Potential employers and landlords may also learn that you declared bankruptcy by looking at your credit record and deny you a job or apartment. *Bankruptcy is often not the fresh start that many people think it is.* The federal bankruptcy law that was passed in 2005 makes it much more difficult and costly to file for bankruptcy and get the fresh start you might want from filing for such relief from creditors.

However, there *are* advantages, but there are also myths and misconceptions about what bankruptcy means. I spoke to Lewis Siegel, a bankruptcy lawyer in practice in New York City, about these points. "There's one rumor that people go into bankruptcy to beat or defraud their creditors," he told me. "I won't say it doesn't happen, but this represents a tiny percentage of the people who are at the end of their means and why they're seeking to file. By the time most people get to a bankruptcy lawyer, they've gone through all their savings, pensions, retirement funds; they're in debt and at their wit's end. They're usually borrowing from one bank card to pay another."

There are also misconceptions about ruination for the future. The stigma about declaring bankruptcy has changed in the last twenty or thirty years. For a long while, it meant that creditors would not be willing to lend you money again soon after bankruptcy. That has changed somewhat. Bankruptcy is reported on your credit record from seven to ten years, and during that period top-tier banks such as JPMorgan Chase and Citibank won't extend credit. However, secondary lenders like Providian and Capital One will often make credit available within two years after bankruptcy, if you're making a good salary and building up credit in other ways. You can also rebuild your credit record by using secured credit cards, for which you put up a certain amount of money, such as $500, to get a $500 line of credit. After you have paid your bills reliably for a year to eighteen months, you can generally graduate to an unsecured card from the same issuer.

What is the advantage of declaring bankruptcy? Basically, people seek either a discharge of their debts, meaning the debt is no longer enforceable, or they restructure the debt and pay it off under different terms or over a different time period than was originally agreed to. In the U.S. Bankruptcy Code, Chapter 7 and Chapter 13 are the basic forms for consumers. These are the differences:

Chapter 7 is a liquidation proceeding. Here, you give up your nonexempt assets to a trustee—each state differs as to what's exempt or not, so check with your local lawyer. In most states, but not all, you get to keep your clothing, furniture, and certain other items. The statistics are approximate, but, Lewis Siegel told me, "I'd say that probably about 85 to 90 percent of cases are Chapter 7. About 85 to 90 percent of *those* are no-asset cases. Here, you don't give up anything because you have nothing which is worthwhile for the trustee to administer." So, in return for giving up your nonexempt assets, a trustee can sell them off and divide the money between your creditors. Finally, you get discharged from basically all your debts.

There are certain debts that are not dischargeable, such as taxes owed to the IRS. In Chapter 13, you don't have to give up your nonexempt assets. Instead, you make payments to a trustee over a period of at least three years and a maximum of five years. Chapter 13 works if you need to restructure your house loan or car loan or if you have some nonexempt assets that you really want to keep, like the family piano. With Chapter 13, you can pay out its value over a period of time.

What happens after bankruptcy, if you've lost it all? Siegel said of the upside, "Usually, you don't worry about who's calling on the phone and focus on your work instead of worrying how you'll pay the creditors. You're able to work better without credit cards and learn how to live within your means. You can begin again." And the downside? It's hard to get credit for a while, and then you pay higher rates or fees or are asked for a larger down payment if you're talking about a car or a house.

If you can avoid bankruptcy proceedings by taking your budget and restructuring it, that's fine. But if you've cut back in every imaginable way and the amount you owe is monumental, bankruptcy may be one way to get back on your feet. Talk to your lawyer, who can best judge the situation in your state.

I want to end with what all financial experts most like to see with their clients: good credit. You can find your way out of debt and reestablish yourself. It happens every day. Keep the faith. As with any goal, you need to break it down into small components so that it is manageable. Get help you can trust. Have respect for yourself and your hard-earned money!

FINALLY: POINTS TO REMEMBER FOR DEBT DESPERADOES

Face your demons: If you have a problem spending to make yourself feel better or to make you temporarily forget a problem that will still be there tomorrow, deal with it. Know why you're getting yourself in debt.

Learn to control your spending. Before you buy something, ask yourself, "What better use can I make of all or most of this money?" The object is to shift your thinking so you build up your capital, not add to your expenses and exhaust your resources!

Get help and a plan to pay off your debts. Lose your fears of getting credit counseling to sort out your debts. Contact either the Consumer Credit Counseling Services (CCCS) in your area or a high-quality national credit counseling agency, such as the Debt Relief Clearinghouse. The clearinghouse refers you to the agency best able to solve your debt problems.

Stop the life- and money-draining effects of negative compounding. Always pay more than the minimum payment on a credit card. Otherwise, you're just treading water, not paying off your debt.

When you finally see the end of your debts and learn how to live within your means, your life changes for the better! Eventually, it gets easier to save and invest, rather than shop and spend.

RESOURCES FOR DEBT DESPERADOES

Are you determined to win the battle with debt and finally see the fruits of your hard work? Do you need somewhere to turn for information on what to do next? If you're a Debt Desperado, you probably need some help cleaning house. Rather than merely sweeping your debts and money problems under the rug, focus on clearing up these problems for good. Here are some really helpful sources to turn to.

Books

The Bankruptcy Kit, by John Ventura (Dearborn Publishing, 30 South Wacker Drive, Suite 2500, Chicago, IL 60606; 800-245-2665; www.dearborn.com/trade). Explains the entire bankruptcy process, from dealing with creditors to the discharge hearing.

How to Get Out of Debt, Stay Out of Debt, and Live Prosperously, by Jerrold Mundis (Bantam Books, 1540 Broadway, New York, NY 10036; 800-733-3000; www.randomhouse.com/

bantamdell). This book is based on the principles of Debtors Anonymous. It is practical and offers doable solutions.

Talk Your Way out of Credit Card Debt, by Scott Bilker (Press One Publishing, PO Box 563, Barnegat, NJ 08005; 888-775-4410; www.debtsmart.com). Some tried-and-true ways to lower your bills.

The Total Money Makeover Workbook: A Perfect Plan for Financial Fitness, by Dave Ramsey (Thomas Nelson, PO Box 141000, Nashville, TN 37214; 800-251-4000; www.thomas nelson.com). Helps you get out of debt and into shape financially.

Your Guide to Personal Bankruptcy Without Shame, by James P. Caher and John M. Caher (Henry Holt, 115 West 18th Street, New York, NY 10011; 212-886-9200; www.henryholt.com). Offers good tips on the legal aspects of bankruptcy as well as alternatives and rebuilding.

Publications

DebtSmart E-mail Newsletter (www.debtsmart.com). This free newsletter is available online and provides money-saving techniques, credit counselor recommendations, and strategies for solving credit problems. The author of the newsletter, Scott Bilker, has written several books on credit including his latest, *Talk Your Way out of Credit Card Debt* (see above).

Organizations

American Bankruptcy Institute (44 Canal Center Plaza, Suite 404, Alexandria, VA. 22314; 703-739-0800; www.abiworld.org). Central clearinghouse for information on bankruptcy, including legislative news, bankruptcy court opinions, statistics, sales of assets from bankruptcy courts, and much more.

Association of Independent Consumer Credit Counseling Agencies (11350 Random Hills Road, Suite 800, Fairfax, VA 22030; 703-934-6118; www.aiccca.org). This association of nonprofit agencies maintains a Web site where consumers can go to find a debt counseling agency in their area.

Debtors Anonymous (General Service Office, PO Box 920888, Needham, MA 02492; 781-453-2743; http://debtorsanonymous. org). National organization with local support groups established to help people who consistently take on too much debt.

Debt Relief Clearinghouse (67 Hunt Street, Agawam, MA 01001; 800-779-4499; www.debtreliefonline.com). Organization that refers you to the best agency available to help you pay off unsecured debt such as credit cards, student loans, medical bills, overdue tax bills with the IRS or state agencies, or prevent home foreclosure.

The National Consumer Law Center (77 Summer Street, 10th Floor, Boston, MA 02110; 617-542-8010; www.consumer law.org). This nonprofit organization specializes in consumer issues on behalf of low-income people.

National Foundation for Credit Counseling (801 Roeder Road, Suite 900, Silver Spring, MD 20910; 301-589-5600; www.nfcc. org). This association of nonprofit agencies runs a Web site that is devoted to helping people with their credit problems. Among other things, that site, http://www.debtadvice.org, offers a budget calculator, a directory for consumers to find a counselor, and an online forum for people to chat about their financial matters and share information.

Web Sites

Ftc.gov. Learn about your credit rights in the consumer and statutes sections of the Federal Trade Commission's Web site, including coverage on the Fair Debt Collection Practices Act.

Myvesta.org. This site has many resources for consumers with debt or credit problems. It includes links to talk to a debt expert and to get your credit report, information on scams, and numerous downloadable publications.

CHAPTER 6

The Coasters

*Do you feel pride in how you've made and managed
   your money so far?*
*Can you rebound from a past money mistake, such as
   a bad investment, learn what went wrong, and
   not let it stop you from investing in the future?*
Do you think the future will take care of itself?

A man once came up to me at a seminar I gave on how to feel
secure as you manage your money and said: "Here's my idea of
secure. I've got it made if I don't mess up!" This forty-five-year-
old Cleveland man went on to explain that because he had
enough money, his business was doing well, he was out of debt,
he wasn't facing any lawsuits, and he had enough life insurance, he felt secure. But, he then added, "Until you mentioned
it, I hadn't thought much about retirement. Maybe there goes
my idea of 'safe'!" I thought, I've just had a classic encounter
with a Coaster Money Type!

Can you ever save too much or be a little too cautious about
investing? Ostriches may leave stable financial management to
others and be unsure of how to answer, and Debt Desperadoes
might say no and wish they could finally be in a position to save
too much. But if you're a Coaster, you're likely to both identify

and understand what this man was talking about: You're vigilant and complacent at the same time. On the one hand, you're on top of your income and outgo, and believe you've got every aspect of your money issues covered. You've been vigilant, and feel secure. On the other hand, you may hear or read about an aspect of someone else's healthy financial picture and realize you haven't been as vigilant as you thought you were. You've been too complacent!

There are also Coasters among you in a subgroup called Optimists who take that sense of security to a different plane. If you're more of an Optimist, you can be complacent at times, but your driving philosophy is that security is a given, and a financial state you deserve. All in all, yours makes for an interesting Money Type with loads of potential.

THE COASTER REVEALED

Your Money Type is the most financially stable individual—as a Coaster, you're someone who is both coping and thriving. Coasters are in a better position than many and don't have dramatic problems, but a few financial changes can make a huge difference in your future. When there's no money crisis, I know how the status quo becomes more attractive to you than change—but *standing still and having tunnel vision about money is actually riskier* than you want to believe. I'll get to the reasons very shortly.

While you have your own dynamism, as a Coaster, you can use a bit of a push and a lot of inspiration to get you more actively involved in managing your money and increasing your net worth. So let's look at this thing called the status quo: I know how Coasters love it and how vigilantly they work to maintain it. But life is not as predictable and static as you wish it were, and what you haven't prepared for today can be damaging to your finances in the near future. Think of how money affects you when financial emergencies happen. Or marriages fracture. Or your company's pension fund goes bust. The status quo you thought was the path to contentment can erupt into a rocky road full of potholes. Today you may describe yourself as "comfortable," but tomorrow you might be living dangerously *by not having done enough financial planning and having implemented your plans.*

Whenever I talk to an Optimist, the Coaster's offshoot, I'm struck by his or her overriding belief that can take complacency to another level. Optimists believe that nothing can go wrong because you will ultimately get what is rightfully yours, which you deserve. Most Optimists are baby boomers, the generation born after World War II, specifically in the mid-1940s to early 1950s. Another generation of Optimists who share this money style were born in the 1960s to 1970s. You may be older or younger than the typical Coaster/Optimist, but you share the philosophy that money will come to you and that everything will turn out just fine.

Older Optimists grew up in a period of astonishing change and growth in America. Yours was the first generation to come of age in generally widespread economic prosperity. Younger Optimists grew up in the technology age, and many of you, like Bill Gates and the more successful dot-com and Internet wizards, literally changed the world. No matter what your age, Optimists have a lot in common with one another across generational lines: Both types grew up in periods of economic growth when there were rarely, if ever, money troubles at home. Later, when you went out into the work world, you expected that sense of "having without question" to continue. Not surprisingly, Optimists tend to be comfortable taking bigger risks than Coasters.

Coasters, more than Optimists, focus on feeling safe and secure—getting there and doing what you can to stay there. In general, this is what you mean by these terms. To you, *safe* indicates job security and your ability to keep a stable financial structure in place—but not necessarily a very high income.

Your debts are under control, and your mortgage is probably paid off or is low enough to be manageable. The money you have in the bank may cover enough of your expenses for at least a year. Generally, your head is above water. You're prepared for some eventualities, that is, you have both health and life insurance, a pension fund or retirement plan that's building up, and some investments. If Coasters have any specific financial worry, it's most likely about budgeting to send the kids to college.

So you feel safe, coasting along quietly and sure that if you wanted to invest more or check on better retirement or college funding plans, you'll get around to it.

If you describe yourself as *secure*, you strive to stay on a continuum that maintains security. Every choice you make is meant to keep you secure. So, for example, you'll have greater cash assets than would a safe-feeling Optimist. You probably have more property and securities that require your attention and a calculator. When you're feeling secure, you have money put away to get you through a dry spell or a health crisis for twelve to twenty-four months. If you own a house, it's nearly or all paid for, and you're well on your way to building a comfortable nest egg for the future. You have some room for play without, so to speak, worrying how much the tickets cost. You can travel, buy season tickets to football or the opera, and take on smaller fix-it projects for the house and rebound quickly from the expenditure. When you see your assets totaled up, the numbers make you feel secure—economically and psychologically.

Most Coasters stop here or hope to get to this point. However, I want to encourage all of you to keep your money earning for you! The results will bring you a greater sense of comfort.

Optimists may do *some* financial planning, but for the most part, you live as if life will always be good, safe, *and* secure, and do not question it. If there is a setback, you feel assured that if you wait things out, things will come back around, but your optimism may be based more on wishful thinking than reality.

The Coaster: Your Strengths

At your best, you're organized, responsible, and focused on stability. Because you're vigilant about your finances, you tend to be fairly well educated about money and market trends. Your type is most likely to read about money and what's happening with it in the world—you'll certainly check out magazine or newspaper financial columns, and pick up books that attract you about money matters. Coasters like being in the know. In fact, some of you are inspired to venture out into businesses of your own and become bigger risk-takers than most of your Money Type. But when you do, you will still behave conservatively, always holding on to your inclination for stability above daring.

You are more likely to have decent insurance coverage and to have done some retirement planning. Coasters are hard workers and don't wait for magic to make their income grow. Coasters are good horse traders. Since you're such middle-of-the-road types, you develop a smart sense of proportion, build good working relationships, and do what you need to stay feeling secure. You have most of your financial ducks lined up, and this gives you a sense of pride.

At their best, Optimists have good self-esteem and accomplish a lot with that confident view that prosperity and good fortune will come their way. You're willing to take financial risks and seek out new opportunities to both create and invest in, most notably, companies your generation virtually invented, Internet businesses and the dot-coms. You can be successful innovators, always looking for an improved future and new ways of making money.

The Coaster: Your Weaknesses

Coasters like to tell me that there's no downside to living carefully and not making any drastic voluntary moves that could threaten it. I like to reply, "Not really!" I see too many Coasters who are not doing enough for themselves. I agree that you're doing a good job, but adopting an attitude of complacency—your real number one weakness—can turn out to be a strike against you.

Coasters are too content to just paddle along. Overly conservative Coasters may not be aware of it, but some of you can be frozen in time, certain your investments will still pay the same dividends and interest—and ignore the effect of inflation on your money—and give up opportunities to do better and add to your holdings. While you keep your nose to the grindstone, you're developing a side effect: tunnel vision. In this case, you cannot see beyond the financial boundaries you've so carefully constructed, and you focus unflinchingly straight ahead.

Coasters worry about making a change, especially when the status quo feels so good. I've known Coasters who've turned down higher-paying jobs, fearing that a career change would jeopardize what they have. If your financial motto is "Slow and steady wins the race," here's where it can turn into "Stop and stagnate blocks your path"—and backfire on you. While you think you're doing what's right and best, you may actually be creating financial setbacks.

Optimists are less conservative. You rarely believe that the world will cheat you of your money, but rather, that the world will *inevitably* provide for you. Although you've often achieved prosperity through your own efforts, you can feel too entitled to it—you "deserve it all." Unfortunately, this attitude of entitlement doesn't prepare you well enough for financial setbacks, and you don't have enough of a safety net in case of a financial downswing. When you assume the money will always be there, you wind up unprepared for either small changes or crises. You may be unwilling to adjust your lifestyle or spending habits when you do encounter financial adversity, putting yourself in further jeopardy. Some Optimists get trapped by the dynamic of positive thinking. It's almost as if you fear that not thinking positively is tantamount to a moral lapse and a betrayal of your values.

While I salute both Coaster types for your ability to be stable and secure, I want you to be a lot more prosperous. You can do this by having a little wider vision and taking a few more risks. You'll see how shortly.

Let me introduce you to a few Coasters whose money management style and life goals may be similar to yours.

"Help! I'm in a Holding Pattern, and I Can't Get Out!"

At age forty-four, Nancy, a Houston-based divorced mother of two looks set for life. Nancy has been employed by the Small Business Administration for twenty-six years, having worked her way up the ranks. In six years, she'll be eligible for a much anticipated retirement and young enough, at fifty, to fulfill her dream: opening a restaurant. Nancy has always known financial security, and she's worried about shaking up her security by going into business for herself.

Nancy and her three younger brothers grew up in a traditional middle-class Virginia home where stability and conformity were the dominating values. This ideology always felt right to Nancy, and she never had an inclination to rebel when she was growing up. Her parents never had money problems, and she couldn't imagine living any other way. Her family tended to live kind of frugally, counting pennies and banking what they could, and were generally close, protective of one another, and caring.

Nancy credits her father, a career army officer, for influencing her choice of jobs: working for the civil service. It was a career track Nancy happily ran starting at eighteen, right out of high school, while at night she went to school and earned a business degree. The civil service route made sense to Nancy, who reasoned that she wouldn't have to worry about waves of corporate change or mismanagement, or of having her job outsourced overseas and being put out of work. "I'm grateful to my father for pushing me and my brothers down this road," she told me.

"It may be conservative, but as a result, we're all good with money."

Meanwhile, Nancy married a career army officer and had two daughters. The marriage ended in divorce, and Nancy devoted herself to supporting her daughters and herself as best she could. Smart and determined to succeed, she rapidly moved up through the ranks at her government job, winding up in a key supervisory position.

While her girls grew into adolescents, Nancy stayed at her job, which she liked for its security but not its predictability. Even so, she stayed, admitting that she got lazy about doing what she thought she really wanted to do—own a coffee shop or, better, a restaurant. She liked cooking, the creativity of coming up with a menu, and the friendly ambience—so unlike working all day in a bureaucracy. Nancy was also a bottom-line person, and she also liked the discipline needed to run a restaurant profitably. She'd even taken part-time, second jobs at both kinds of eateries over a five-year period. In fact, Nancy came away assured that she could run a restaurant more successfully than the owners she worked for. But, as Nancy put it, she's terrified to "push herself into that risk category." Despite her procrastination and her fears, Nancy is still lured by the idea of going into her own business.

When I spoke to Nancy, she said she considers herself responsible, yet, she told me, hesitating a moment before continuing, "it embarrasses me to say it, but just maybe I haven't done enough in case of emergencies." Instead, she explained, she "coasts" with existing investments, and she does not take advantage of investment opportunities that she hears about. If a crisis occurred, she told me, she'd need to dip into her investments or seek help from her father. And then there is the tantalizer that seems too out of reach for her—the lure of a second career where she is in business for herself.

Can she afford to make the change? Since her pension will pay her bills without worry, she feels that at fifty she'll be young enough to start another career. Nancy says, however,

NANCY'S FINANCIAL SNAPSHOT

Nancy excels at her job and earns a solid living, and makes careful choices to live within her means. Here's what her money picture looks like:

- She earns $95,000 a year, which includes bonuses, in a managerial position.

- She has a thirty-year fixed mortgage on her new, smaller $178,000 home, purchased after her daughters left for college.

- One of her two cars is paid in full, and she carries home, auto, and life insurance, and has a mutual fund brokerage account. "I like to dabble in investments," she says.

- Her savings account is modest, and her credit card debt, all accumulated by making big purchases related to moving to her new home, is about $12,000. Upon my advice (in an earlier correspondence with her), she transferred the balances to lower-interest cards, reducing her debt.

- As a public employee, her retirement pension plan is guaranteed. She also has a 401(k).

that indecision is "hanging her up." What she's really feeling is a crisis of confidence about moving from a bureaucracy into the private sector. A part of her wants to work with a small business. "I can write a fabulous business plan in my sleep," she relates. "I have all kinds of talents and skills. Give me a mess, and I'll straighten it out. I'm not worried about being good at what I do. But I'm not sure if I shouldn't keep doing what my parents do—play it safe and never look back. I feel I'm doing well with what I have right now, but I want more. I worry that I'm too close to retirement to make any changes, even ones that could significantly improve my financial picture."

When I asked her what her goals are over the next six months, Nancy told me her priority is to see her daughters through college. With their graduation and her retirement around the corner, she may be coasting, but she adds, "I've got to face my future, and soon! Am I going to have a business or not?" Finally, she promised herself that she would do more research on owning a restaurant. Going into business means taking risks, but it also means taking a chance on herself and really testing her business skills.

Clearly, Nancy is more concerned with keeping the status quo than in moving forward with her life, which has always traveled uneventfully along a financially secure continuum. Such a personal history tends to create an understandable conflict for a Coaster personality when the idea of change is introduced—even if she's the one doing the introducing. How sincere is her dream of being in business for herself, or is she flattering herself that she could "do better" than the restaurant owners she worked for? She's toiled for a lifetime to lock her idea of security into place, but the new and the unknown are still a bit threatening. But at least she's still dreaming.

Martin is a different breed of Coaster, who is also stuck and in need of some real encouragement—and self-confidence. This is why:

"My Single-mindedness Won the Race!"

Nancy would have benefited from meeting Martin to get a boost of encouragement about being an entrepreneur. Martin is an interesting man. He reminds me a little of a Striver, but he's bent on achievement as a good thing, rather than flaunting what success buys. Strivers, remember, like to make sure others know the degree to which they are successful—that's part of the drive to make it. Martin is a toned-down version of the Striver mentality—not at all a rare breed—in Optimist's clothes. He's just like others of his Money Type in that he works diligently to maintain security above all. But he's unlike his Coaster counterparts in that he pursues achievement more aggressively, believing positively that he has the future sewn up.

When I first met Martin at a business convention, he told me that he was living his dream. I always like to hear that, but I also heard something else in his tone: an edge of doubt. I wondered what it was and asked him about it in a later phone call. He told me that an old problem of his was on his mind again: competition with his brothers. Here's what happened to this Optimist:

Now a southern California entrepreneur, at thirty-nine, Martin is a self-made man with a successful import business. Martin believes his sharp money savvy will allow him to maintain the comfortable lifestyle to which he has become accustomed. In a way, he also believes that being his own boss inspires him to keep succeeding.

MARTIN'S FINANCIAL SNAPSHOT

"Right now, I live below my means," Martin admitted while quickly acknowledging, "Obviously, I also live really well." He told me that his income is higher than his outgo and that he could "easily afford bigger and better." Married with three children, Martin unabashedly gave this overview of his finances:

- His net worth is $750,000.

- He's building his dream house on a lake.

- He's about to make a deal for sixty acres of land.

- When I brought up the subject of investments, he told me he was conservative but not averse to taking some risks.

Martin attributes his entrepreneurial drive to his parents, who volunteered for the Peace Corps in the idealistic spirit of the 1960s. When their two years of service ended, they moved to Arizona, where Martin's father started a business marketing crafts on a global scale. The business provided the family a comfortable lifestyle in a sprawling three-bedroom home. Martin, the youngest, was considered the jock in the family, the C student with personality and energy. His brothers were A students, who would go on to earn business school degrees.

Martin grew up feeling that he'd never measure up to his brothers' potential success and that he would always lag behind them. Yet, despite or because of feeling he wasn't as good as his brothers, Martin fought to be better. He had that inner fire to succeed, and he wouldn't let himself think that he couldn't get what he wanted. He was, he said, "thinking positively." And his thinking worked. When Martin graduated from college, to everyone's surprise, he decided to follow in his father's footsteps. He was determined to succeed as an entrepreneur and eventually run his own business.

Over the next five years, Martin worked his way up at two import-export firms, traveling widely and learning what he needed to know before going out on his own. Meanwhile, he watched as his brothers took corporate jobs and worked their way up, notch by notch. He never wanted to work for a company and be at the mercy of corporate culture or live with the fear being professionally redundant. Rather, he felt motivated by a drive he calls "the essence of being an entrepreneur." He meant that by working for himself, his fortune was his own to make or break. After a brief partnership with his father, he started his own venture, turning to the market of his generation—Asia—and prospering. By the time he was thirty, Martin was sure he'd made the right career choice. Not only had he done well, he had wound up outearning his brothers.

Now he insists he is worry-free when it comes to financial planning and providing for the years when most people retire. "I don't plan on retiring," he told me. "I like being productive,

I want to continue being active creating things." His aspirations remain high, he says, but he is driven by success rather than the accumulation of wealth for its own sake or, he insists, for the status money can bring.

I wondered if his lack of concern about a potential economic fall was a sign of the overconfidence of the Optimist's modus operandi, or youthful success. Or whether it harked back to his fear of losing the race to the finish line with his brothers. Martin talks with an entrepreneurial pride that barely conceals a certain superiority over his brothers, who, it turns out, are perfectly happy working in corporate America. "I don't begrudge my brothers their success," Martin told me, "but then again, as the son who wasn't expected to succeed as much as I have, I feel as if I've fooled them all. At this point, I hope I'm no longer competing with my brothers. What I make of my life and how I manage money is my business, and has nothing to do with them."

Martin was definitely a very *secure* Optimist, in business for himself and totally dependent on his own judgments and an interested market. Were his ideas of investing in himself and in that plot of real estate (see his financial snapshot) realistic, given the economy's vulnerability to sharp swings? I asked him if he didn't want to invest a chunk of his money in blue chip stocks—essentially conservative vehicles, albeit with a good long-term payoff. Martin brushed aside these suggestions by not addressing them, leaning instead on his role as entrepreneur as his bottom line. In his Optimist's view, he can keep making money, bring out new products, whatever they may be, and maintain his status quo. Given his druthers, the sky's the limit.

Nancy and Martin may be in different tax brackets, but they're both stuck in an emotional quandary about money. Nancy keeps her dreams at arm's length, fearful of shaking up her security by becoming an entrepreneur. Martin is fueled by a need to succeed and fearful of losing what he has by investing in anything or anyone but himself. He is also hooked just enough on the belief that thinking positively about a financial

HOW NOT TO FALL SHORT AT RETIREMENT

Here are a few points to think about so you don't run out of money in your retirement:

- According to Andrew Huddart, CEO of mPower.com, which provides online retirement advice, most people need about 70 percent of their final pay going into retirement to maintain their present lifestyle.

- If you sock away only 10 percent of your salary in a 401(k), you may be out of money by the age of seventy.

- According to the Employee Benefit Research Institute, the average person in his or her sixties has a 401(k) balance of $105,822.

- You may have to either put more money away or work longer before you retire.

venture can help make it come true. Both of them, though, avoid change more than they care to admit.

All is not lost for these two Coasters—or for you, if you relate intimately to their key issues. Here are a number of steps that will get you on the road to being unstuck from where you are now.

MAKING CHANGES: THE EMOTIONAL PATH

When I think about Nancy and Martin, I see hardworking people seeking a good life. But I also see people who are a little overwhelmed by having to make some big choices. It's never easy to move away from a comfortable situation—the drive for *security* being both the guiding light and the passion of the Coaster-Optimist personality—but in these times, it's necessary to take some risks.

How can Nancy, Martin, or you, if you're a classic Coaster, shake up your world just enough to increase your assets and benefit your financial future? First, Coasters help themselves most by relinquishing any counterproductive financial behavior that smacks of complacency. Are you clinging too dearly to what you know about saving and investing and not daring to go beyond your usual borders? Or like Martin, do you think you're a one-man band and seek only your own limiting financial counsel—and like many Optimists, think the money will always be there or get there?

Why change how you think about money if everything seems fine?

I don't like to say it so bluntly, but sudden demands on your money can trigger *fear*—a fear of not meeting an important bill. Consider this: If a payment is due for your teenager's first year of college and you don't have the money to fund it, or you've come up short on a down payment for the house you want—well, you cannot feel either good or complacent any longer. In this case, fear, or certainly active worry, can be a better motivator to spur you to think about getting yourself into better financial shape.

There are any number of ways to deflate your complacency *and* transform your "fear factor" by exercising just enough financial pluck.

You would do yourself an enormous favor by being willing to take a few steps out of the box and doing more! How? Let me start with Nancy's challenging issue—an overidentification with her parents' values, while at the same time feeling conflicted because she wants something different for herself from what they have. Maybe this is partially your story, too. It takes a shift in thinking, but it's really possible to break through this kind of emotional dilemma. It shapes up this way:

Your Future Doesn't Have to Duplicate
Anyone Else's Past!

Nancy is a woman who easily and comfortably shares a dominant trait with her ultraconservative parents—the drive toward conformity and security. In fact, when her father retired from the army and her mother from teaching, they each took a civil service job, still insecure about working in the private sector.

While in her heart Nancy may be saying, "I am them and they are me," her reasoning mind persists in delivering another more daring message about using money more creatively than history says is possible in her family. She hears herself saying, "I am them, but *I'm also me*. It's okay to make a decision that suits me and that I know I can achieve. I'm not betraying my parents if I try something new." This idea is creating a conflict for her. And what if you want to dare to be different and have more, while also holding on to security? You may be saying something similar to yourself, such as, "My family always managed money *this* way, not *that* way. We're conservative. Do I dare take a gamble?"

Do you share Nancy's lifelong inclination to hew to the status quo? If so, it probably reflects back on how your parents raised a family without breaking the bank, and at the same time took care of themselves in their old age. It's likely that your parents played their cards close to the vest and never stretched to take any risks. And now, like Nancy, you probably so identify with your parents' values that you feel compelled to follow their lead. But it goes deeper.

Coasters like Nancy are understandably worried about building a more satisfying life for themselves than the one their parents had. Taking risks and taking a stand, which means you must defy the family's traditions, is hard for you. Yet the truth is that neither you nor Nancy will get what you want by continuing with your family's tentative approach to money. Psychologists tell me that when you grow up in a family that is so fixed on regimentation and takes no risks in any sphere, your behavior may reflect their fears of having nothing. You may not have grown up in a home in money trouble. You may not be in money trouble now, but you can't figure out how to live better and get ahead because you're used to moving in careful, tiny steps. Change is on the way.

Try this shift in thinking:

The good news is that you can change your family history by *following your own lead, without jeopardizing your security* to make improvements. Rather than blindly abiding by your father's, mother's, or some family dynasty's code of behavior, understand that you do not have to duplicate anyone's idea of what to do with your money. Rather, you can make some small changes that can get you closer to what *you* want—not what others want for you or what you believe you must do to please others—and still feel secure.

One way to start being your own financial person is to look at your own talents and passions, and decide if you're using them in your best interests. Take Nancy as an example. What small-business-owner-to-be doesn't need the advice and expertise of a skilled writer who says she can do business plans "in her sleep"? I could easily see Nancy applying her business skills in the private sector and earning extra income. Yet people like Nancy are understandably frightened of the unknown.

Unless you try something, you won't know what you can or cannot do. But if you have a desire to create a more satisfying life for yourself than the one your parents led, you need to make the unknown *known*. No one can make that shift but you. Keep your financial safety nets, and take a step out into change. You don't want to go from zero to sixty, so to speak, but accelerate slowly. Rather than jump into fulfilling a big dream, grow your confidence by starting small. You don't even have to tell anyone in your family what your plan is. Speak only to people who are supportive of you, and don't hope to convert naysayers.

So, back to Nancy as an example for you. Nancy is unable to take the leap to restaurateur, her dream, with its complicated factors involved in being a success. She's stuck because she can hear her father's voice in her head reminding her of how she *will* lose money—and no one in their family loses money! Instead, she could make the move to working with a consultancy firm. This doesn't compromise her pension income and allows her to keep up her earning potential. Over the next five years or so, she should be able to set up any number of plans that insure her against financial crisis. (You'll read exactly how to do this in the following Financial Path.)

Most of all, when you make this shift in thinking, you need to get as comfortable as you can while making little changes that do *not* follow along in your parents' footsteps. Ignore the lifelong silent message from your family, "It is better to do things safely and not dare to reach out for more." If you have dreams, work at them! You are your own person. If you really were like your parents, you would have stopped dreaming a long time ago.

Not Wanting to Better a Much Loved Parent

Psychologists suggest that Nancy fears hurting her father, whom she so admires, by striving beyond *his* capabilities. This is not an uncommon emotional conflict provoking guilt that many Coasters (as well as other Money Types) confront and may not like to talk about. Here's Dad or Mom who has worked so hard and whose values you believe in. Here you are, in a position to exceed that parent's aspirations and income. Some Coasters, a woman like Nancy, for example, have always been a "good" daughter and a "good" girl. And as much as she's indecisive about venturing into the private sector, so is she feeling that guilt about distinguishing herself from the family. Is there a resolution to this issue for Nancy or for you?

The truth is that there are parents who chide their children for wanting more and pursuing different lives. They tell you how they feel betrayed, abandoned, or belittled by their more successful children. They are likely to discourage your interests and argue for you to "follow tradition," whatever that may be. And then there are parents (like Nancy's) who are your cheering section throughout your life and who worry about your never being in financial jeopardy. Their devotion to security may seem so rigid that you fear you'll threaten the relationship by wanting something different.

Do you need to put your own financial aspirations aside to remain not only a child in your parents' eyes but a "good" child?

Try this shift in thinking:

If you do or can possibly outearn a parent you admire and love deeply, don't punish yourself by feeling as if you betrayed them! Instead, pat yourself on the back. Your parents have done a good job raising you, have given you values, and have taught

---

ARE YOU ON TRACK?

A Roper Public Affairs survey of 1,500 Americans revealed that saving for retirement is by far the major financial goal, but, ironically, most of us *do not know what we have to do to reach that goal satisfactorily*!

Asked whether they know how much to save or invest to attain their goals, just under half of the respondents who are saving for retirement know how much they should be putting away. The same is true for people who are saving to buy a house—and the number is worse for other financial goals, such as "saving for a rainy day," having enough for a major home renovation, paying for children's education, or buying a second home.

you how to manage money and take care of yourself. This is good parenting, so thank them, and walk on your own. When you separate from parents, you're different only in that you're your own person, while still his or her child.

My bet is that Nancy's father, for example, worries about what he's always worried about: undisturbed security and the insecurity of business risks. My advice to Nancy and to you is: Don't give up your chances for increased financial success because you believe your money will show up your parents. If you make it, they should be proud. If they're a little envious, be kind and they'll eventually deal with it. I can't imagine that a parent isn't strong enough to accept a child's greater financial success and wish them well!

I only hope you take the higher road for yourself, and keep your eye on your destination.

The Favored Son Dilemma: When the Child Voted Least Likely to Succeed Proves a Different Point

I thought about this thing called complacency, so typical of Coasters, and realized that Martin was expressing it more as an Optimist would. Martin felt he had an obligation to think positively, not only about himself but about money. For him, peace of mind resided almost entirely in knowing he was running a near-million-dollar-business on his own. He was letting his money ride on his own decisions in his own business and brushing off the idea of investing in other profitable businesses. However, to acknowledge that others may know as much (or more) about money as he does reminded him of his past. For him to give in to feelings of self-doubt was tantamount to giving up on himself and wooing failure instead.

His complacency had his name on it. But under "Martin, entrepreneur" were the unwritten words only he could read: "I made it, but my brothers are still smarter. Can I keep the success going?"

If you were the son or daughter who was thought to be "most likely *not* to succeed," but you did succeed, you probably grew up wondering if your parents knew something about you that you didn't. Why did they see you at the bottom of the heap? In a crisis of confidence, you still hear their remarks in your head about your not measuring up to a sibling. But your track record as a grown-up in business says you are not only as good but better! What do you do? You don't want to fail and thereby prove them right, but part of you (the kid in you) may want to fail so you can't keep proving them wrong. Stop here and give yourself a break.

Let me go back to Martin for a minute. On the surface, Martin speaks proudly of what he's done, but therein lies that darker inner anxiety. His brothers have major jobs in corporations, and on the surface he jokingly looks down on them, calling them "wage slaves."

While Martin was succeeding, he was also becoming a little arrogant, making himself the all-around expert on money management, a one-man band. In a way, watching what happened to others who lost money in the stock market was a bit of an ego boost for him. Martin admits that he felt superior when his brothers lost a lot of money in the market by thinking, "Aren't I smart to have stayed out of those investments!" This rationale allows him to talk about his great achievement—building a business and being Mr. Entrepreneur in the family.

Martin's essentially fine, but he has to stop competing with his brothers and, most importantly, accept himself. I would ask you to consider this advice for yourself, if this issue threatens to undermine your financial stability. How?

Try this shift in thinking:

If you're someone who needs to show your siblings how capable you are, and are thereby putting yourself at risk, you're not operating in your best interest. There comes a point when sibling rivalry makes no sense, and jockeying for position within the family pays you back in nothing but frustration. Give yourself credit for what you've done and how far you've come. Here, truly, is where you can apply your Optimist's inclination for thinking positively. Ask yourself if you've denied or diminished financial advice because you equate "expertise" with the experts who have it—that is, your siblings who've got the grad school degrees. All people who want to help you are not your siblings in disguise. If you've done well for yourself so far, you no longer need to let your siblings make you feel unsure of yourself.

If you understand this situation, step back and get some perspective on who you are. Have you basically forged your own achievements, despite others expecting less of you? Have you tended to live with the family teasing you about how you didn't measure up to a sibling's potential? But have you always known that you have the stuff to succeed? And did you do it, despite what your parents believed or what your brother's (or sister's) potential was supposed to be? Good for you.

For example, look at what Martin is doing: He's so determined to prove he can succeed without a business school degree or financial advice—which both represent what his brothers have and do—he may be heading for financial problems. He puts nearly all his eggs in his own basket, and furthermore, he's afraid to look at what can potentially happen. He coasts along, believing that things will take care of themselves and he'll remain in fine shape. In actuality, he knows that his brothers, with their pensions, are likely to be financially secure. He's scared to look ahead, as if it would stop the roll he's on.

Sometimes, while playing it shrewdly and carefully, you avoid seeing the broader view of what can happen to your money because you're stuck emotionally. Even more to the point, some Optimists make thinking positively about what they have the power to do the ultimate virtue. To this end, you judge yourselves weak, vacillating, or complaining if you have a negative thought about yourself. What happens is that you can develop a kind of tunnel vision where you stop growing financially and emotionally. Instead, understand your goals, aspirations, and what you want the focus of your financial future to be. And understand, of course, what is of least importance—worrying about bettering your siblings.

What's interesting about Martin's attachment to thinking positively is that he always faces the truth about finances. My bet is you do, too. Unlike the Ostrich, who prefers to hide from money issues, the Optimist takes them on. So, thinking positively doesn't make you into someone who goes off in a dreamworld where goodness and beauty prevail, and where money is deemed unimportant. Rather, you take positive thinking too personally, even as it dominates how you make decisions. Allow that you can make mistakes, but be aware of them and what happened. Failing to take action when you need to can lead to real disaster.

MAKING CHANGES: THE FINANCIAL PATH

When I check which Money Type is most likely to contact me for financial information and advice, I'm always surprised that Coasters-Optimists—the most balanced of the group—win out. This is meaningful. I get a lot of correspondence that's full of detailed information about where your money is going, and nearly every note reflects a genuine pride in feeling, generally, as if you've made the right decisions. This is great. But because every note also contains requests for advice on improving your finances, I want to shake things up a little for you.

My goal for you is *more* security and prosperity, which can be achieved only when you either take a little more risk with investments and/or, ironically, invest in yourself. I'll tell you how shortly. Because your Money Type is essentially a good money manager, you can make the kind of changes that will ultimately pay off. But to make any change in your life, you need a goal, a plan, and, to really get you going, *motivation*. A goal such as accumulating more money to have a cushier retirement has a built-in motivator—getting to sixty-five and knowing you don't have to worry about feeling secure as you age.

For a Detroit woman who contacted me, a better retirement was important, but her heart was in making money creatively outside her salaried job. She wrote, "I don't want to get to sixty-five without doing something more with money than saving it." When this Coaster finally had an opportunity to test her ability to take a risk for the first time—and finally connect with her "inner entrepreneur"—life changed in ways she'd only dreamed about. You may see yourself in her story and understand how you can fulfill a financial dream that you thought would always be out of reach.

Breaking Out of the Mold While Staying in Good Financial Shape

When Amy e-mailed me the first time, this forty-four-year-old single mother wrote that, since her divorce, she's become even more of a "savings queen" who would like to expand her financial interests.

As with many Coasters, Amy believed her savings plans would take care of everything, but she knows she's fooling herself. At first glance, Amy's monthly money management pattern looked sensible.

But if Amy has a financial flaw, it's that she saves too much. She's debt-free, but her disposable income is at a premium, especially with a teenage son.

She sounded so much like many Coasters who work to sustain a certain level of security and go no further. Then came a sense of needing change, but how? Amy reads voraciously about money, personal finance, and investing. "I'd love to do lectures for people with modest-to-middle incomes," she wrote, "but it's not enough to talk about going into municipal bonds. Money is the most exciting thing in the world. People are so afraid of it. Sure, it intimidates me, too—no doubt about it. I

AMY'S FINANCIAL SNAPSHOT

- She earns about $43,000 a year as a supervisor in a non-profit rights organization.

- 15 percent of her weekly salary goes into a 403(b).

- $300 a month is automatically deposited in an education fund for her son.

- $150 from each paycheck goes to pay the property taxes on her home.

- She paid off a fifteen-year mortgage in ten years, using the funds from her alimony payments to own her house free and clear in two-thirds the time.

- She has three credit cards she rarely uses.

dream about going into business but fear losing what I've knocked myself out to save."

Destiny then dealt Amy a winning hand, and all she had to do was pick up the cards. First, her ex-husband sold a parcel of land that six family members had invested in ten years earlier. Amy's share of the proceeds was $8,000. She put the money directly into her savings account until she could decide what to do with it for the long run. Then a close friend who had a profitable turnaround by refurbishing a fixer-upper home asked Amy to go in with her as a partner in another house she was looking at in an up-and-coming area. Amy's friend hired an excellent carpenter-handyman on the first house, who is also interested in going in for a share on another house.

Amy's first inclination, she wrote, was to assure herself this deal wasn't for her. "I can't afford to be in debt because I save too much," she explained. But out of curiosity, she took a ride with her friend to look at the house. She could see the potential. Then she read everything she could about real estate and partnership deals. Amy's friend was giving her another week to decide whether to buy in for $15,000. That meant pulling $7,000 out of her savings account and adding it to the windfall from her husband. She ended her e-mail to me with, "I'm panicked and I'm stuck. I'm better off investing in blue chip stocks, right? Any advice on how to proceed?"

Placing Unfair Limitations on Yourself

What's so interesting about Amy is that she has a powerhouse streak that she's squelched and is expressed only in her dreams. While she says she reads *voraciously* about money and how people make it, I picked up something else in how she talks about herself—that she also reads about money *vicariously*. That is, she's reading about how to grow money and how *others* invest and live out their financial goals. Then, in her fantasies, she puts herself in their place and is moved by the stories. But she hasn't taken the important leap: Amy has to stop thinking of herself as someone for whom money will always be limited and expand her expectations—and believe she *can* go to the next economic level and succeed comfortably.

Something else is operating here. Many people, Amy included, tend to equate financial success with big-money deals, access to a secret "network" whose members get in on the ground floor in moneymaking ventures—or the simple, safe system that adds and subtracts the sums in their bank accounts. The truth is, moneymaking opportunities are all around you—and around Amy—through people whose expertise can be a valuable source of that sought-after access. If they're willing to share their knowledge and ask you in to a venture, check it out carefully. Amy's neighbor is just such access to opportunity.

It's clear to me that Amy's task is to broaden her vision for herself. Then she can accept that she's entitled to more. But to make any life change, she needs to clarify and understand where she was. Since Amy had only one week to make her decision, I could not make it for her, but I did suggest that she answer four questions. (Now I would suggest she read Chapter 2 of this book and answer the questions there. Answer these for yourself, too.)

1. Did your family tell you what they thought you would be capable of earning or having? Have you lived out *their* image of you, in spite of yourself?
2. Can you imagine making a lot of money and not feeling as if you are selling out or doing something wrong?
3. What do you want to do with your life in terms of earning potential?
4. What excuses do you give yourself to not make changes? Write them down, and then think of solutions to overcome these excuses. (Understanding the excuses that hold you back gives you the power to fight them.)

Amy shot her answers back to me, and I'll sum them up for you: Part of Amy's thinking about *saved* money being equal to security comes from her upbringing. Her father, a shopkeeper, passed his fear of losing everything along to his four daughters, all of whom are either Coasters or Squirrels. But Amy, the oldest child, somehow, by temperament over teaching, loved making money as much as she feared not saving any. This influenced her choice of career—working in the nonprofit sector where the struggle for funding a cause is a way of life. Her office buddies believe that working for profit or liking money means you "sell out" and lose sight of your values. (This is an unfortunate and inaccurate belief.)

So, here's Amy, a passionate closet entrepreneur, surrounded by naysayers. Except for her friend who knows in her gut that Amy is the right partner at the right time for refurbishing and reselling houses. And Amy's excuses for not going beyond the cult of savings? Amy told me that when she looked over her excuses, she was surprised to learn how negatively she thought about life. She said, "I thought saving meant something positive. I have money. I have accounts with my name on them, therefore I am! I see I talk about money and life in terms of *what is missing* and *what I don't have*. No way to live life. I thought, it's now or never. It wasn't easy. I was shaking with dread, as if I were jumping out of a plane and wondering if my parachute would open. With a few hours to go, I called my friend and said, 'Let's do this deal and don't let me change my mind.'"

About seven months later, Amy e-mailed me to say that the refurbished house sold, and she made $20,000 over her $15,000 investment. This is a significant increase over her 2 or 3 percent interest savings accounts. This success has both inspired and encouraged her to continue her quest to be an entrepreneur, one positive small step at a time. My sense is that Amy will break through her outdated ideas about money and her limitations, and enjoy her work and her profits as she deserves to do.

Now, let's tackle the three essentials for you:

Setting Up a Worry-Free Future

If you want to look into the future and see yourself financially worry-free, you will need to sit down and do some serious retirement planning. Take a chunk of a few weekends and think it out. Talk to your family. Pull out your calculator or set up a software program, such as Quicken, that helps you through the process. It may be tedious, but when you're done with your worksheet, you'll have a great sense of satisfaction.

You'll need to do some realistic projections of what you'll need for the future. The younger you are when you start planning for retirement, the better off you'll be. In fact, a survey done by Vanguard, the mutual fund giant, reported that *only one-third* of us are on track to have a retirement income equal to 70 percent or more of what we now earn, *one-third* are likely to see 50 percent of their income, and the others are way behind, saying they're not saving enough for retirement.

I'll break it down a bit more for you.

Planning Ahead: How Much You Need to Save to Have a Worry-Free Retirement

Financial planners typically estimate that you'll need 60 to 100 percent of what you spend now for your retirement. How much you'll need depends on how lavish your dreams are. If you're like most Coasters or an Optimist like Martin, you have a rough idea of where your money goes. You need, however, to be specific. If you're completely clueless, get a notebook and begin keeping a diary of all your spending for a few weeks. Keep track of monthly bills, groceries, movies, transportation, trips to Pizza Hut for take-out dinner. Glean information from your checkbook and your credit card statements. After several weeks, you'll be able to produce an average monthly figure for expenses.

To help you get started, copy and use the Monthly Budgeting Worksheet on page 87 to get a good grasp on your current needs. You'll also see what's most likely to change by the time you retire: Your children will be out of the house and on their own, and your mortgage will be mostly or all paid off, although there will be taxes and you won't have the expenses associated with working to contend with. While you're striking things off the list, realize there will be new expenses on the horizon. You'll have time to travel, continue your education, golf—even start a small home business. What will your to-do list cost you?

Now, for a rough idea of your expenses in retirement, use the Retirement Expenses Worksheet on the following page. This simple worksheet is designed to adjust your working years' level of expenses to your retirement years' level of expenses and to factor in a long-term inflation rate of 4.5 percent. The savings called for in item 2 include all regular savings plus contributions to retirement plans such as 401(k)s and individual retirement accounts (IRAs). The worksheet's sample figures assume an annual income of $50,000, an annual savings of $5,000, a 70 percent level of retirement spending, and twenty years before retirement. I've included two other worksheets as well, the Capital Accumulation Worksheet and the Annual Retirement Savings Worksheet, which together will give you a pretty complete picture of how to plan for a comfortable retirement.

A few words on the inflation factor: Although inflation's been a relatively tame beast in the past decade, it could rear its

RETIREMENT EXPENSES WORKSHEET

	Example	Your Situation
1. Present Gross Annual Income	$50,000	$_____
2. Present Annual Savings	$ 5,000	$_____
3. Current Spending (Subtract item 2 from item 1)	$45,000	$_____
4. Retirement Spending Level (between 60 and 80% depending on your assumptions of lifestyle)	70%	_____ %
5. Annual Cost of Living (in present dollars) if You Retired Now (Multiply item 4 by item 3)	$31,500	$_____
6. 4.5% Inflation Factor (from table below)	2.4	_____
7. Estimated Annual Cost of Living (in future dollars) at Retirement (Multiply item 6 by item 5)	$75,600	$_____

Years Until Retirement	Inflation Factor
40	5.8
35	4.7
30	3.7
25	3
20	2.4
15	1.9
10	1.6
5	1.2

CAPITAL ACCUMULATION WORKSHEET

	Example	Your Situation
1. Estimated Annual Cost of Living (in future dollars) at Retirement (item 7 from Retirement Expenses Worksheet)	$75,600	$
2. Annual Pension Income	10,000	
3. Inflation-Adjusted Pension Income (Multiply item 2 by appropriate inflation factor in Retirement Expenses Worksheet)	24,000	
4. Annual Social Security Benefits	15,000	
5. Inflation-Adjusted Social Security Benefit (Multiply item 4 by appropriate inflation factor)	36,000	
6. Inflation-Adjusted Pension and Social Security Income (Add items 3 and 5)	60,000	
7. Amount by which Expenses Exceed Pension and Social Security Income (Subtract item 6 from item 1)	15,600	
8. Needed Capital (Multiply item 7 by 20)	$312,000	$

ugly head again. You'll have to consider the impact of inflation on your estimates for your retirement cost of living and your investment returns in retirement. Your retirement kitty can cover your lifestyle comfortably if inflation stays mild, but be aware of what an upsurge in inflation could mean. The impact of inflation increases over time, and you have to take into consideration not just the expected rate of inflation but such things as how many years you have until you retire and how long you expect to be in retirement.

ANNUAL RETIREMENT SAVINGS WORKSHEET

	Example	Your Situation
1. Capital Needed to Fund Retirement (item 8 from Capital Accumulation Worksheet)	$312,000	$_____
2. Current Investment Assets (value of stocks, bonds, mutual funds, etc.)	$30,000	$_____
3. 7.5% Appreciation Factor (from table below)	4.2	_____
4. Appreciation of Your Investment Assets until Retirement (Multiply item 2 by item 3)	$126,000	$_____
5. Other Assets Required by Retirement Age (Subtract item 4 from item 1)	$186,000	$_____
6. Savings Factor for Years Until Retirement (from table below)	0.0231	_____
7. Savings Needed over the Next Year (Multiply item 5 by item 6)	$4,296	$_____

Years Until Retirement	7.5% Appreciation Factor
40	18
35	12.6
30	8.8
25	6.1
20	4.2
15	3
10	2.1
5	1.4

Years Until Retirement	
40	0.0044
35	0.0065
30	0.0097
25	0.0147
20	0.0231
15	0.0383
10	0.0707
5	0.1722

WHEN TO TAP SOCIAL SECURITY BENEFITS

Just as deciding when to retire is a major decision, so is deciding when to tap your Social Security benefits. People ask me whether it's smart to start dipping into the benefits as early as age sixty-two. You can, but know the financial upshot. If you collect before sixty-five, your benefits are reduced five-ninths of 1 percent for each month before your full retirement age. So, if your full retirement age is sixty-five and you sign up for collecting Social Security when you're sixty-four, you'll receive 93 percent of your full benefit. At age sixty-two, you would get 80 percent. Note, however, that the reduction will be greater in future years as the full retirement age increases.

There are advantages and disadvantages to taking your benefits before your full retirement age:

- The downside is that your benefits are permanently reduced. For example, people who took early benefits at sixty-two in 2003 have their checks permanently reduced by 20.8 percent.

- The upside is that you collect benefits for a longer period of time. And if you're strapped for cash, you may have few choices other than turning to Social Security.

This is the second big money issue for Coasters to manage:

Planning Ahead: How Much You Need to Save to Pay for Your Children's College Education

If you're feeling overwhelmed by what four years of college for just one child can cost, you are not alone. While some Coasters begin saving and planning for this expense when their children

It's a big decision. Contact Social Security for more information.

The age at which full benefits are payable is increasing in gradual steps from sixty-five to sixty-seven. The following table lists the steps:

Age to Receive Full Social Security Benefits

Year of Birth	Full Retirement Age
1937 or earlier	65
1938	65 and 2 months
1939	65 and 4 months
1940	65 and 6 months
1941	65 and 8 months
1942	65 and 10 months
1943–54	66
1955	66 and 2 months
1956	66 and 4 months
1957	66 and 6 months
1958	66 and 8 months
1959	66 and 10 months
1960 and later	67

Source: Social Security Administration

are born, most do not. Rather than dwell on how much money you might have saved, start planning today and don't look back. I have a few ideas that will definitely guide you toward meeting college costs securely.

Your first step involves getting a rough idea of just how much money you'll need to spend annually, quarterly, or monthly. With that in mind, you can create a realistic savings plan that you can live with. College costs don't just include full-time or part-time tuition, but can include special fees (depending on the

APPROXIMATE YEARLY SOCIAL SECURITY BENEFITS, DEPENDING ON EARNINGS AND WHEN BENEFITS BEGIN

Age in 2004	Age When Benefits Begin	Estimated earnings in 2003 and benefit at entitlement (NRA)							
25	67	Earnings in 2003	$ 5,898	$11,796	$17,693	$23,591	$29,489	$35,387	$87,000
		Yearly benefit amount	7,541	10,740	13,943	17,141	19,513	21,013	25,063
35	67	Earnings in 2003	9,778	19,557	29,335	39,113	48,891	58,670	87,000
		Yearly benefit amount	7,541	10,740	13,943	17,141	19,513	21,013	24,890
45	66 & 10 mos.	Earnings in 2003	11,060	22,120	33,180	44,240	55,299	66,359	87,000
		Yearly benefit amount	7,541	10,740	13,943	17,141	19,513	21,013	24,890
55	66	Earnings in 2003	10,443	20,886	31,328	41,771	52,214	62,657	87,000
		Yearly benefit amount	7,541	10,740	13,943	17,141	19,513	21,013	24,512
65	65 & 4 mos.	Earnings in 2003	6,898	13,796	20,695	27,593	34,491	41,389	87,000
		Yearly benefit amount	7,204	10,268	13,331	16,394	18,587	19,732	21,905

Source: Social Security Administration

Note:

1 The assumption underlying the above benefit estimates are similar to those used for the Social Security Statement. These estimates reflect no increase in the cost of living or average wage and earnings level after December 2003. However, earnings after 2003 follow scaled earnings patterns as age increases.

2 Scaled earnings patterns starting at age 21 are assumed for all but the maximum worker. These scaled patterns reflect the relative earnings level by age experienced during 1991–2000. For the maximum worker, earnings start at age 22 and are assumed to be equal to the OASDI benefit and contribution base through 2003. (For 2003, this amount was $87,000.)

college), books and supplies, and, if your child is away at school, room and board.

For a rough idea of how much college might cost and how much you must save, you have a few choices. You can ask a financial planner to calculate the amounts. Or you can use one of the software programs on the market or the many calculators on college financing found in related Web sites to figure it out for yourself. (See a few of these sites in the Resources section at the end of this chapter.) You can also find similar exercises available in such software as Quicken and Microsoft Money.

I've put together a sample worksheet that will help you estimate both college costs and your savings needs (see page 123). The entries assume your child is two years old when you start saving, that he or she will enter college at eighteen, and that you'll continue to save all through your child's college years. Also included is the estimate that college costs will escalate 5 percent a year. It also assumes you earn 8 percent per year after taxes on your investments and are in the 31 percent federal tax rate bracket. To complete the worksheet, you must know the current annual cost of a school your child might attend. Your best bet is to call the college or check out the figures on the school's Web site.

Above all, you will see by trying various combinations of factors on the worksheet that the earlier you start to save, the less you must put aside each month or each year. And, of course, the longer you wait, the more you must save every month. *A rule of thumb is to set aside between $2,000 and $4,000 a year if you begin when your child is born.* If you start saving when he or she is in the second or third grade, you'll need a reserve between $4,000 and $8,000 a year.

Setting Up a Savings Plan Targeted for College Costs

When people ask me about college savings plans, the first thing I tell them is to *save consistently*. There's economic power in putting aside at least $50, or even better, $100 a month. Check the chart below, Money Accumulated by Investing $100 per Month, to see what I mean.

In the left column, find the number of years until your child enrolls in college. Across the top, you can see how your money will compound at different after-tax rates of return. If you save more than $100 a month, multiply these numbers by the appropriate multiple of $100. For example, if you save $400 a month, multiply these numbers by four. If you save less than $100, do the math that fits your saving profile.

An Option to Help You Pay Off College Loans: Reverse Mortgages

Coasters-Optimists may want to investigate this option, if paying off college costs is still an ongoing financial issue. A reverse

MONEY ACCUMULATED BY INVESTING $100 PER MONTH

# of Years until College	Rates of Return 5.5%	7%	8%	9%	10%	12%
1	$ 1,236	$ 1,246	$ 1,253	$ 1,260	$ 1,267	$ 1,281
2	2,542	2,583	2,611	2,638	2,667	2,724
3	3,922	4,016	4,081	4,146	4,213	4,351
4	5,380	5,553	5,673	5,795	5,921	6,183
5	6,920	7,201	7,397	7,599	7,808	8,349
6	8,546	8,968	9,264	9,572	9,893	10,576
7	10,265	10,863	11,286	11,730	12,196	13,198
8	12,080	12,895	13,476	14,091	14,740	16,153
9	13,998	15,073	15,848	16,672	17,550	19,482
10	16,024	17,409	18,417	19,497	20,655	23,234
11	18,164	19,914	21,198	22,586	24,085	27,461
12	20,425	22,602	24,211	25,964	27,874	32,225
13	22,814	25,481	27,474	29,660	32,060	37,593
14	25,537	28,569	31,008	33,703	36,684	43,642
15	28,002	31,881	34,835	38,124	41,792	50,458
16	30,818	35,432	38,979	42,961	47,436	58,138
17	33,793	39,240	43,468	48,251	53,670	66,792
18	36,936	48,323	48,329	54,037	60,557	76,544

mortgage permits you to convert your home equity into cash without selling your home or giving up title to it. Whether you have a good or bad credit rating does not affect the loan in any way. Essentially a loan, a reverse mortgage provides funds to you in a lump-sum, onetime payment, a line of credit (the most popular method), or fixed payments for life. To apply for a reverse mortgage, you must be 62 or older and own your home free and clear. The money you get can be used for any purpose whatsoever, from eliminating the balances on your grown children's outstanding student loans, to funding home improvements or paying off medical bills. You can begin to pay yourself back without having to sell your precious asset because, in effect, the lender makes payments back to you.

The older you are, the more reverse mortgage money you can receive, but other conditions affecting the loan amount also apply, such as your equity in the property, the value and location of the home, and current interest rates. Many older Coasters-Optimists find a degree of financial security with this plan, especially since it makes funds available during the retirement years.

The loans to you do not have to be repaid until the death of the last surviving borrower. Even then, your heirs are not required to sell your home but can choose to pay off the loan using other sources and retain title to the property. No payments on a reverse mortgage are due, however, until the borrower ceases to occupy the house as his or her principal residence.

The mortgage is offered by many banks and financial institutions and comes in a choice of three types: *single purpose, federally insured,* and *proprietary.* Briefly, a single-purpose reverse mortgage is designed for one specific purpose, such as home repairs or payment of property taxes, and is the least costly of the three. Proceeds from a federally insured reverse mortgage, known as a HECM (Home Equity Conversion Mortgage) can be used for any purpose. Available throughout the U.S. to any homeowners 62 and over, these FHA-backed loans are more costly than single-purpose programs. Proprietary reverse mortgages are the most costly and provide a large loan-advance if your home is worth a lot more than the average home value in your area. This kind of reverse mortgage is backed by private companies rather than by government agencies.

To learn more about these mortgages and if you can benefit from them, check the Resources section at the end of this chapter. To start, you can contact the National Reverse Mortgage Lenders Association (www.reversemortgage.org) or click on "Shopping for a Reverse Mortgage" on the AARP (American Association of Retired Persons) Web site, www.aarp.org/revmort.

Finally, here's the third wake-up call for you, and it's so important: insurance.

Protecting Yourself and Your Loved Ones, Part 1: Insure Yourself!

You may have to pull Ostriches out of their hole to make them become aware of what they need to do with money, but you Coasters-Optimists *are* an aware Money Type—however, you're often *not* motivated enough to do the right thing. You may not be adequately prepared for emergencies, thinking, "I'm healthy, I'll be fine, and nothing will go wrong."

Coasters-Optimists are vulnerable to not having enough life insurance. How much do you need? There's a rule of thumb that's useful, if imprecise: You should buy insurance equal to six to ten times your gross annual family income. If you're supporting a big family and paying out a big mortgage, go for the higher figure. If you have a working spouse and lower housing costs, you're probably safer at the lower end of the range.

There are six different kinds of insurance: life, health, disability, homeowners, auto, and long-term care. A classic case of not having enough life insurance is someone coasting along, doing okay, and then the breadwinner dies. Coasting comes to a halt, and the survivors may receive a few hundred thousand but need a few million. Plan to have enough insurance so that if you die, the people depending on your income are protected and don't have to change their lifestyle radically.

The world of insurance can be a bit confusing, and as a result, many people pay for more insurance coverage than they actually need. The insurance industry is notorious for using jargon and complex presentations that baffle most people. What you don't know about insurance can potentially hurt you in two ways:

1. You pay too much for a policy that you could have bought much cheaper had you understood how to compare both insurers and policies, and
2. The coverage you purchase may be too much or too little for your needs, or it may duplicate existing coverage in some areas and leave you unprotected in others.

The result is that you put yourself in unnecessary jeopardy, and you could be ruined financially if you have a large claim that isn't covered. I want to help you through the insurance maze just enough to be sure you're clear about what all those policies mean.

What to Know Before Buying Insurance— Knowledge Is Security!

Since there are a number of issues to think about before buying insurance—such as types of insurers, different ways insurance is offered, rating systems, types of insurance—let me direct you to some general information sites (see Appendix for exact sources) and provide some helpful guidelines here to get you started or back on track if you already have a policy and need to make changes. There are insurance rating systems where you can get important information on the company from which you buy your policy. You want to get some idea of the insurance company's financial condition. Make sure it is stable and strong enough so you know it will be there to pay claims if you ever need it to.

There are five principal independent firms that rate insurance companies' financial strength (addressees, phone numbers, and descriptions of their publications and services are in the Resources section). The four traditional agencies are A. M. Best, Fitch, Moody's Investor Service, and Standard & Poor's (S&P) Corporation. The newer entrant in the field, Weiss Ratings, is considered a maverick by the insurance industry because it uses a different and far more conservative method of assessing insurers' financial conditions.

Two Important Insurance Policies to Start With

While there are six kinds of insurance that you should have, let me stress the three biggest ones: life, health, and disability insurance. I want to specifically emphasize life and disability insurance here, which many people put off buying. I assume (and hope!) you have some sort of health coverage.

SIX POINTS YOU NEED TO KNOW BEFORE BUYING AN INSURANCE POLICY

When anyone asks me how to choose a life or health insurance policy, my answer is: It depends on your personal situation. This includes how much you can afford, your preferences regarding long-term care options, and the level of risk you're willing to take. Keep these important factors in mind:

- Make sure you understand what the policy covers and what it doesn't.

- What conditions are required to qualify for coverage?

- How long will you need coverage?

- For health insurance, what is the daily maximum dollar amount of care the insurer will provide?

- What are the renewal terms? (The best policy is one that is guaranteed renewable, which means the insurance company cannot cancel the policy unless you fail to pay the premiums.)

- Does your policy keep up with rising costs so that you are protected from inflation?

(The United Seniors Health Cooperative recommends long-term care policies that automatically increase benefits at the rate of 5 percent annually. Compounded inflation protection is recommended for people applying up to the age of 70 and simple inflation for those applying after 70. Though this coverage will cost you more, it will likely pay off in the long run. To be able to afford the extra coverage, you can choose a policy with a shorter benefit length or a less comprehensive policy.)

No one said that picking insurance policies was going to be fun, but when you need it and it pays off, you'll be happy you bought the right ones.

Life insurance: Life insurance is designed to protect the survivors of the insured, which is not to say that a life insurance policy yields no advantages while you're around. Nevertheless, the main reason to purchase a policy is for the death benefit, which you hope your dependents collect far into the future. There are four basic types of life insurance: term, whole life, universal life, and variable life. The debates about which is best rage on, so you must decide what's best for you based on how much coverage you need, how big a premium you can afford, and whether you want insurance only for its death benefit or also for its saving potential. Term insurance pays off only when you die; whole life, universal life, and variable life insurance are variations of cash value insurance, which combines a death benefit and an investment fund.

If your family or other people depend on your income, you need life insurance to help them live without your income if you pass away. The insurance contract requires that the insurance company pay your beneficiaries a set amount, called the death benefit, if you should die for almost any reason (suicide is usually excluded for the first few years of the policy). Your beneficiaries can receive the money in one lump sum free of federal income taxes. The funds should be enough to replace your paycheck, cover the beneficiaries' daily living expenses, and pay your final medical bills and burial costs. Also, the insurance proceeds should be invested to provide beneficiaries with income for long-term needs such as retirement, estate taxes, or college costs.

So how much insurance is enough? My suggestion is for you to figure this out long before you listen to any insurance agent's sometimes confusing pitch or the details of various policies. Assessing how much is enough isn't a simple process because each family is different and there's no easy formula to work from. You may want to consult an independent insurance advisor, a financial advisor, or run through some of the exercises available on software like Microsoft Money or Quicken.

Here are the differences between types of insurance: With term insurance, for which you can pay a relatively low premium, the policy pays off only if you die. There's no cash value and no investment fund, and you can buy a lot more in death benefit. Cash value policies cost more, but a good part of your premium goes into an investment fund, which grows the cash value over time—and which you can borrow against or use to supplement your retirement income. With whole life insurance, the insurance company does all the investing for you, typically in bonds, real estate, and some stocks. With variable insurance, you get to choose where your money is invested among various stock and bond fund options. With universal insurance, your money is typically invested in a money market account, which grows based on current interest rates.

Disability insurance: Though you might think it unlikely that you'll ever become disabled either on the job or outside work, you are mistaken. According to the American Council of Life Insurers, someone aged thirty-five is six times more likely to become disabled than die before reaching age sixty-five!

If you miss work for a short time, your employer will probably provide short-term sick leave. You might also collect benefits from workers' compensation if you were injured on the job. Other governmental programs, such as veterans benefits, civil service disability, or black lung insurance for miners could also kick in. If you were injured in a car accident, your auto insurance pays you a certain amount of cash for a limited period. And if you are a union member, you could be eligible for group disability coverage. You qualify for Social Security disability benefits if you become severely disabled.

But even if you collect from several government programs, you probably won't receive enough money to live comfortably. You could wind up spending your hard-earned retirement savings just to make ends meet. Because you don't want your dreams to evaporate because of an unexpected illness or accident that puts you out of work or limits your earning capacity, it's crucial to get individual long-term disability insurance. If you qualify, you can receive between 50 and 80 percent of your regular salary, depending on the policy, plus cost-of-living adjustments in some policies. Companies don't pay 100 percent of your salary because they want you to have an incentive to go back to work.

According to the American Health Care Association, the most important service a policy should cover is custodial or personal care. A good long-term-care insurance policy covers all levels of care, especially personal care, and all settings, including facility care, community adult day care, assisted living, and nursing facilities.

As with other types of insurance, you want to check on the financial health of the insurer. Do a little digging to find out about the firm's reputation, shop around for price and quality, and you'll probably want professional guidance for this significant decision, perhaps from your existing insurance agent, your financial planner, or other financial advisors.

Protecting Yourself and Your Loved Ones, Part 2: Estate Planning—What to Know About Passing Down Your Legacy

Optimists aren't the only Money Types who are uncomfortable when they think about leaving this earth. No one likes to think about passing on, but what you do need to think about is what you will leave behind, and who will get it. What you should at least decide about now is whether you want to control how your estate is settled or if you want to leave it to the probate court, which might distribute your property in a way that wouldn't suit you.

If you think estate planning is daunting, then think of how much more daunting it would be if your worldly possessions were distributed, but your estate had to pay thousands of dollars in onerous estate taxes that easily could have been avoided. On the other hand, if you make the effort to maximize the basic estate planning procedures, your relatives and/or friends for whom you care deeply will receive a far greater inheritance. Even though you won't benefit personally after your death, you will live with the satisfaction of knowing you have done all you could do to pass on the fruits of your life's labor to your loved ones.

I want to take the intimidation factor out of estate planning, especially if you think you have nothing to pass on, or you are concerned about how much a lawyer will charge you to draw up a will and other estate planning documents. For the two-thirds of all Americans who do not have a will (or, as lawyers call it, dying intestate), the probate court takes over and can dominate survivors' lives for years. Instead, do yourself and others you care about a favor and get this aspect of your financial life completed to your satisfaction.

Why do it? Estate planning settles not only the disposition of possessions and money but also other major life decisions, including child custody. Because estate planning may be a mystery to you, let me outline some of the key areas covered by the term:

- Choosing who gets how much of your money and possessions that remain after the costs of settling the estate are subtracted.
- Preparing a strategy to give away many of your assets as tax-free gifts while you live to minimize the assets socked by estate taxes when you die.
- Selecting a guardian for your children if they are younger than age eighteen. This guardian, who may be an individual or a couple, would take your children into their home and raise them, so you must feel as certain as possible that they would bring up your children in a manner in which you would approve.
- Selecting a trustee to administer any trusts you may establish.
- Nominating an executor of your estate, who should be an independent person you trust, to carry out the provisions

of your will faithfully. Often, this is a lawyer familiar with your family.

- Deciding what should be done with your body after you die. For instance, you may want it donated for medical research or cremated. Also, specifying how and where you want to be buried. Some people even limit what they want spent on their funerals.
- Appointing a successor custodian for the assets of a child or grandchild if you currently act as a custodian for a Uniform Gifts to Minors account. If you don't specify the successor custodian, a court will decide for you.
- Planning to make gifts of either money or property to your favorite charity, university, or religious institution. Without your specific written instructions, no such gifts can be authorized by the executor of your estate.
- Preparing for the time you are unable to care for yourself. You can prepare what are called advance directives giving instructions on what kinds of health care you want provided or withheld in the event you cannot communicate your wishes. You can specify in a living will, for example, whether you want extraordinary treatment to keep you alive if you go into a coma. You can also appoint someone you trust with a health care power of attorney to make difficult decisions about your medical treatment if you are unable to make these decisions yourself.

Most of all, by taking care of these decisions in a calm, unhurried fashion far in advance of your death, you avoid any need for a hastily drawn up document or, even worse, a deathbed will, which most likely will be contested later. People always bring up the cost of doing estate planning. Usually the process involves lawyers, financial planners, insurance agents, and accountants, but it does not have to involve all these professionals; you can do it yourself. There are several easy-to-use computer programs, such as Living TrustMaker, Quicken Family Lawyer, or Quicken WillMaker, which ask you questions, then format your answers into legal documents that protect you and your estate against almost every eventuality.

I hope I've gotten you inspired to improve your Coasterhood by doing more for yourself.

FINALLY: POINTS TO REMEMBER FOR COASTERS

Because you don't see any money crisis in your life, don't coast on the status quo. Remember, in this economy, *standing still and not investing more energetically is actually riskier* than you might want to believe.

Coasters do best when they break through the complacency that marks your Money Type. If *fear* of loss is a better motivator to get you into better financial shape than a hot stock tip, then do whatever gets you to act.

To make any change in your life, you need a goal, a plan, and to really get you going, motivation. A goal such as accumulating more money to have a cushier retirement has a built-in motivator—getting to sixty-five and knowing you don't have to worry about feeling secure as you age.

Take care of the big three by planning ahead: Know how much you need to save to have a worry-free retirement, know how much you need to save to pay for your children's college education, and protect yourself and your loved ones—insure yourself adequately!

Think about estate planning. It helps you take control of your money now, and how your legacy will be distributed—as you want it to be.

RESOURCES FOR COASTERS

Imagine that you're on a lake in a rowboat. Sure, you could probably eventually get to the other side by letting the current move you along. But if you fueled the ride with some of your own energy and paddled, you'd travel a lot more efficiently and reach your goal faster. As a Coaster or Optimist, your greatest challenge is to avoid getting stuck in a still or stagnant sea. Check where you are and where you're going. For example, have you put enough aside for your children's college education? Do you have a will? Is your estate plan in good shape? And while you may be healthy today, have you considered long-term-care insurance for the future, when you might need it? Some of the following resources will be useful as you prepare to meet these goals.

Books

AARP Crash Course in Estate Planning: The Essential Guide to Wills, Trusts, and Your Personal Legacy, by Michael T. Palermo (Sterling Publishing, 387 Park Avenue South, New York, NY 10016; 212-532-7160; www.sterlingpub.com). A crash course in estate planning and writing your will.

The American Bar Association Guide to Wills and Estates, Second Edition: Everything You Need to Know About Wills, Estates, Trusts, and Taxes, by the American Bar Association (Random House, 1745 Broadway, New York, NY 10019; 212-782-9000; www.randomhouse.com). A how-to guide.

Missed Fortune: Dispel the Money Myth Conceptions—Isn't It Time You Became Wealthy?, by Douglas R. Andrew (Warner Business Books, 1271 Avenue of the Americas, New York, NY 10020; 800-759-0190; www.twbookmark.com). Advice goes against the grain, but some of you Coasters may find it refreshing.

Plan Your Estate, by Denis Clifford, Cora Jordan. (Nolo Publishing, 950 Parker Street, Berkeley CA 94710; 800-728-3555; www.nolo.com). Easy-to-understand and useful book.

The Retirement Nightmare: How to Save Yourself from Your Heirs and Protectors: Involuntary Conservatorships and Guardianships (Golden Age Series), by Diane G. Armstrong, Ph.D. (Prometheus Books, 59 John Glenn Drive, Amherst, New York 14228; 800-421-0351; www.prometheusbooks.com). Focuses on how you can protect yourself from heirs.

Insurance Company Ratings Services

A.M. Best Company, Inc. (Ambest Road, Oldwick, NJ 08858; 908-439-2200; www.ambest.com). Publishers of insurance information, including financial data, industry news, and insurer ratings.

Fitch Ratings (1 State Street Plaza, New York, NY 10004; 212-908-0500; www.fitchibca.com). Ratings company that currently maintains coverage of 3,100 financial institutions, including 1,600 banks and 1,400 insurance companies.

Moody's Investor Service (99 Church Street, New York, NY 10007; 212-553-0300; www.moodys.com). Source for credit ratings, research, and risk analysis. Publishes credit opinions, deal research, and commentary.

Standard & Poor's (55 Water Street, New York, NY 10041; 212-438-1000 or 212-438-2000; www.standardandpoors.com). Provides independent credit ratings, indices, risk evaluation, investment research, data, and valuations.

Weiss Ratings Inc. (15430 Endeavour Drive, Jupiter, FL 33478; 561-627-3300; www.weissratings.com). Provides research and ratings on more than 15,000 institutions, including life, health, and annuity insurers, property and casualty insurers, HMOs, Blue Cross Blue Shield plans, banks, and savings and loans.

Organizations

American Academy of Estate Planning Attorneys (4365 Executive Drive, Suite 850, San Diego, CA 92121; 800-846-1555; www.aaepa.com). Use this site to help find an estate planning attorney and learn about estate planning.

American Association of Retired Persons (AARP) (800-209-8085; www.aarp.org/revmort). They offer a hard copy or online booklet called *Homemade Money: A Consumer's Guide to Reverse Mortgages*.

American College of Trust and Estate Counsel (3415 South Sepulveda Boulevard, Suite 330; Los Angeles, CA 90034; 310-398-1888; www.actec.org). A professional association of trust and estate lawyers that will refer you to a qualified estate planning attorney in your area.

America's Health Insurance Plans (601 Pennsylvania Avenue, NW, South Building, Suite 500, Washington, DC 20004; 202-778-3200; www.ahip.org). National association of health insurance companies. Web site has consumer guides on long-term care, disability insurance, and managed care. Also has links to health insurers and facts and figures about insurance.

CollegeNET (805 SW Broadway, Suite 1600, Portland, OR 97205; 503-973-5200; www.collegenet.com). Lets you search for and file applications at more than 1,500 colleges. You can also search for scholarships and financial aid information.

College Savings Bank (5 Vaughn Drive, Princeton, NJ 08540; 800-888-2723; www.collegesavings.com). Sells the College-Sure CD, designed to let parents prepay college education costs, either in a lump sum or in smaller amounts over time.

Department of Housing and Urban Development (HUD) (888-446-3487; www.hud.gov). Offers calculators and other tools to help you decide on whether a reverse mortgage is right for you.

Fannie Mae (800-732-6643; www.fanniemae.com). Get information about HECMs and Home Keeper Mortgages, and a list of lenders who offer them.

Financial Freedom Senior Funding Corporation (800-500-5150; www.ffsenior.com). Proprietary type (privately held) reverse mortgage company, offering programs such as Financial Freedom Equity Guard and Cash Account Plans, which are available in limited areas.

National Center for Home Equity Conversion (NCHEC) (651-222-6775; www.reverse.org). They offer calculators and other tools to help you decide on whether a reverse mortgage is right for you.

National Reverse Morgage Lenders Association (202-939-1765; www.reversemortgage.org). Provides a list of reverse mortgage lenders in each state and has detailed information about reverse mortgages.

Sallie Mae (12061 Bluemont Way, Reston, VA 20190; 888-2-SALLIE; www.salliemae.com). Provides information about higher education, including planning for college, financial resources, and applying for and managing loans.

Web Sites

Estateplanning.com. Find a professional or a seminar in your area.

Fastweb.com. A site where you can find colleges and search for scholarships that your child has the best chance of winning. Choose from 600,000 scholarships, some of which you can apply for online.

Finaid.com. Provides advice about financial aid, including paperwork you'll need to apply. Answers questions you might have and offers calculators to help you figure out how much school will cost, how much you need to save, and how much aid you'll need.

Long Term Care Quote (www.searchltc.com). Independent Web site to help you pick the best long-term care insurance policy for your needs and budget. You can also contact the agency at 800-587-3279.

Nolo.com. Leads you, step by step, through the process of writing a will. It will also help you with general estate planning issues, various kinds of trusts, and funeral arrangement plans.

Reverse.org. Explains reverse mortgages and helps you find a reverse mortgage lender.

Reversemortgage.org. Explains your reverse mortgage choices. The information on the site is provided by the National Reverse Mortgage Lenders Association, which is an educational resource, advocate, and public affairs center for reverse mortgage lenders and related professionals.

Savingforcollege.com. Site offers a plethora of college planning advice and information about 529 plans and the Coverdell Education Savings Account. The site provides answers to frequently asked questions and walks you through opening an account.

CHAPTER 7

The High Rollers

*Does taking a risk give you an emotional rush that
you find exhilarating or addictive?*
*Are you torn between wanting to play the long shot
and playing it safe with your money?*
*Do you believe that the only way to get what you
want in life is by taking risks?*

If I asked you what you would do to insure a life free of money problems, what would you choose? When I put the question out, the first answer I get is almost always, "win the lottery" followed by "hard work." As enjoyable as it is to dream about a life free of money troubles, in reality, neither choice is a sure shot. Lottery winners are known to blow their huge winnings, rather than invest them or use them wisely. Hard workers can lose their jobs, their businesses, and their safety nets. But then there are the people who will answer a third way: "Believe in your hunches and figure out how to make them pay off."

When you find a hard worker, innovative thinker, hunch-player, and childlike dreamer all wrapped up in one, you're talking to a Money Type called the High Roller. And if you answered yes to two or more questions at the head of this chapter, chances are good that you are among this very complex type.

Because you tend to be imaginative, gutsy, and willing to put yourself on the line for what you want, I won't ask you to minimize or jettison the qualities that inspire you. I can help show you that you don't have to be a financial daredevil all the time. Instead, you can be a cautious risk-taker some of the time. By being more calculating with money, you can indulge yourself in taking high risks in a more limited way, but mostly protect your interests and build up your assets. Take a look at how:

THE HIGH ROLLER REVEALED

Your Money Type is a first cousin to the Striver type—you're part of a sector of people who seek what's bigger and greater in life. Like the Striver, you have an inclination for being an entrepreneur—you like being in charge of making the decisions about where your money goes. However, your tendency is to gamble on your hunches and take greater risks to achieve your goals than would the other types. This may be so for two reasons: You trust your instincts about the risk paying off and leading to a profitable, ongoing business. Or, on the flip side, you see the risk being big enough to pay off by giving you one moment in the sun. You secretly believe the winning big risk will make up for what you fear are your limited and losing capabilities.

For many of you, *gamble* is the operative word. What really distinguishes you as a High Roller is that you are by nature a gambler to one degree or another. Some High Rollers like to invest in the highest-risk stocks, while other High Rollers avoid the stock market and prefer games of chance at the casino. Sometimes you win, and sometimes you lose. Other High Rollers invest only in themselves and gamble on building their own business. Since you have the highest risk tolerance of any of the Money Types, part of your belief system is feeling sure you *will* win and beat the odds. You may not even stop betting on your "win" when you know failure could mean financial disaster.

There's another quality to the High Roller that makes your type unique. If gambling is at one end of the High Roller's profile, then the innovative High Roller, with loftier visions of achievement than winning at games of chance, is at the other end. American history abounds with stories of High Roller risk-takers, some of whom survived their gambles and built empires. Like these more dynamic and effective High Rollers, you may have the stuff to convince people you will be successful and get them in on the action. Other High Rollers become crash victims of their own mismanagement, ignorance, or greed. These may be people who fear they don't have the goods to be successful other than by investing everything in the "big deal" or the toss of the dice. Not sure of their career goals, or smarts, they may keep hoping for that magic circumstance to pull them through.

In fact, some High Rollers may also become charismatic leaders. It is usually a High Roller with a wild, creative, or life-changing idea who attracts partners, employees, followers— and other risk-takers who are willing to back them financially. Think back, and you'll be able to name people who were willing to bet on an idea and take others with them to the ends of the earth to make a dream come true. Think Christopher Columbus or Lewis and Clark or Henry Ford. Think of Bill Gates or Steve Jobs, for example, and their idea of bringing the personal computer to everyone. Taking the risks and putting in the effort to make their ideas come to life were their primary goal—a classic High Roller trait for the more idealistic of you. Making phenomenal amounts of money was important but secondary to the goal.

Not that High Rollers don't love money, and a lot of it. How you deal with money can be your saving grace or your downfall. This will depend on whether you operate dominantly from your strengths or your weaknesses.

The High Roller: Your Strengths

Chief among your strengths are a high tolerance for risk taking and a belief in your vision. Once you have a goal, you go for it without a second thought. High Rollers are smart at looking at the marketplace, figuring out what's needed, or where the next area of growth will be. New concepts and inventions intrigue you, and you're always thinking of new ways to use them and profit from them. You are known for creating new products, even if they're variations of things that exist. When your vision is backed up with a plan, your energy in combination with your tenacity can be powerful.

You're ambitious and competitive, and like the challenge of competing with others and coming out on top.

The High Roller: Your Weaknesses

Billionaire investment virtuoso Warren Buffett was once asked about his investment strategy, and he answered, "I don't try to jump over seven-foot bars. I look around for one-foot bars I can step over." In this statement, Buffett, who is known to live modestly despite his enormous wealth, probably offers High Rollers some of the best advice: To prosper, be shrewd, but be more conservative. Of all the types, a High Roller is most likely to get into trouble by habitually leaping over seven-foot bars— taking risks without a safety net.

This need to leap when you can stroll is part of the core dynamics of your type: High Rollers seek the rush of daring the universe to take them down. You fit into what has become in many ways an addictive society—whether the addiction is, for example, to food, drugs, or making money. Maybe it's bravado or anger or a need to prove yourself to be tougher, smarter, or faster, but whatever your motivation, more times than not it brings you loss, not gain. It's this same attitude that makes you think when entering a high-risk deal or tossing the dice at a casino, "This is my lucky night." Unlucky nights are more frequent.

If you have one dominant weakness, it is that you don't like facing the downside of risk and will deny it can affect you. You want to believe your project will be funded, your business will take off, your tech stocks will quadruple in value. The downside of denying the potential consequences of high-risk ventures or of gambling is that you can get wiped out. Sometimes, you are the kind of High Roller who feels, in fact, that the only way you can get what you want is the one big break—not from your hard work or know-how, but by chance.

Bankruptcy and even suicide are not uncommon among High Rollers who are finally forced to give up or who give up on themselves. Psychologists tell me that these suicide victims were people who never had much confidence in themselves and relied on the luck of the market. They were probably people who said, "I did it once. I don't have the smarts to do it again."

While you have the tenacity to keep trying despite losing money, which is a good trait, another weakness is not managing money better the next time out. That is, you're a little stubborn about learning how.

The High Roller and the Type T Personality

Entrepreneur magazine published a feature on Frank Farley, a Temple University psychologist who profiled a Type T personality—the T standing for thrill seeking. Farley wasn't referring to reckless behavior or mindless gambling, but to the thrills this type gets from great but focused risk taking. What are Type Ts like?

Type Ts love to take risks in order to make things happen. "All human progress depends on these people," Farley said. He identified a number of traits that signify how these personalities distinguish themselves. Every High Roller has a few of these T personality traits:

- Motivated by variety, novelty, and change.
- Eats challenges for breakfast.
- Thrives on uncertainty and unpredictability.
- Dislikes too much structure and too many rules.
- Believes he can control his fate.
- Tends to show independent judgment and likes to make up his own mind.
- Seeks intense experiences.
- Is curious about how much and what she can do.
- Often doesn't acknowledge that she's taken great risks or any risks, while others would say she's taken enormous risks.

How do High Rollers play out their inclinations and to what effect? I spoke to two people who most clearly typified your Money Type. When you read their stories, you'll learn, as I did, what drives them to take risks that can be far more costly than they want to believe.

Hooked on Playing the Stock Market—And Going for Broke

Betsy e-mailed me recently, with a challenging, even provocative, opening line. She wrote, "This is embarrassing for me to write about, but my marriage almost hinges on your answer." This, essentially, was the issue: Betsy loves playing the stock market. She's made *and* lost hundreds of thousands of dollars over the last few years, and in her words, she "can't seem to break even." Because of her recent losses, she and her husband, George, argue about money "on a daily basis." I knew I was communicating with a hard-core High Roller when Betsy asked my advice on sinking money into a hot tip she named—rather than ask me how she could downshift to more conservative investments. I'll tell you more about this shortly.

I was interested in Betsy's High Roller thinking and later e-mailed her to ask more about her. I learned this about her life: Born in Los Angeles, this thirty-two-year-old was raised by a high school shop teacher and a mother who ran a two-seat beauty salon in their home. Betsy's older sister was studious and ambitious, and eventually got a law degree. Betsy, two years younger and with a more outgoing personality, did well in school, but she was always compared negatively to her fair-haired sister—especially by her mother. In fact, her mother told Betsy she'd grow up to be a failure unless she toned down her high-spirited behavior. Betsy always felt that she couldn't live up to her sister's achievements, and after graduating from college, she decided to live her own life and not worry about being like her sister, "the perfect one."

Betsy may not have been as studious as her sister, but she had a few traits her sister didn't: a tolerance for the adrenaline high of high-risk ventures, a taste for gambling, and a love of pop culture. She also had something to prove. She eventually worked her way up to vice president at a small public relations company, where her accounts include gourmet food products. "The work has its upside," Betsy told me. "It pays well enough and I get a lot of perks, but it also has a downside. The work is stressful, and I don't really like talking about food all day. Since my husband gets home late and travels a lot, I do my own thing at night. I've got my laptop and a list of all the stock market sites—and a direct dial to my broker early the next morning. All I think about is making a lot of bucks."

I asked her to tell me more about how her stock picks were threatening her marriage. Betsy wrote that her husband of five years is most disturbed by and resents what he calls her "crazy gambling" in the market. Overall, George feels she has no respect for his financial needs—security and moderation. Even though Betsy earns over $100,000 a year in salary, it was becoming clear that she was using her profits in the market to unconsciously make up for the shortcomings her mother had told her she had. A fairly stable marriage and a good job were being put in jeopardy as Betsy continued to play the market. She told me by way of explanation, "I earn nearly as much as George. I'm investing *my* money, not his, but he still won't understand and wants me to quit."

Betsy's irate because she feels George has no right to call the shots on money he hasn't earned. The financial losses are hers, and so far, they haven't affected their standard of living. Betsy thinks she's got a right to keep investing in high-risk stocks, and that by chastising her for it, George is being "cheap."

Her latest e-mail to me included this comment: "I heard about this hot tip. If I'm right on this pick, George will thank me. If I'm wrong, it's my loss. Why can't he understand that how I invest is perfectly sensible for the long run? What I'm doing is really good for both of us. Someone has to take the risks or you wind up with nothing!"

Going for Broke, and on Someone Else's Money

In recent years, surveys show that about 80 million people own stock, which amounts to nearly 50 percent of all households in the United States. Everyone knows someone who made money and then lost money when one "sure thing"—the dot-com phenomenon—burst its bubble. In fact, in the two and a half years following the collapse of the dot-coms, stock market losses for Americans were estimated at about $8.5 trillion.

Betsy was among them. The problem is not about investing per se or playing the stock market—both are essential to the economy. The problem is a potentially self-destructive and reckless attitude about investing—the downfall of many a High Roller.

I get so many e-mails, letters, and calls from High Rollers who think very much the way Betsy does. I know she's not alone out there, sitting at her computer and clicking on the many stock market and brokerage sites, checking prices, buying, selling, or trading—sometimes on an hourly basis. This can become a High Roller's favorite at-home addiction, as it has for Betsy.

Let's get to the bottom line. There's a reality factor about investing that Betsy has not yet had to deal with, but it is a driving force in a High Roller's thinking: If you cannot afford to invest with your own funds or take a loss, don't invest. If, like Betsy, you want to score big simply to prove a point, ask yourself if the possible loss is worth it to you and those you care about. It's unrealistic to expect that your spouse will shrug off the loss as yours and that it won't affect the marriage. Betsy has tunnel vision. She only wants to see the benefits of taking a risk, and she wants her husband to share her point of view by ignoring how self-destructive her investing habits have become.

To Betsy, some success in public relations made her a bit too sure of herself, believing she could conquer *any* field and make money. Some High Rollers think that doing well in one field confers blanket expertise in all areas, including money. I felt Betsy, like many High Rollers, was a bit in love with the idea of herself as invincible, which was probably a cover-up for feeling wildly vulnerable and inadequate. But unfortunately, that bravado included the idea that she had a flair for the market. When Betsy wrote me about wanting to invest in her hot tip, believing it was "perfectly sensible" for the long run, I knew she was doing a frantic dance with the stock market. She was about to spin out of control.

If she were a wildly successful investor, I'd tell Betsy to keep doing what she was doing. Instead, Betsy is really trapped in the past, using money to insulate herself from her real feelings, being overstimulated by money games. Her mother told her she'd grow up to be a failure unless she became more "perfect" like her older sister, but she succeeded by being herself. Betsy fought for a career and marriage to a stable man who loved her. Yet, by being a High Roller, she was about to jeopardize her marriage, confirming what her mother told her she would always be: a loser who was not worthy of respect or love.

Betsy is better than this, and I told her so.

And her financial thinking is not sound, whether or not George really is cheap. Is playing the market this way worth her self-esteem and her marriage? I don't think so.

You Don't Want to Bet the Farm!

Who is most likely to bounce back after a business loss? A study of Harvard Business School graduates who started their own companies singled out a significant factor that distinguished those who were eventually successful and those who weren't: When successful graduates failed the first time, the study pointed out, "they still had money left over."

While Betsy looks to the market to satisfy her urge to be a player and win big, Ben takes a different approach to winning big in life. Ben is a born High Roller, and once he decided to be his own boss, he pursued achievement aggressively. This entrepreneur had decades of success, until his casual attitude about money collided with his costly high-risk projects. This is Ben's story:

When You Believe That Betting on Yourself Is the Best Deal

"Picture an animated cartoon of someone running through a wall and leaving the outline of his body as he crashes through," Ben told me. "That was what I felt I had—the ability to run through a brick wall and come out alive and still on the run." Then Ben told me he had suffered a big financial setback and that his business was in jeopardy from his taking one risk too many. So after decades of crashing through brick walls and trotting off with millions, this High Roller unfortunately crash-landed, leaving a heap of damage that he will have to repair. "After all my success," he added, "I had to face the fact that I wasn't smart enough with money." His story is an interesting one.

Now sixty years old, Ben revealed some complex emotional connections to money that began when he was a boy. The youngest child of factory worker parents, Ben grew up in a stable home in an inner-city Boston neighborhood. Ben did well in school, but his inclination was to hang out on the street, "buddying up," he said, "with other boys who were smarter than me about life and could teach me something. I wanted to be an equal." He learned enough one day when he was eleven years old to come home with over $100 won gambling in a street game. The win would mark some of his conflicts about money for life.

Ben told his father about winning the money, but his father was not impressed—he was furious. He dragged Ben down the hall of their building, opened the incinerator door, and tossed in the money. "You know what that taught me?" Ben said, laughing. "To never again let my father know what I was doing. I thought, what the hell is wrong with him? He should have put the money in his pocket and made believe he threw it down the incinerator. Burning it up didn't stop me from playing again."

Ben may have described himself as a street kid, but he got through college and graduate school, albeit with no plans for his future and a lot of optimism. Through a connection, he got a job with an over-the-counter brokerage firm. Within a year, working on commission only, Ben was earning a minimum of $3,000 a week—in 1966. "Suddenly, money was pumping out of a machine," Ben said, "but I put very little value on the money itself. It didn't matter to me. It was money from wheeling and dealing and getting people to invest. But it taught me that my salesmanship was a skill that could take me places."

Then Ben's firm got into trouble with the SEC and went bankrupt. Ben got job offers from other brokerage firms, but instead of accepting one, he made a life-changing decision: to never work for anyone again and to start his own company. "I decided to create the products I'd dream up," he told me. "I knew I could bet on myself and my imagination. That's where my heart and head live. My skill is in getting the best people to make my vision come true, and I fight with them hard enough to get it out of them. I've done books, records, and all sorts of high-quality products. I don't gamble anymore, I don't invest in the stock market, I don't buy myself expensive toys—I take big risks with my ideas."

I asked Ben if he had investors for all his products and what kind of deals he made. I wanted to know how his High Roller tendencies got him into trouble. "One of my diseases was using my own money," Ben answered. "That was the pitfall. Not everyone you work with will have your vision. I paid out huge amounts of money to get what I wanted and took the risks on projects I believed in. I had to make them happen—even if it meant jeopardizing financial security." Ben amended his comment by telling me that he made sure the most important situations in his life were covered: that his sons went to good schools; that he could support his wife, a writer who worked on her novels at home; and that the mortgage was paid on a "nice place to live." Other than these essentials, Ben said, he never thought about the future. That beast came back to bite him.

After a few high-cost projects tanked—Ben having burst through one brick wall too many—he lost millions and is about to declare bankruptcy. Ben admits that he should have been smart enough to bring in a business manager. Now he was standing in the rubble. He said he'd had many opportunities to hire experts but had decided against it, "assuming I could play all the roles." He said, "I am not a master of understatement, and I lived that way. So, yes, I could have managed money much better. I went along making money but never really thinking about it. It's hard to believe, but it's true."

"It's Only Money!"—If I Lose It, There Will Always Be More

What struck me about Ben—and I've heard this so many times from other High Rollers—is the contradiction in how he talks about money. One minute he's offhand about it ("I don't do this work for money—I have to create things."). Another minute, he's a businessman who estimates how much his time is worth ("I only take on projects that I see making me seven figures."). Yet another minute, he's proud of his work selling well and earning him a lot of money ("I've made millions."). Overall, he's a High Roller who is conflicted about what money means to him. And whether or not he acknowledges it, he is still ruled by a defining moment with money.

Such a defining moment in your early life can be an influence on whether you become a High Roller. And in his case, Ben may still be watching the father he loved burn his winnings and soothing himself by thinking, "Who cares—I'll win more, and I won't tell him!" While his father thought he was punishing him, Ben was angry that his father wasn't more impressed with his achievement or at least accepting of it.

He hasn't gambled since he graduated from high school, but Ben gambles on himself, and like all professional gamblers, he plays to win. By betting on himself first, he has a wide measure of control. That Ben has an "I'll show them!" attitude in business is not surprising. And he *does* show them—his work for the most part has been high-quality and profitable. He can't control the outcome and the sales every time, but he can control the product and keep most of the profits. And although he always feared having someone come in and destroy what he has—as if by his father's hand again—by not trusting others to help him manage money, he made his fears come true.

When a High Roller Makes It

People always ask successful High Rollers what they did to make it. Specific factors may change from story to story, but successful High Rollers share a number of characteristics in driving hard to get what they want: They seek high risk, but it is *risk with a purposeful and realistic goal*—it's not risk for kicks or for ego. Bill Cullen, CEO of Glencullen Motor Group, the Renault distributorship for Ireland, a $400 million annual revenue firm based in Dublin, is such a High Roller. His whole success story is in his book, *It's a Long Way from Penny Apples*, but here's how he started, according to an article in the *Robb Report Worth*:

"Cullen grew up in a family with little money, the oldest of fourteen children. He was raised with strong moral values and business acumen learned from his hard-working mother, who was a street vendor. He planned his career moves carefully, from working at a Ford dealership to when, at the age of forty-four, he said, 'he took an implausible gamble that would pay off handsomely.'

"Cullen bought a dying forty-two-company conglomerate in 1986 for just $1, plus the assumption of $25 million in debt—with a 24 percent interest rate. The primary company in the group was the Renault distributorship in Ireland. Cullen said, 'I was able to turn this company around and earn a profit of a quarter-million dollars *a year later*.'" (My emphasis.)

Impressive work.

Can High Rollers change? Of course. But to do so takes some planning, some effort, and a belief that pulling back a bit on your risk taking can pay off. You'll need to break some habits that have become second-nature and consider other ideas about managing money. I have a few ideas for you that I know can be put into operation and will change, for the better, your relationship with money. It begins by understanding how you feel about it.

MAKING CHANGES: THE EMOTIONAL PATH

Since money for a High Roller is equated with emotional intensity, thrills, daring, and living on the edge of the unknown, I know how much of a struggle it may be for you to shift down to the world of moderation. But you can do it, if not painlessly, then surely step by step. The point is for you to change any High Roller habits that are getting in the way of your living securely. And if truth be told nowadays, what could be more thrilling than feeling secure and free?

There are a few actions to think about as you begin this ride toward some moderation:

Why Do You Need the High?

As with most High Rollers, including those of you who tell me you gamble on yourselves, the inner connection to feeding on risk is probably about a payoff greater than money—power or attention or acclaim. It's not really the acquisition and management of money, as you might think. Those connections began early in your life. Recall Ben's story and the image of those bills going up in flames and his offhand way of talking about money.

What's your story? Summon some of that High Roller courage and face any money demons that still whisper in your ear and get you into money trouble. Refer to Chapter 2 to help you answer questions about your past, your philosophy of money, and what you want from life.

Try this shift in thinking:

Listen to what you say to yourself about money, spending, and living on the edge, and what makes you take risks that get you into trouble. Connect the risk taking to early experiences that might have given rise to such behavior. Trace your tendency to being a High Roller and pinpoint where it came from. Here are a few questions to start you off:

- Do you believe that taking a big risk is the only way to find success?
- Are you a High Roller by example? That is, did you have High Roller parents who took big risks and were success-

ful at it, and did they want you to do the same? Or did they lose a lot, and do you feel it's your job to be successful to show them how it can be done?

- Are you a High Roller by choice? Did you grow up feeling deprived in some way and dream about easy money making you happy? Did you ever say to yourself growing up, "I won't struggle like my parents. I want to strike it big, as fast as I can."
- Did you, like Ben in the previous story, endure a traumatic event connected to having and keeping money? Did you lose money or something of value? Was it deliberate or by accident?
- Are you attracted to the image of the High Roller—as being tougher, slicker, smarter, and more glamorous than the average working person?

Psychologists say that the first step toward healing old wounds is awareness. Once you face your demons, you can begin to vanquish them.

Can You Put the Brakes on Your Addiction to Thrills?

High Rollers live financial high-wire acts for the thrill. Remove the net, and you're even more excited. Money and heated emotions seem to go together for you, and those feelings also include deep anxiety about how you manage money. This, you're less likely to admit. And Betsy, to whom I introduced you earlier in the chapter, is in real emotional turmoil. Part of her problem is the inability to decelerate the need for thrills and even her anxiety about living with few extreme highs and lows.

You may set money goals for yourself that you need to attain by taking big risks. As Betsy's behavior shows, living on the edge is preferable to what she thinks is boring, such as her husband's more conservative handling of money. If, like Betsy, you think of investments as exciting or boring, you've connected with them emotionally. Those very descriptors give you away.

Betsy has a sophisticated, demanding job and clearly has what it takes to succeed. The same may be true for you. There's no question that she can become a smarter participant in the fate of her finances, as you can in yours!

Try this shift in thinking:

High Rollers are perceptive and creative. You could apply some of that perspicacity to your own situation: *You must tone down your emotional connection to money* so that it is not all about rebellion, daring, or anger. Secondly, you will have to examine why you need to be in charge, in control, and appear powerful to others by taking bigger risks. Do you, like Betsy, want to show someone up as "cheap" or "boring" for not having the same passion as you do for risks? Or are you like Ben, taking big risks on your own skills and judgments? Justifying your actions by saying, "Everyone in my life is conservative, and I'm the one who takes the risks," is simplistic thinking. Everyone is really a risk-taker and risk-avoider. We take or avoid risks in different domains, physical, intellectual, emotional, or financial.

I was talking to Olivia Mellan, the Washington, D.C., psychologist I mentioned earlier, about the impulse your Money Type has for thrill seeking. She said, "Someone once asked me if there was something in the brains of men that made them bigger risk-takers than women. I'm not a brain biologist, but the way women and men are raised would explain some of those differences. Men are raised to compete and win and value risk taking, women a lot less so. We also live in an addictive society, and many people like the thrill of the ride and are addicted to an adrenaline high."

Biologically speaking, High Rollers need to step back from the edge and go for the calm gained from brain endorphins, not a pounding heart from the rush of adrenaline. That is, don't let enthusiasm about a high-risk investment pull you in over your head emotionally as well as financially. Allow yourself to appreciate the more conservative ventures and breathe easy.

I gained some more insight about this type's attraction to thrills from Olivia Mellan. High Rollers, she said, need to get a grip on the "addictive urge for peak experiences and the soft belly pleasure of being stimulated by a deal they love." If this sounds viscerally intense, it is precisely why many of you have a tough time walking away from high-risk ventures: danger, newness, and conquest. You like being titillated by risk, and want to think it's a warm and loving relationship. Unfortunately, most high-risk relationships end with your being left behind.

Here's the truth: Practical matters count, and when they stabilize your life, you feel better. Why lose your shirt? Practicality serves what is possible, not what is pie in the sky. When you tone down your emotions, you can let practicality provide a more sober evaluation of the risks you want to take.

I worry about High Rollers like Betsy who are addicted to gambling or high-risk investments—and who keep losing their money and their property. Find help at Gamblers Anonymous. Participating in meetings is one way to show you care about yourself. Eventually, you can repair your self-esteem to the point where you can accept yourself as a worthy person, without having to be a financial daredevil.

Until you can get yourself into a group, do yourself a big favor: Avoid "slippery places," that is, anywhere you can slip up. This could be the racetrack, weekends in Atlantic City or

WHAT IS THE SUREST ROUTE TO WEALTH?

A *Money* magazine survey once asked their readers what they believed was the surest route to wealth. Not surprisingly, 59 percent said hard work was the answer, while 39 percent hoped to beat the astonishing odds against them and answered, "winning the lottery."

Las Vegas, hanging around other High Rollers—or being in contact with stockbrokers who specialize in high-risk investments. Lose their phone numbers.

MAKING CHANGES: THE FINANCIAL PATH

My mission for you is to show you how to manage your money without squelching your creative or risk-taking impulses. In a few words: *Scale down your High Roller instincts for at least one year*. I do not want to suggest that you stop taking risks, but rather, show you how to keep a certain amount of cash on the side. Then you can *limit* how much money you put into riskier ventures and establish some security, too. When you see how much more money you have at the end of the year by limiting your risks, you can go on to a second year of scaling down. Read through my suggestions and take them one at a time. I know these steps work.

Before you begin downshifting on your high-risk tolerance factor, you will need to prepare yourself. To stay grounded, there are a few adjustments in thinking that will help you lower your anxiety level, at least about where your money is going. If there is a theme for you, it is to consider moderate risks, rather than high risks. But to make changes in your finances, you have to make a shift in your thinking. To get yourself going, think in terms of *beneficial change and increased profits*, real action and movement, and not limitations.

Set Realistic Limits and Stick to Them

High Rollers lead with their emotions, but successful investing requires a rational mind. Both Betsy and Ben would benefit most by knowing what their limits are and giving it a number, such as how much money they can really afford to lose without affecting their lifestyles. Next, they need a financial advisor they trust, not a stockbroker with an ax to grind, to help them make investment decisions—with and without their spouses. This advisor should be qualified and have a broad base of investment knowledge, as well as an understanding of both Betsy's and Ben's goals for greater financial success and stability.

Ben is facing bankruptcy and may not have much cash to invest, but in Betsy's case, a good advisor can help her determine what percentage of her cash reserves or portfolio can be allocated to higher-risk investments. Most of all, Betsy would benefit from discovering the appeal of lower-risk investing. High Rollers must reallocate some of their money from the top of the Investment Risk Pyramid to the middle (see page 297). An advisor can help Betsy evaluate the ground rules of high-risk ventures: that is, some will fly and some will not. She should educate herself by calculating the risks and not buy on impulse.

Can a High Roller see the light and live more moderately without feeling the pain? While many stay in financial orbit until catastrophe explodes around them, others can regulate their risk taking and prosper. However, huge financial loss need not be the only impetus for finally getting the downside of High Roller behavior in balance. Some High Rollers who are just starting out can control the adrenaline highs of the big risk/big payoff stakes, get perspective on investing, and develop into a more cautious risk-taking High Roller. Debbie is such an example of how some High Rollers are both born and made.

Upping Your Chances for a Payoff–Taking Educated Risks

Debbie first contacted me about two years ago to ask my advice about managing her money, because, she said, "I know we're wasting a lot of money by not having any investments. We're not putting our money where we can make a profit. CDs are too conservative. We don't know much about the stock market.

Where can we invest so that we have some freedom? My husband is too tight with money, but I believe in taking risks. My husband panics when I mention investments." I suggested medium-risk investments, like corporate bonds, and asked her to check out the real estate market in her area and to do so vigilantly. Since then, she and her husband have changed, even blossomed.

Debbie, with a higher risk tolerance, put her mind to developing her High Roller tendencies, but she kept them in check. Debbie may love risk, but she always exercises caution. While she and her husband, Joe, have a way to go before they can be considered players, they are in the game to stay.

"We grew up having nothing," Debbie says of their backgrounds. "I grew up on welfare, and Joe's parents divorced when he was very young—and his mother always struggled to make ends meet. Such an early life really opens your eyes to what money can do," Debbie told me. "I grew up promising myself to make as much money as I can and never put my kids through what I had to endure, always wanting for something. Even though we had so little, my mother's mantra was 'Find a way to save, save, save.' She believed this was how people got rich. I knew there had to be a better way to build your assets than saving." Debbie, the High Roller of this North Carolina couple, eventually found the way that would best suit her—real estate.

Debbie and Joe put themselves through college, determined to succeed. Debbie got a job as a paralegal in a small local law firm, and Joe eventually got a doctorate that helped land him a job in hospital administration. At the same time, Debbie was reading about investment strategies and had contacted me for advice. She told me that at first, she dismissed my suggestion of the real estate business. But inspired by a friend's success, she took the leap. Debbie was soon immersed in the competitive, sometimes cutthroat world of real estate. She'd found her metier.

Now more or less a stay-at-home mom, Debbie and Joe live on Joe's salary and put her real estate earnings into investments—a combination of rental properties that they buy and flip, lease to purchase, and straight sales. After two years, Debbie and her husband are pinning their future on her start-up success. Joe works with her on a limited basis, but it's Debbie, the would-be High Roller entrepreneur, who makes most of the choices. They've been smart choices so far, and she's excited by where she hopes real estate can take them. "We've paid off student loans, credit cards, and other debts, and substantially reduced our fifteen-year mortgage," she said. They sold their first home two years ago, bought for $130,00, at a $45,000 profit. They reinvested the profits in their business. Last Christmas eve, they got a nice gift—they sold their second home, which they'd bought for $270,000, and made a $78,000 profit. They used the money to pay off the home equity loan. On New Year's Day, they moved in with Debbie's sister while their new house is being built. It will cost them $100,000 less than their first house, and it will reduce their debt.

"I want to put our money to work for us, but every now and then, Joe says, 'You've lost your mind,' when he hears what I've chosen to do next!" Debbie says of her Squirrel husband. "Over the last two months, I bought three rental properties, all financed through a home equity loan. Each of the rentals has a positive cash flow of $500 a month. But my husband, a bit of a penny-pincher, worries. But I tell him you have to take some risks. You have to use your money wisely, but you have to ask yourself if you want to live month to month or eventually have real holdings, real assets. It's all about working as a team and having a vision of what you want to get."

Debbie's goal is to have eight to ten rental properties and to continue using Joe's income to pay bills, put money into retirement accounts, and have some fun traveling with the kids. Now Debbie is taking a bigger step up—she and Joe have bought two great beachfront properties, which together are valued at $500,000. They'll hold them for a year or so, then sell.

"You can't get anywhere without a risk," Debbie says, true to her Money Type. "It gets you the reward. You know, if a deal falls through, it falls through. We'll do much better next time. I've never walked away from a moneymaking opportunity. I hope I never do." She clearly loves the thrill of the deal, and the sense of satisfaction and contentment. "I dream about owning more developed property and more undeveloped land, and I have to control myself from going crazy," she added. "All I have to do is remember what 'nothing' feels like—most of my childhood—and tone down. Real estate has changed us, but we're stewards of that money, and we take it seriously."

She doesn't play hunches, nor is she drawn to get-rich-quick schemes. Success is thrilling for her, but not to the point where she's reckless with money. An unusual High Roller, Debbie doesn't believe in luck. She told me finally, "Success is all about education and hard work, striking when the iron is hot and taking the risk. I don't see a downside. That may be overly confident to some people, but it works for us every time."

I've put together a number of painless money-saving, cautious risk-taking ideas for you. These ideas still allow you to take advantage of your instincts for innovation and trends while showing you how to hold on to more of your money and make sure it works for you.

Don't Blow Your Retirement Fund—401(k) Mistakes to Avoid

Without question, the 401(k) for many of you is the primary source of funds for your retirement kitty. Some High Rollers dip in or cash out, or do not manage their 401(k), thinking it will take care of itself. Here's where you can be self-protective and practical. If you blow your 40l(k), you can pretty much kiss your dream retirement goodbye. Let's look at some of the top mistakes you should avoid.

Failing to rebalance your portfolio: You certainly don't want to move in and out of your investments as a day trader does, but you also don't want to not give your initial selections another thought until retirement day. Financial gurus say that once a year you should take a hard look at your holdings: How have they done? What's happening in the market? What's changed in your life? See what, if anything, needs adjusting or pruning. In many cases, it makes sense to cut back on some of the big winners of the past year and put some money into the losers, because otherwise you are just following last year's trends when they may be about to change. Get help from a financial advisor if you can't do it yourself.

Cashing out when you change jobs: You feel good about that new job you're starting soon, but don't lose your head and see the money you've got in the fund suddenly as disposable income. The $30,000 or so that you've saved is not the ticket to paradise or a fancy sports car or the makings of a new investment on a hot property. For one thing, by the time you pay the mandatory 20 percent federal withholding tax, the IRS's 10 percent penalty if you are under fifty-nine and a half, and state and local taxes—call it the case of the disappearing kitty.

It's far better to roll over that money into an IRA, but be careful. If you roll over the money into an existing IRA, you won't be able to parlay that money into a new 401(k) later. This may not matter if you're sixty-five, but it's a different story if you're thirty-something. How to handle your current 401(k) is probably a question best addressed by your financial advisor. But generally, the benefits from rolling it over to your new employer's 401(k) are the ability to borrow the funds in the future and the low or no transaction fees when investing. The benefit of rolling it over to an IRA is that your investment options are not limited by what your new employer offers.

Putting your eggs in one basket: You don't want to load up on your own company's stock (25 percent of your portfolio in your company's stock should be the max), nor do you want too many mutual funds that look like cousins by investing in essentially the same stocks or bonds. You want a broad mix of assets to protect your growth opportunities. You'll need to spend the time to learn what you have in your portfolio, but unfortunately, many people don't take the time. A recent survey showed that half of their respondents spent *six hours or less* a year managing their portfolio. That kind of inattention will do nothing to boost your stash. Take advantage, too, of any employer-provided financial planning and investment advice, especially if it's free.

Think in Terms of Saving for Lower-Risk Long-Term Goals

Someone once said, "You need long-term goals to keep you from being frustrated by short-range failures." How true! Your inclination is to favor short-term thinking and flashy deals, so I want to encourage you to take a chunk of money and invest it toward a long-term goal. Do not touch it, except to add funds.

To begin with, you'll need to fill out a financial plan (see Cash Flow Worksheet on p. 72, which can help you figure out what you need to know about your money and where it goes). Of course, your plan will need an actual goal to shoot for: This can be a retirement fund, upgrading, remodeling or buying a new house, paying for a child's college education, traveling, or relocating. Create a real picture for yourself of what you want— High Rollers are imaginative, and you see what you want clearly, which allows you to make impossible things happen.

What is your long-term goal? We're going to aim for what is considered the average time to achieve a long-term goal: ten years. Whether you'll be shooting for the most common long-term goal—a financially secure retirement—or funding extensive travel in the future or being sure you can afford medical care in your later years, you'll need to do a little math to figure out some estimated costs. You'll find the following Long-Term Goals Worksheet helpful in getting a sense of those numbers.

Next you want to do a little math to figure out how much cash you need to save or invest to reach the goal. To make it easier, I've created a table that tells you how your money will grow by rate of interest and number of years—the ultimate amount of course determined by how much you put in. First,

LONG-TERM GOALS WORKSHEET

Goal	Priority	Date to Accomplish	$ Amount Needed
Buy Retirement Home	_____	_____	_____
Buy Vacation Home	_____	_____	_____
Continue Education	_____	_____	_____
Do Community or Charity Work	_____	_____	_____
Establish Long-Term Health Care for Self and/or Spouse	_____	_____	_____
Establish Retirement Fund	_____	_____	_____
Help Older Parents	_____	_____	_____
Make a Charitable Bequest	_____	_____	_____
Pay Off Mortgage Early	_____	_____	_____
Start a Business	_____	_____	_____
Start a Second Career	_____	_____	_____
Travel Extensively	_____	_____	_____
Other (specify)	_____	_____	_____
Total $ Needed			$_____

take a look at the chart, and then read the simple instructions on how to use it, which follow.

The left column shows the *number of years* you have until you need the money for your goal. The next four columns show the *divisors for four different rates of return* that you can safely assume it is possible to earn, on average, over a long period of time. These rates of return assume you have adjusted for the

DETERMINING THE MONTHLY SAVINGS
NEEDED TO REACH A GOAL

	Divisors (By Rate of Return)			
Years to Goal	2%	4%	6%	8%
1	12.1	12.2	12.3	12.4
2	24.5	24.9	25.4	25.9
3	37.1	38.2	39.3	40.6
4	49.9	51.9	54.1	56.4
5	63.1	66.2	69.8	73.6
6	76.5	81.1	86.4	92.1
7	90.2	96.6	104.1	112.3
8	104.2	112.7	122.8	134.1
9	118.4	129.5	142.7	157.7
10	133.0	146.9	163.9	183.4
11	147.8	165.1	186.3	211.1
12	163.0	184.0	210.1	241.2
13	178.5	203.6	235.4	273.7
14	194.2	224.0	262.3	309.0
15	210.4	245.3	290.8	347.3
16	226.8	267.4	321.1	388.7
17	243.6	290.4	353.2	433.6
18	260.7	314.3	387.3	482.2
19	278.2	339.2	423.6	534.9
20	296.1	365.1	462.0	592.0
21	314.2	392.1	502.9	653.8
22	332.8	420.1	546.2	720.8
23	351.8	449.3	592.2	793.4
24	371.2	479.6	641.1	872.0
25	390.9	511.2	693.0	957.2

effects of inflation and taxes, and are known as real after-tax yields. The higher the rate of return, the more risk you have to take in your investment choices to achieve your goal.

To use the table, take the amount of money you will need to pay for your goal and pick an *assumed* rate of return. Then find the divisor for the number of years you've allocated to reach the goal. Simply divide your dollar goal by the divisor, and you have figured out the monthly amount of savings needed to reach that goal. The divisor automatically calculates the effect of compounding of interest, which can become a powerful force over time.

Here's a hypothetical case. Say you're shooting for a $100,000 nest egg for your retirement in twenty years. Start by thinking years and percentages. Look down the years column to the twenty-year line and, assuming a real after-tax yield of 8 percent, move across to the 8 percent column. You find that the divisor is 592. Now divide your $100,000 goal by 592 and you wind up with the $168.92 a month you need to save to reach that goal. Simple!

Part of your investment strategy is to assemble a portfolio of stocks, bonds, mutual funds, and bank instruments that will get you where you want to go. One of the main risks you must overcome in a long-term plan is the slow but steady erosion of the worth of a dollar because of inflation. A good investment strategy will keep your dollars growing faster—something you relate to a lot!—so that when you need to spend them, you will have enough. Another element of investing is finding a *lower* level of risk with which you will feel comfortable.

Give Yourself a Safety Net—Lower-Risk Investments You Can Live With

Once you have prioritized your goals, you want to track your progress. This way, you'll know exactly where you stand and what it will take to achieve what you've set out to accomplish financially. Beginners at investing tend to start out with most of their money in cash instruments. These are investments that are safe from loss of principal—checking, savings, and certificate of deposit (CD) accounts at banks, savings and loans, and credit unions, money market funds, and Treasury bills (T bills).

Higher-Yield CDs

These are bank, savings and loan, or credit union instruments that allow you to lock in an interest rate for a specific period of time. If you withdraw your money before the CD matures, you face an early-withdrawal penalty set by each bank—often three months' interest. The most popular CDs mature in three months, six months, and one year, although banks offer some with up to a five-year maturity and various other customized and designer CDs. Banks don't charge fees to buy a certificate. All interest from CDs is taxable in the year it is received, even if it is reinvested. Remember to calculate the effect of those taxes when comparing potential CD returns against other alternatives like tax-free money funds or municipal bonds.

However, and I think this will be of greater interest to you, you can buy higher-yield CDs, and you won't have to buy one from your local bank or any bank in your state. Many banks accept out-of-state deposits by wire or mail. The highest yields around the country are publicized constantly in major financial newspapers as well as on Web sites from companies like Bankrate (www.bankrate.com). You can subscribe to their newsletter, *100 Highest Yields* (11811 U.S. Highway 1, Suite 101, North Palm Beach, FL 33408; 800-243-7720).

Bonds

There are many kinds of bonds to fit many investment needs, from the ultra-secure Treasury bonds or U.S. savings bonds issued and backed by the U.S. government, to slightly more speculative government agency securities. The latter includes issues from agencies like the Farmers Home Administration (FmHa), Federal Home Loan Mortgage Corporation (Freddie Mac), and even the U.S. Postal Service. Though they do not carry the full faith and credit of the U.S. government behind them, you can be fairly certain that Congress would make sure these agencies don't default on their debt.

The bond market is complex, and impossible to cover in this space in greater detail, but let me give you a few basics. While bonds are interest-bearing vehicles that are considered safer and more conservative than stocks, they don't have the same kind of long-term growth potential. When you invest in a bond, you're essentially loaning the issuer of that bond your money in return for a fixed rate of interest for a specific amount of time. Normally, you receive interest payments every six months, and when the bond matures, you receive your original principal, no matter how much the price of the bond had fluctuated since it was issued. Which bonds are for you?

Going up the risk ladder are mortgage-backed securities, then municipal bonds issued by states, cities, counties, towns, villages, and taxing authorities of many types. There are international bonds, corporate bonds, zero coupon bonds, considerable bonds, and the most speculative of all, high-yield or junk bonds. If the process of choosing individual bonds seems too complicated, bond mutual funds might be right for you. Resist an urge to jump into junk bonds, which offer the highest risk, and choose bonds in the midlevel range, such as corporate bonds, Treasury bonds, or zero coupon bonds.

What I want to emphasize is that investing in bonds is one of the key vehicles available to help you achieve your financial goals. They allow you to lock in a set rate of income for a long period, which can give your financial plan a rock-solid foundation—something you are seeking. Also, if you want to trade bonds more actively, you can earn capital gains by buying them when their prices fall and selling them when their prices rise, just as you can do with stocks.

Become a Landlord—Invest in Rental Real Estate

Real estate speculation, or buying foreclosed properties and reselling them, may sound like classic High Roller options, but I won't suggest going down this road with you. Investing in real estate for profit is definitely tricky and can take a great deal of time and expertise, but may offer lucrative rewards as well. Real estate has the advantages of appreciation potential, tax benefits, and substantial income if you participate in rental real estate. The real estate market is also subject to the influence of national trends, such as changes in tax laws and interest rates, as well as local trends in economic growth and supply and demand for similar properties.

When seeking advice about investing in real estate, make sure you know or can research your source of knowledge. The field is rife with self-promoters promising instant riches for "no money down." Their so-called seminars are, in fact, high-pressure sales pitches. Stay clear. These scam artists show off their wealth to impress you—and get you into their game by promising you financial success or financial freedom. Many of them get to flash their millions by giving bad real estate advice, not taking it—a very low-end High Roller. If you wish to invest legitimately in real estate, you have several options. I'm going to recommend rental real estate for you.

This means you become a landlord, which has its advantages and disadvantages—but it's the kind of prospect that could suit your High Roller personality. If you own a good property, it can appreciate handsomely over time and provide solid rental income. In addition, you can reap substantial tax benefits, such as writing off losses up to $25,000 against other income, if you meet certain IRS restrictions.

However, few people think of being a landlord as fun. Tenants complain. You are responsible if the plumbing breaks down in the middle of the night or if the furnace conks out in the dead of winter. Not every renter pays his or her rent on time. You must constantly guard against vandalism, and sometimes you have to evict a tenant. Also, in some localities, rent controls prevent you from raising rents enough to cover increased expenses and upkeep.

The key to successful rental real estate is to buy properties in good locations to attract the type of tenant who takes care of his or her unit and is so happy living on the property that he or she never objects to yearly rent hikes. Easier said than done. But the deal can get better.

When looking for profitable rental properties, you might begin in working-class neighborhoods, where prices are more reasonable and tenants are more reliable than in the elite neighborhoods of town. To find a bargain, you could focus on properties with problems that are relatively easy to resolve. The problem, be it asbestos removal, a leaky roof, or some other repair, might scare the current owners so much that they will sell at a large discount from the property's real value. Before buying, determine how much it will cost to resolve the problem and estimate the rent you could collect once the place is in tip-top shape.

Another way to get the best possible value when buying rental real estate is to look for a building that sits on a lot providing extra land that could be developed. You might be able to add onto the building, erect a new home, or even sell part of the land to offset your purchase cost. Before you contemplate such a strategy, however, determine whether you will need a zoning variance to subdivide the land.

Cover Some of Your Bases with Insurance

The idea is to create a solid conservative base. You need to be insured. There are six types of insurance you need to make sure you are covered by: life, health, auto, homeowners, disability, and long-term care.

Before you buy insurance, consider this: The field of insurance can be difficult to understand, and as a result, you may wind up paying for more insurance coverage than you actually need. The insurance industry is notorious for using jargon and complex presentations that baffle most of us. What you don't know about insurance can hurt you in two ways: 1) you may pay too much for a policy that you could have bought much cheaper had you understood how to compare insurers and policies, and

2) the coverage you purchase may be too much or too little for your needs, or it may duplicate existing coverage in some areas and leave you unprotected in others. You could be ruined financially if you have a large claim that isn't covered.

Before buying a policy from an insurance company or contact one of its sales reps, check the firm's financial condition. Five independent firms rate insurance companies' financial strength, A. M. Best, Fitch, Moody's Investor Service, Weiss Ratings, and Standard & Poor's Corporation—their contact information is in the Appendix. Always understand exactly what you're paying for before you sign any document. Don't hesitate to ask questions of agents, brokers, direct marketing salespeople, or insurance advisors—whoever is selling you your policy. It's your money and your legacy on the line, so be confident that you know your policy's benefits. (You can check the chapter on Coasters to get more information on what to know before buying a policy.)

FINALLY: POINTS TO REMEMBER FOR HIGH ROLLERS

Life is really not a matter of black-and-white, all or nothing, win or lose. Rather than living at the edge financially, move toward the middle. The moderate position will be more likely to provide financial security for you.

Do not set impossible or out-of-reach goals for yourself, which you would need to achieve by taking big risks with money. Use your strengths—imagination, vision, tenacity—to set goals, and your common sense to back them up with the help of a sharp, disciplined money manager.

If you seek high risk, be sure it is risk with a purposeful and realistic goal and not a risk for kicks or for ego.

Be realistic, cautious, and practical—don't put money into a venture purely on an emotional impulse.

Shift from favoring short-term thinking and flashy deals to taking a chunk of money and investing it in a long-term goal. Do not touch it, except to add funds. It will pay off for you.

RESOURCES FOR HIGH ROLLERS

Your best bet is to stop living on the edge and cool down. Think through your decisions, desires, and actions more carefully. A little risk is healthy, but too much can hurt you. To help you cultivate the impulse to look before you leap, investigate these resources.

Books

Built to Last: Successful Habits of Visionary Companies, by James C. Collins and Jerry I. Porras (HarperCollins, 10 East 53rd Street, New York, NY 10022; 212-207-7583; www.harper collins.com). Identifies eighteen "visionary" companies and sets out to determine what's special about them. A good read for the budding entrepreneur.

How to Be a Quick Turn Real Estate Millionaire: Make Fast Cash with No Money, Credit, or Previous Experience, by Ron LeGrand. (Dearborn Trade Publishing, 30 South Wacker Drive, Suite 2500, Chicago IL 60606; 800-245-2665; www.dearborn. com/trade). LeGrand shares his technique for building wealth in real estate.

Investing in Real Estate, by Andrew James McLean and Gary W. Eldred (John Wiley & Sons, 111 River Street, Hoboken, NJ 07030; 201-748-6000; www.wiley.com). Now in its fourth edition, this practical guide will help you invest in real estate such as houses and small apartment buildings to generate cash flow and build current wealth.

Rich Dad Poor Dad: What the Rich Teach Their Kids About Money—That the Poor and Middle Class Do Not!, by Robert T. Kiyosaki with Sharon L. Lechter, CPA (Warner Business Books, 1271 Avenue of the Americas, New York, NY 10020; www. richdad.com or www.twbookmark.com). In this classic bestseller, Kiyosaki and Lechter present a unique perspective on how to accumulate wealth, both in real estate and in other ways.

Publications

Entrepreneur magazine (2445 McCabe Way, Irvine, CA 92614; 949-261-2325; www.entrepreneur.com). You can subscribe to a hard copy of the magazine, or just spend time browsing through the Web site, which is filled with useful (and free) articles, how-to guides, and other information. Topics include how to start a business, running a home-based business, franchising, and financial management.

Worth magazine (http://worth.com). This publication has sections that deal with entrepreneurship, investment opportunities, philanthropy, and trusts and estates.

Organizations

Alliance 1 (11700 West Lake Park Drive, Milwaukee, WI 53224; 414-359-1040; www.alliance1.org). An international nonprofit organization dedicated to improving family life through services, education, and advocacy. Member agencies throughout the United States provide family counseling services, and more.

Gamblers Anonymous (PO Box 17173, Los Angeles, CA 90017; 213-386-8789; www.gamblersanonymous.org). This group focuses on helping compulsive gamblers stop gambling. There are no dues or fees; the only requirement is a desire to stop gambling.

Institute of Consumer Financial Education (PO Box 34070, San Diego, CA 92163; 619-239-1401; www.financial-education-icfe.org). This group aims to help people improve their spending, increase their savings, and use credit more wisely. Their Web site has a spenders' quiz, credit card tips, and links to other helpful sites.

International Franchise Association (1350 New York Avenue, NW, Suite 900, Washington, DC 20005; 202-628-8000; www.franchise.org). If you're thinking of buying a franchise, this is one Web site you don't want to skip. It offers online courses and answers frequently asked questions. It also offers links to other services that franchisees and potential business owners might find of interest.

National Association of Real Estate Investment Trusts (1875 I Street NW, Suite 600, Washington, DC 20006; 202-739-9400; www.nareit.com). Offers information on investing in REITs (real estate investment trusts), a glossary of terms, and updates on the industry.

National Council on Problem Gambling (216 G Street NE, Suite 200, Washington, DC 20002; 202-547-9204; www.ncp gambling.org). Offers a twenty-four-hour national hotline (800-522-4700), as well as resources and places to go for help.

Options Industry Council (The Options Clearing Corporation, One North Wacker Drive, Suite 500, Chicago IL 60606; 888-678-4667; www.optionscentral.com). This nonprofit group educates investors about the benefits and risks of stock options. You can choose from twelve online courses or attend a free seminar in your area. The Web site answers frequently asked questions about options and provides an options pricing calculator, as well as the names and numbers of brokers to call for more information.

CHAPTER **8**

The Squirrels

*Do you believe that the only way to feel financially
secure is to hang on to every penny?*
*Does worry about money ever stand in the way of
you enjoying what you have?*
*Do you live with an unrealistic fear that financial dis-
aster is looming just around the corner?*

In putting this chapter together, I recalled a story I read about a
woman whose inclination toward thrift fit the Squirrel type
perfectly, if to an extreme. The woman's name was Anne
Scheiber, and she left an astonishing legacy—one that shocked
everyone, including her heirs.

Capsulized, her story would go this way: Former IRS auditor
who always lived her life as if she did not have enough money
for her next meal dies at the age of 101, leaving $22 million to a
college and medical school. Her few intimates describe her as
pathologically frugal, a woman whose only joy came from
accumulating money.

These are a few more revealing details of this Squirrel. Anne
Scheiber grew up one of nine children and with a fear of being
left destitute, a result of her father's financial losses and early
death. On her own from the age of fifteen, she eventually

wound up in Washington, D.C., working as an auditor for the IRS. She got a law degree at night, but instead of going into practice, she stuck with what she thought was the more secure government job. Scrimping and saving was already a way of life for her.

Her IRS experience would soon pay off for her in ways beyond incremental salary raises. Scheiber was smart. When she pored over other people's tax returns, she decided that the surest way to get rich was to invest in stocks and bonds. And she decided to get rich, too.

She retired from the IRS in the early 1940s and moved to New York City with $5,000 in savings. Scheiber found a broker and sank her savings into her stock picks. She moved into a rented studio apartment, living on her meager pension and Social Security. While her money was growing, Scheiber's life became even more narrowly focused—nothing mattered to her but making money.

By 1970, she was a multimillionaire, but she still lived in her studio rental apartment, with paint peeling off the walls and the furniture she'd bought in 1944. She wore the same black coat and hat every day, no matter what the season, spending none of her money to improve her life or even to indulge in simple human pleasures. Every cent went into investments.

While she was alive, no one but her broker and her lawyer knew how much money she had—she swore them to secrecy—and how sad a woman she really was, despite the millions. One of her nephews said that the richer she got, the more bitter she became. When Scheiber died in 1995, still in the same shabby studio apartment, the money she could never enjoy would be happily put to good use by her heirs. And when the story of this rich eccentric broke, not a few financial analysts examined the record of how she increased a $5,000 investment by 439,900 percent.

Anne Scheiber may have been described as brilliant but weird about money, but she was certainly bursting with the same kind of vulnerabilities and fears of her Money Type, a Bag Lady version of the Squirrel. (I'll introduce you to another, more identifiable Bag Lady type later in the chapter, and show you how to deal with the emotional issues surrounding money more satisfactorily.)

Which brings me back to you. Would you say you are predominantly a Squirrel who prefers thrift over spending? Do you think you may have some of these overly frugal, self-sacrificing Bag Lady tendencies in dealing with money? Answering yes to two or three of the questions at the opening of the chapter pretty much identifies you as a Squirrel.

I get thousands of e-mails and letters from your Money Type, so I have a good idea about what your money concerns are: maximizing your assets without taking much risk. If I have any goals for your Money Type, the first would be to encourage you to take a few risks by putting some of your money into higher-earning investments. (More on this later.) My other goal is for you to keep your passion for accumulating money, but additionally, to give yourself the pleasure of enjoying what you earn. You're essentially good with money, so let it be good to you!

What are Squirrels all about? Let's take a look.

THE SQUIRREL REVEALED

Squirrels love money and worry about it with the same depth of emotion. Of all the Money Types, yours is the most fearful of losing it all. As a way to avert financial disaster, you would devote your life to safe saving habits and job security. Of course, there's an emotional component to this often irrational fear that with one wrong move, you'll be destitute. A wrong move can mean anything under or beyond your control—from a parent or spouse losing a job, to a business failing, to a death, to a bad investment, to a swindle. Sometimes the fear has a basis in fact—a financial disaster is part of your history and you don't want it happening again. You are artists at preparing for disaster! When your motto is "If anything can go wrong with money, it will," you're not going to take the kind of risks you need to take so your money can earn higher returns.

Like your animal mascot, the Squirrel, you operate out of an instinct to prepare for shortages and hard times. You build a stash so that you not only survive on a daily basis, you thrive over the long run. Of course, this is tactically smart: thrift, foresight, planning, and frugality keep you going without worry. But as a Squirrel, the same instinct that says, "add it to the pile," is also driven by the fear that demands, "and now, lock the door so none of it gets taken." If any Money Type goes overboard about not investing or spending more aggressively, it's you.

As for Bag Ladies, a variation of this Money Type: You live in a safe and insular world as long as you have assets. Real bag ladies are on the street and represent not only the fear of losing one's assets, but of being abandoned and having no one to turn to for something as basic as a room with a bed and a meal.

Overall, you have energy and courage, so give yourself a break and consider my suggestions for how you can really build your assets! They will pay off for you.

The Squirrel: Your Strengths

While Squirrels sometimes get a bad rap because they're not easily parted from their money, they should be commended for how well they manage what they have. As a Squirrel, you're probably comfortable with a budget, happy to use pennies-back store coupons, and know where to find the best deals in town. Squirrels can be so disciplined about not spending money that you can resist sales, bargains, and deals. In fact, you can emphatically say no to a child pleading for money to buy stuff and stick to your guns. You're not a soft touch, the way the Striver or High Roller parent might be.

You're an ace at balancing your checkbook—and anyone else's—and you probably have a job where you can demonstrate your expertise for order, organization, and establishing (and living within) limits. As a classic Squirrel, you'll easily live within your means and don't need to prove anything to others through your possessions. Privately knowing you have enough money or material things is satisfying enough for you.

The Bag Ladies among you live in a safe and insular world as long as they have assets. Many Bag Ladies have managed to accumulate real wealth but by definition without much enjoyment or satisfaction. You have persistence and follow-through and, of course, native caution. No one can match your talent for getting more out of a dollar—whether it is through investing or in making what you purchase last a long time.

Above all, Squirrels are pragmatic—practical and realistic about money, but to a fault.

The Squirrel: Your Weaknesses

As a Squirrel, you typically live way below your means, clipping coupons—which ironically can be a strength. But the downside is that you take few or no vacations and do not enjoy what you have, rarely treating yourself to the affordable good life.

Then again, there are Squirrels not unlike the man I recently met at a seminar I was giving on investing. At the end of the evening, he came up to speak to me. He told me he and his wife own a great four-bedroom house in Westchester County and they've finally paid off their mortgage. So, just as they reached retirement age, they have a house worth over a million dollars and no liquid income, but, the man said, smiling, "We've got no debt!" While being out of debt is in fact a good thing, in this case, Squirrel thinking has undone it.

As a Squirrel is disposed to accumulate assets, so is he inclined to resist debt. This Squirrel couple's decision to pay off their mortgage ten years ahead of time is a good example of what *not* to do. They were proud of having paid off their mortgage, but doing so didn't really enhance their overall money picture. The rush to say, "We have no debt," reflects an anxiety about owing money, not commonsense money management. Their weakness was in succumbing to the anxiety and putting it in charge of their money. They would have done better had they paid off their mortgage slowly and put the extra money toward investments that would have grown for them. They would have had liquidity. Being this debt-averse made them house-rich and cash-poor.

Like this couple, too many Squirrels just don't test reality about money. The looming thought about eliminating debt, for example, cancels out any other possibility. When this happens, you aren't open to and cannot make more intelligent choices—and take smarter risks. Nowhere is this more evident than with a variation of the Squirrel, the Bag Lady.

Motivated by a deep-seated fear of loss, Bag Ladies, sadly, cheat themselves. The fear of becoming destitute, or a bag

---

WORRY ABOUT MONEY

Is money a headache that worrying about makes worse? An article in *Men's Health* magazine called "Mental About Money" quoted Susan Galvan, the executive director of the Kinder Institute of Life Planning, a financial planning firm, on the subject.

A common male money hang-up, she says, is the belief "I don't earn enough." Galvan says it's more important to decide what you want in life to make you happy and then figure out how much cash you need to get there—rather than assume it is the pursuit of money itself that will make you happy. It's more useful to develop a saving-and-spending strategy based on what you want out of life. "*When you focus on money,*" she says, "*you will never find fulfillment. Money is the support system, not the primary goal.*"

lady—a person without resources and not in control of her life—turns people who are usually comfortable into hoarders who live way, *way* below their means. Bag Ladies are usually women (but men qualify here, too!) who are doing okay and have no reason to fear losing it all.

Ruled by an irrational fear that with one wrong move they'll be on the street, at their worst, Bag Ladies can't enjoy what they have. Since Bag Ladies fervently believe *everything* can go wrong, they prepare for disaster as a way of life. They don't allow themselves to see a truer or balanced money picture because their focus is on the possibility of loss. By seeing imminent disaster, they take few risks and tend to keep money in low-interest savings accounts and CDs, which ironically can lead them to lose out on the opportunity of enjoying greater prosperity and security.

Let me introduce you to a few classic Squirrels who are still stuck and unsure of what to do. When I talked to them and heard their stories, I realized they were courageous individuals who had forgotten they had more control over their money and their choices than they believed. I saw how to help them and make them a little less Squirrel-like, without their stepping too far out of character. Take a look:

"I Won't Go Through Losing It All Again!"

When I spoke to Tina, she and her family had just come back from a trip to Florida and a weekend at Disney World—a much deserved vacation for all of them. I asked if they'd had a great time, and she hesitated a moment before answering, "All I could think about was the $4,500 it cost us!" Finally she admitted, "After a few days, I could actually begin to enjoy myself. I was glad we'd made the plans." I knew I was talking to a classic Squirrel who's more likely to focus on expenditures than on the value of the experience the money is making possible.

Her own financial well-being—as well as her husband's success—doesn't ease her mind. And it's not just spending for vacations that worry this forty-four-year-old Tulsa woman. Tina's feelings about outgo plumb much deeper. Her fears center on being left financially ruined, her apprehension a remnant of a very real and life-changing specter from her childhood. "I'm not burying coffee cans full of cash in the yard," she assured me, but given her family history, she could very well be tempted to pick up the shovel.

Growing up with all the privileges a child could ask for, Tina had a good life until the good life crashed. She was only eleven years old when her businessman father was stricken with a disease for which there was no cure. He could never work again, and his savings and investments didn't pay for his medical care or for maintaining anything near the family's level of upkeep. Tina's grandmother bailed them out. Her father's illness and the sudden downshift in Tina's family's circumstances changed her life drastically, forcing her to grow up quickly. "I saw how your world can collapse under you in a heartbeat and how you have no control," she said. "All I could think about was money and the question 'how much?'"

By her early teens, Tina vowed to avert financial catastrophe any way she could. She paid her own way through college by taking out student loans and working weekends at a bar for the higher salary—to get "more bang for my buck"—rather than taking a lower-paying job as a teaching assistant. Frugal and staunchly risk-averse, Tina was determined to graduate with an MBA degree, which would guarantee her a better job. She didn't think about being fulfilled by a career, but by how much it would eventually pay off. In the back of her mind, she was always waiting for the next shoe to drop—someone or something beyond her control stopping the source of money.

Tina's aspirations landed her in an executive suite in a financial services firm. "In the days before I was married, I lost money on some stocks. I learned you don't die from losing $1,000, but it still hurt like crazy. I got really gun-shy." Then she married and had a son. She and her husband, Doug, were each earning six-figure salaries and wanted for nothing. Then their second child was born with a serious disability. "The morning I came back from maternity leave, my boss told me he thought I should get my home life together," Tina said. The other shoe had dropped. She lost her job, and the family income was cut in half.

That was two years ago. Mostly a stay-at-home mom now, Tina teaches a few classes at a local university on a part-time basis.

Tina told me she'd like to lose the sense of trepidation that being a Squirrel creates for her: "I look back on my childhood and still see my father's face in despair, a picture of how much

---

TINA AND DOUG'S FINANCIAL SNAPSHOT

This upper-middle-class family is not feeling a financial crunch with one spouse working full-time and the other working part-time. Their profile looks like this:

- They're debt-free, with only $90,000 remaining on their $400,000 mortgage. They owe nothing on their credit cards.

- Tina's van is paid off, although Doug still has car payments.

- A $40,000 mutual fund will help cover future college expenses.

- Tina and Doug have rolled over 401(k)s from prior jobs, and they think they'll be fine when they retire.

- Ever frugal, Tina shops for the family's clothing or household items only when they need replacing, and she favors buying what's on sale and at discount retailers for food and other necessities.

losing *can* hurt. I don't want to relive that." Tina said that her father's not being able to make money took away his will to live even more than his illness did. "I felt helpless because I couldn't stop the turn of events or make my father better so he could continue bringing in money," she said. "Everything was taken from him. I'll do anything to prevent knowing such loss again."

Learn from Catastrophe–Don't Let It Rule Your Life

Tina's innocence ended with her Striver father's tragic fate and her Squirrel-like habits clicking into place. For her, squirreling away every cent and living ultra-frugally are safety measures meant to avert another frightening financial catastrophe. So far, Tina's done well for herself, but she's stuck looking back *and* looking over her shoulder for a surprise that will strip her assets again.

Logically, she knows that by walking with ghosts who remind her of loss she can see only what they see—imminent financial disaster. I know she's ready to do what too many Squirrels cannot do: give themselves the power over money and not allow money to hold such power over them. Every Squirrel can do this!

Alan's case is bit different, but he shares a number of Squirrel qualities that tend to limit his possibilities.

"I Was Raised to Be Grateful for Getting By and Ashamed for Wanting More!"

Alan is a recently retired Michigan man who is an interesting Squirrel type. He worries about money, he tells me, not for himself but for his only daughter, Sally. He's afraid he won't have enough money down the line to help this divorced daughter, whose poor money management skills worry him to excess. As for his own life, he claims it's satisfactory, although he would like to figure out a way to earn more. Alan says he's living below his means, but he promises me the situation is not uncomfortable. The truth is that Alan is a Squirrel in denial about what would make his life better.

Alan is a resilient man who grew up in a home where money was always tight. His father died young in an accident, but his mother always was optimistic and never complained. Alan said he grew up feeling poor and like an outsider. Yet his mother's teachings made him resilient and hardworking. The fear of extreme poverty and losing everything sharpened his natural Squirrel inclinations. "My mother preached the importance of always having a job and never to get into a situation where I'd need help with money. And to get an education. Her advice grounded me."

When Alan was about fourteen, his grandmother moved in with them. If Alan was suddenly made aware of how money changes life when his father died, his awareness was sharpened with his grandmother in the house. "My mother took care of her, but I know there were times when she resented it. There were times when I resented it. There was a lot of bitterness in the house because we just didn't have a lot of money, and less room." Alan dreamed of being an architect, but by the age of seventeen, he'd convinced himself that such a profession would be too unstable and full of negative what-ifs—what if he didn't have clients, what if his clients couldn't pay. He didn't want a life that would in any way leave the door open for money struggles. "I decided I'd always have a job and a healthy bank account," he said.

As Alan's early family life made him a Squirrel, so would his wife's outlook on money reinforce his feelings. "She was always interested in keeping up appearances. I don't have to have the biggest and the best, but Barbara did," he explained. Barbara owned a mall boutique, but she wasn't a good businesswoman and couldn't manage money. They lost their home and all their savings—everything Alan worried about. "I lived my fears," he said. "Then we got divorced. I had nothing—I was down to zero. I slowly worked my way out of that with my pack rat tendencies. I started by having amounts automatically deducted from my paycheck and deposited into a credit union account. I didn't want to be tempted to spend those few dollars."

Some of Alan's Squirrel behavior can be traced to a thirty-five-year career in a government job, where there are no bonuses or other similar financial rewards. He's relied on several good promotions and the related salary increases to improve his standard of living. When I ask him what he'd like to change about his financial picture, he answers in a flash: "More money."

"I'm not feeling deprived. It's hard for me to envision a real crisis, unless I lost everything," Alan told me. "I could probably

---

ALAN'S FINANCIAL SNAPSHOT

At age sixty-two, Alan has retired and has the following assets:

- A $75,000 pension and Social Security.

- A 457 plan—essentially a 401(k) for municipal or government employees—which he enrolled in several years before retirement. He has since moved a portion of that into an IRA.

- A brokerage savings account at 2.35 percent, which is funded by direct withdrawals from his checking account.

- Since everything ultimately will go to his daughter and grandchildren, he set up a 529 college plan for his two grandchildren, unsure that his daughter would do it for them.

- A small amount of money in a mutual fund and in a CD. But he shies away from the stock market, considering it "too risky."

invest my money better, but I don't know where to begin. And there's that fear in me about doing it. I know I have cash in the bank, and that's comforting!" One reason Alan has cash in the bank is that he rarely spends money on himself. He doesn't take as many vacations as he'd like to, usually deciding to bank the money. Instead of going away, he travels across town, moves in with his daughter, and baby-sits for his grandchildren. Alan is stuck.

"I don't know what to do next," he said. "Any ideas?"

I have some thoughts for Alan, and for Squirrels out there who think as he does:

Increase Your Expectations—And Go for It!

Alan never had much growing up in a family that, unfortunately, thought of themselves as poor. It doesn't take much of a leap from thinking you're poor to *being* poor. If you think you are, you're right. At one point, Alan remembered that when he was a teenager, growing up in a two-bedroom apartment with his mother and his grandmother, he jokingly called his house "secondhand land." By the time he started working and he was more sophisticated, he called home "the land of limitation." How meaningful.

While his mother's good-humored protectiveness was the one positive aspect to his home, he also knew that his parents had no idea of how much they could have. They believed in limitation, as if to say, "More money and prosperity is not for us. It is for other people." Alan, though, followed his mother's advice and took a civil service job, instead of doing what he wanted to do—become an architect. As his mother had low expectations, so did Alan. His choice depressed him then, and it depresses him now.

Choices, though, are not fixed and predetermined. They can be changed by changing your point of view!

I have a number of ideas that should tantalize Squirrels to gain a little confidence in taking a slightly bigger risk to increase their nest eggs. First, though, we need to look at what's really going on in the hearts and minds of Squirrels in terms of their relationship to money.

MAKING CHANGES: THE EMOTIONAL PATH

My mission for every Squirrel is to help you understand that you deserve to enjoy your money now and that such pleasure will not lead you into disaster. What's stopping you is what is stopping both Tina and Alan—emotional baggage. I know some Squirrels regard saving and amassing money as a virtue. And it is. But it's not virtuous to cheat yourself out of a better life by holding on to ideas about money that keep you fearful or limited. While it takes a little work for you to sort through your feelings about money—which, hopefully, you began by answering the questions in Chapter 2—I'm confident that you can conquer your demons and start making small changes to increase your net worth. Think about what might have influenced the negative aspects of your Squirrel money habits. These are issues you need to defuse.

As psychologists always say: It's not the event that matters, but how you respond to it. Some people collapse in despair and depression over loss. Some Squirrels have been known to commit suicide when they lose their money; others say, "If I made it once, I can make it again," and go on. To make a change, even a tiny one, you need to respond to money differently. Tina and Alan lived through their own versions of catastrophe and loss, and they each wound up with a different emotional wound. Tina is haunted by her past and walks with the ghosts, while Alan lives in a state of limbo. Here's what happened to them. You may see yourself in their situations.

Face Your Demons and Walk Away the Victor!

What's true for Tina is true for all of us. We're products of our history, and there's no denying that traumatic events will shape our behavior. In a very real way, Tina learned to cope with her family's financial loss and was able to move on. She has a positivity to her that is primed for change. The same is true for you.

As I see it, anyone who still feels so hurt by a past event concerning money has some work to do to relieve that pain for good. There are really two tasks to work out: to understand and forgive yourself and your parents for the life you might feel was taken away from you and them. Secondly, psychologists tell me, you may be feeling guilty about being in a safer financial position than your parents were when they were the age you are now. Because of that guilt, you may be unable to give yourself the pleasure of enjoying your hard work and take the next step to smarter handling of money.

Try this shift in thinking:

If you identify with Tina's story, it is time to relinquish painful past experiences over which you had no control and never will. Believe that what you have now is the best of yourself, and you do have control over that. You control your choices *now*. What could give you greater confidence? You owe it to yourself and to the people who care about you to drop the burdens of the past. They're too costly and return nothing.

When people suffer huge changes in circumstances as children, like Tina or even like the IRS agent whose story opens this chapter, the repercussions can be intense and, even more damaging, long-lasting. If financial upheaval shaped part of your childhood, you probably remember the feelings you had or behaviors you acted out when disaster struck—behaviors of which you are now ashamed. You may still experience panic about money, not unlike the way you felt when your world began coming apart those many years ago.

If you are someone who has had a financial disaster in your past, it is wise to sit down and record how you feel about money. For Squirrels who are still hurting from a past experience, ask yourself these questions:

- Is your feeling about money connected in any way to a feeling of grief or fear? Is there a particular incident that made these feelings so vivid for you that you made them a way of life?
- What did your parents tell you that you could have? More than you wanted or less than you wanted?
- Do you have more money now than your parents did at your age?
- Do you feel guilty about being financially comfortable? Did your parents make you feel guilty about asking for anything that cost money?
- Did you make a decision about your own financial life during the first year of a traumatic event? What was it? Did you stick to it?
- Has your life suffered needlessly in any way because you will not spend money you can afford?

A shift in thinking will finally resolve the conflicts in your early life, the emotional battles that must be resolved. It will finally get rid of an enormous, long-standing burden—believing that life and money are limited. Secondly, you can see exactly how your relationship with your parents affected your ability to handle money. Conflicts in such relationships can cast a long shadow over how you deal with money. In a Squirrel's case, the conflict will push you aggressively toward clinging to what you have.

Taking inspiration from Alan's story, the next emotional task for you will be a bit different. Here, you may feel that history must repeat itself and that a parent's financial limitations will inevitably show up as your own. If that's so, consider this:

Think Bigger, and Believe That It Means You!

Do you think big (or bigger) about money or do you think small? Most Squirrels dream big, but live too small. This rut in the Squirrel's Emotional Path runs deep and bumpy. Time to smooth the road and move on! Here's what I mean: Many Squirrels who are raised in homes where counting pennies was once a factor for survival, literally see money only in terms of pennies later on. This is thinking small, and because of it, your real emotional task is to come to terms with the negative messages you were taught that have nothing to do with reality now.

Alan, for example, got a depressing message from his mother about making do that he took with him through his own adult life. This idea of simply getting by as a good thing limits creativity, personal growth, and experiences. Did you hear similar messages that said, "All you can expect from life is as little as possible"? Or, "Be grateful for pennies and crumbs"? If your parents seemed downtrodden, you may not see how your life can be any different—even when you earn a lot of money or, as in Alan's case, marry a woman he thought would help him live vicariously. Barbara had the guts to go out on her own and live her dream—and hopefully, make it pay off. When a spouse or partner turns out to be an emotional and financial nemesis, though, Squirrels think that's proof that life tosses them only bad news or the tiniest bits.

Many Squirrels still live in a state of mild deprivation, in their own self-made "land of limitation." While part of it can be credited to your Squirrel tendencies, another part is that you don't give yourself what you need—whether it is an outlet to exercise any squelched creativity, indulging yourself once in a while and not feeling pain about the cost, or learning more about how to put your money to work for you. What's missing in Alan's life is hope, dreams, and joy. Is this true for you, too? You may have grown up feeling crowded, deprived, and downtrodden, but now you're able to begin breaking through to a "land of bounty" and make changes.

Try this shift in thinking:

To move out of the land of limitation and into a land where there is abundance—your fair share of it—you need to believe that such a possible state of money affairs exists. For evidence, look around. Squirrels are realists, right? What do you see?

Lots of people have lots of money gained by lots of opportunities. What are you saying to yourself about where the money is? Rather than feel as if others have and you do not, shift your perspective from feeling limited or deprived to a goal. Decide what you want to have, and plot your course to get it. There is one of those cosmic homilies that says, You attract and bring into your life what you think about. Think pennies and limitation, and it is yours. Expand your possibilities wisely, and you have dollars. Imagine yourself having what you want.

Alan's goal, he told me, for example, is to have "more money." This is the beginning of naming a goal that is not out of reach for him or for *you*. To attain it, you need to envision your plans for making that money (which I can help you with in the Financial Path, coming up), know what you'd do with more money, other than save it or leave it to your family or a charity. By raising expectations of yourself and what you can have, you can finally break through feeling downtrodden or depressed, and break out of that tight little box.

Can the Bag Lady, the most extreme version of the Squirrels, change? You'll see how a shift in thinking about putting money into perspective can make the difference. Darlene is such an example:

Conquering the Bag Lady Syndrome

"I decided to give myself a present for my thirty-ninth birthday," Darlene, a Miami human resources director, wrote me recently. "I decided to stop being a Scrooge and be good to myself. I took some of the money my father left me and put it toward a two-bedroom condo. Talk about miracles! I've been living in a cramped studio apartment since I left my husband and got a divorce. A week ago, I woke up thinking that I can't get to forty still panicking every time I have to spend more than $100. Since I've been working, and even in my marriage, I'd be frantic anytime a big expense came up, whether it was buying a new couch or paying taxes. I'd see the money go and panic that spending x amount of dollars would mean I'd end up broke. I'm still a little worried about paying the mortgage, but I'll deal with it."

Darlene calls herself a Scrooge, suggesting she suffers when she has to see money go, even to pay bills. Darlene is living out her version of the Bag Lady syndrome, clinging to an irrational belief that with one wrong financial move, she'll be destitute.

Women's fear of destitution, some experts think, has to do with financial reality of the times compounded by, as author Colette Dowling says in *Maxing Out: Why Women Sabotage Their Financial Security*, "the head-on collision of traditional cultural norms and the relatively new expectation that women be self sufficient." While women were raised to be dependent on men, they are also expected to be capable money-earners. (The huge issues of women's salaries, how women may outlive their savings, and the financial consequences of fractured marriages are beyond my scope here. But I wanted to bring them to your attention, so you can read up on them and, hopefully, find solutions for yourself, if that's what you need to live better.)

I asked Darlene if her fears about money ever bring on fantasies of seeing herself on the street, all alone. She said, "Of course! I've even called friends at really anxious moments, like when I left my husband and knew I'd never get a penny of alimony. I was between jobs, going for my degree, and feeling vulnerable. What if, I said to myself. What if I can't make it? I asked my friends if they'd let me stay over on their couch in case I wound up with nothing and no place of my own. That's how bad the threat of no money can make you feel. But," she added, "I have to say that I'm feeling more confident now. I have an inheritance and enough money in the bank to never be on the street, and I know how to keep the money safe. I have a job and a second income. I'm ready to grow up and leave some of those terrible fears behind me."

If this touches you, be aware that the Bag Lady syndrome isn't an uncommon worry among women. In fact, you may be, ironically, in the peak of your earning years. Even though you have money and are far from destitution, the downside of feeling like a Bag Lady is that unjustified panic over possible money loss makes you extremely conservative. By seeing imminent disaster, you take very few risks with money.

Except for buying a condo, which is a good investment, Darlene put her money into low-risk, low-interest vehicles. I recommended that she apportion some of her inheritance and invest it more wisely—and to find an expert financial advisor to manage it. "I found someone who's made a lot of money for a friend and gave him a chunk of money," she told me. "I'm still worried, but I'm not scared. And that's important for someone like me."

How the Bag Lady Fears Start in Childhood

I was interested in what Darlene kept hinting at: that there was a turning point in her childhood that somehow would forever after mark her as a Squirrel with Bag Lady tendencies. According to Anne Scheiber's reports of her childhood—the Bag Lady multimillionaire whose story opened the chapter—hard times were even harder for girls. When her father died, her mother said all the money would go toward educating her four brothers. She and her four sisters were on their own, which for Scheiber was from the age of fifteen.

Darlene's story was different but as emotionally life-changing. She said candidly, "Thinking rationally, I know that in all probability I'll never be destitute, but emotionally, I'm still healing from a difficult childhood." There was the trauma she calls "the biggie." When Darlene was ten years old, her unhappy mother wanted a divorce, but she was intimidated into staying in the marriage. Her father swore he would leave all his money to an animal shelter—and he threatened he'd make sure Darlene and her mother wound up on the street, with nothing. While he was a fairly successful businessman, Darlene's father was tyrannical and emotionally unstable, and he ruled the roost by using money to express love, rage, caring, or his own fears. Over the next few years, Darlene's father made the same threat more than a few times, "hence," she said, "my bag lady fear."

Ironically, Darlene married an Ostrich type—a man who eventually refused to make any efforts at earning a salary or to figure out why he was so cavalier about supporting his family. After a few years, Darlene left him, finding his attitude about money intolerable. While working at her job in human resources, she went back to school and got a degree in industrial psychology. She now works for a corporation and supplements her income by counseling a few clients privately. Ultimately, her Squirrel/Bag Lady tendencies put her in control of her money. Being able to defuse the stultifying power of those early threats to her survival brought her to a much more prosperous and stable present.

Darlene still works on resolving her view of the past. She knows her father wouldn't have hurt her as horribly as he threatened, but the damage was done. She was nearing forty when she could finally disconnect from that feeling of being a helpless, dependent child at the mercy of a threat. Buying her condo wasn't easy for her, but it was liberating. "I believe you have to protect yourself against someone ever again controlling the money so it will be left to their version of an animal shelter."

The same is true for any of you who grew up in troubled households where money was used as a weapon. Darlene says, "I know there's no reason to hold on to that gut feeling that disaster is around the corner. I can look at what my life is like now. I have a job. I can build up my second career. But I had to learn to say, 'Get ahold of yourself! You're not ten years old, you're thirty-nine and okay after all.'"

Darlene was finally able to break through some of her Squirrel behavior and begin to develop a healthier relationship to money.

The main issue for Squirrels is to get your money out of your stash and get it growing! It takes some self-motivation, but any Squirrel can do it. I've seen it happen for Squirrels thousands of times. Here's where it can begin for you:

MAKING CHANGES: THE FINANCIAL PATH

Let me start with a statistic: The last time I checked, Americans had over $6 trillion in savings accounts, checking accounts, CDs, and money market funds. But, and this is an important but, these many trillions were all in safe money places and earning *maybe 2 percent* interest. So, while your Squirrel logic may argue, "Yes, but it's secure," the reality is that it is $6 trillion that's guaranteed never to grow very much. As someone in the financial world who's interested in how to make money grow, I hope to inspire you to see the potential in smarter and, yes, safer investments that will give you the edge you seek. Now is your chance to make a real difference in what you see on your balance sheet: more money that you have invested wisely.

Remember: You're good at managing money. See how you can manage more by following these guidelines:

Embrace Diversification

It's time to pull some of your money out of those low-interest accounts and diversify—and do it in a knowledgeable way. Squirrels have something in common with Ostriches, in that they hide and don't want to learn about the next tier of investing because they're afraid of what will happen. You can overcome that fear through knowledge. Check specialty investment Web sites and compare information. Go to seminars or talks by financial advisors—many of them are free or low-cost—and ask questions.

Be Willing to Try a New Way of Thinking That Lets You Make Adjustments to How You Save, Invest, and Manage Money

To get more control over your life, be aware of what you say to yourself about yourself in terms of money. This begins with what you think about your relationship with money. Do you hear yourself say, "I'll never have anything," or, "I give up—I'll never make as much money as . . ." or, "Poor people can't think about investing"?

If you believe that saving to the point of hoarding is everything, take another look at whether such saving really provides satisfaction for you and yours. Ultimately, you become more successful when you maximize your abilities to handle money and keep your fears about not having money in check.

Besides a fear of losing all your money, not taking risks is another of your weaknesses. My goal is to help you earn bigger profits on your money, and to do that, you must take more of a risk. You can do it. Here's how: First learn what your risk tolerance can do for you.

Assess Your Tolerance for Risk

Unfortunately, for many Squirrels the word *risk* is just like the word *budget* for a Debt Desperado: It sounds nearly impossible to achieve. "Why would I want to risk my hard-earned money?" you say. "I'm very conservative."

The answer is simple: If you take no risks with your assets, you will be unlikely to earn a return high enough to achieve your financial goals. To paraphrase the familiar saying about physical exercise—"No pain, no gain"—when you get into the money world, the saying goes, "No risk, no return."

Now, I'm not suggesting that you take enormous risk with all of your money. Not every risky investment will earn a high return. If it did, it wouldn't be risky. But by diversifying your assets carefully among high-risk, medium-risk, and low-risk investments, you are assured of ending up with a larger pool of assets over time than if you keep all of your money in low-risk, low-return choices.

Let's talk about risk so that you want to know it, or at least be on friendlier terms. It's tricky enough to predict what's going to happen over the next few months, but it is even more difficult to know what the long-term future holds. Therefore, under normal circumstances, the longer you commit yourself to an investment, the more risk you are taking. But because you are taking more risk, you should be compensated in the long run with a higher return. As you determine your tolerance for risk, you should understand several types of risk. Here are the most important risks you will face:

Playing it too safe risk: As mentioned earlier, if you keep all your money in super-safe CDs, money market funds, and Treasury bills, you run the risk of outliving your assets because your return will not keep you current with inflation. This risk is not frequently recognized, but it is probably the biggest one people take—running in place. By the time you have figured out that you have been too conservative with your investments, it is often too late to build up enough capital to live on.

Lack of diversification risk: This is commonly known as the risk of keeping all your eggs in one basket—a habit many Squirrels cannot break easily. If all your assets are in one kind of investment, like stocks or bonds, you are not protected if that asset falls sharply in value. Even more dangerous is to keep most of your money in just one stock, bond, or CD because if something happens to it, you have no alternate assets to fall back on. Many people's biggest financial mistake is to have too much of their net worth tied up in their company's stock. Even if it is a wonderful company that has a bright future, these people lack diversification. I've gotten many letters from people who feel that if they don't keep buying shares of their company's stock, it is tantamount to betrayal of their employer. You have to protect yourself first!

The way to lower risk in this area is to spread your holdings among different kinds of assets as well as among several individual investments within each kind of asset. One easy way to diversify is to buy a mutual fund, which itself holds dozens of stocks or bonds. Since Squirrels always ask me which investments are safest, I want to show you, literally, how savings and investing vehicles stack up with the Investment Risk Pyramid.

Climbing the Investment Pyramid

Ideally, when striving to achieve your financial goals, you want to select where you put your money wisely so you can profit *and* sleep at night—that is, you want to diversify where you put your money. Squirrels tend to veer toward low-risk and some moderate-risk sectors and avoid high-risk investments. Since I want to encourage you to expand your interests just enough and not have you worry, take a look at the Investment Risk Pyramid, which stacks your options from low to high risk.

Here's how it breaks down: At the top of the pyramid are the riskiest assets, which offer the greatest potential for high returns as well as big losses. The *high-risk* apex includes collectibles; foreign investments; futures contracts; junk bonds; new stock issues; oil and gas limited partnerships; options; raw land; small growth stocks; tax shelters; speculative real estate construction; venture capital; and warrants.

The next tier of the pyramid, the *moderate-risk* sector, includes stock and bond mutual funds, income-oriented limited partnerships, mortgage-backed securities, large growth stocks, corporate and municipal bonds, and rental real estate.

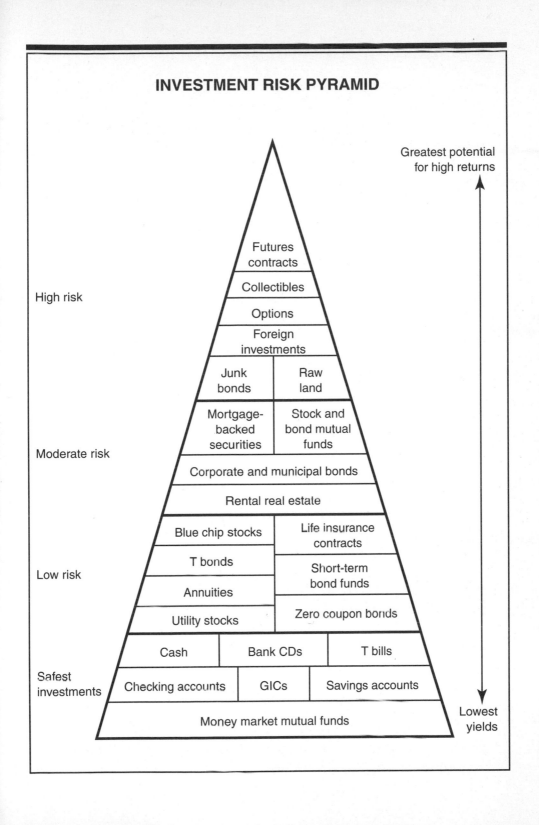

INVESTMENT RISK PYRAMID

Greatest potential for high returns

High risk
- Futures contracts
- Collectibles
- Options
- Foreign investments
- Junk bonds | Raw land

Moderate risk
- Mortgage-backed securities | Stock and bond mutual funds
- Corporate and municipal bonds
- Rental real estate

Low risk
- Blue chip stocks | Life insurance contracts
- T bonds | Short-term bond funds
- Annuities
- Utility stocks | Zero coupon bonds

Safest investments
- Cash | Bank CDs | T bills
- Checking accounts | GICs | Savings accounts
- Money market mutual funds

Lowest yields

The third tier, the *low-risk* sector, consists of annuities, blue chip stocks, Treasury bonds, life insurance contracts, municipal bonds with the highest credit ratings, short-term bond funds, utility stocks, and zero coupon bonds.

The *base* of the pyramid, the safest investments, contains investments with which there is almost no chance of losing your principal. Included here are bank CDs, checking accounts, cash, money market mutual funds, and guaranteed investment contracts (GICs) found in salary reduction plans (401(k)s and 403(b)s), savings accounts, and Treasury bills. Here's where Squirrels tend to get stuck—this safety zone allows for minimal growth that doesn't keep up with inflation rates.

What's your next move? Look at your assets. Figure out what small percentage you can put into higher-risk vehicles. Doesn't it make sense to let your hard-earned money earn even more? You can see exactly where your potential moneymaking investments can come from. Of course, this means taking a risk. I know that as a typical Squirrel, you're thinking, "I'm still not sure!" Before you make any decisions, understand how you really think about risk. Change requiring greater expenditure is a bit tough for Squirrels, but you can do it—even in small increments of $25. You may be overestimating how risk-averse you are and have untapped sources of daring. You now have a chance to find out how much.

Take the Risk Tolerance Quiz to See Exactly How You Feel About Risks

By now, you know that to make your chestnut grow, you have to step out of your comfort zone with money. I've put together a quiz that will give you insight into how much risk you feel you're able to take. Answer each of the questions, giving yourself one point for answer 1, two points for answer 2, three points for answer 3, and four points for answer 4. Then add up the points.

Figuring Out Your Risk Tolerance: A Quiz

A. If someone made me an offer to invest 15 percent of my net worth in a deal he said had an 80 percent chance of being profitable, the level of profit would have to be:

1. No level of profit would be worth that kind of risk.
2. Seven times the amount I invested.
3. Three times the amount I invested.
4. At least as much as I have invested in the first place.

POINTS: _____

B. How comfortable would I be assuming a $10,000 debt in the hope of achieving a $20,000 gain over the next few months?

1. Totally uncomfortable—I would never do it.
2. Somewhat uncomfortable—I would probably never do it.
3. Somewhat comfortable—I might do it.
4. Very comfortable—I would jump at the chance to do it.

POINTS: _____

C. I am holding a lottery ticket that has gotten me to the finals, where I have a one-in-four chance of winning a $100,000 prize. The least I would be willing to sell my ticket for before the drawing is:

1. $15,000
2. $20,000
3. $35,000
4. $60,000

POINTS: _____

D. I have spent more than $150 on one or more of these activities: professional sports gambling, recreational bettor on poker or basketball games I participate in, casino gambling:

1. I have never participated in any of these activities.
2. I have participated in these activities only a few times in my life.
3. I have participated in one of these activities in the past year.
4. I have participated in two or more of these activities in the past year.

POINTS: _____

E. Whenever I have to decide where to invest a large amount of money, I:

1. Delay the decision.
2. Get somebody else (like my broker) to decide for me.
3. Share the decision with advisors.
4. Decide on my own.

POINTS: _____

F. If a stock I bought doubled in the year after I bought it, I would:

1. Sell all of my shares.
2. Sell half of my shares.
3. Not sell any shares.
4. Buy more shares.

POINTS: _____

G. Which of the following describes how I make my investment decisions?

1. Never on my own.
2. Sometimes on my own.
3. Often on my own.
4. Always on my own.

POINTS: _____

H. My luck in investing is:

1. Terrible.
2. Average.
3. Better than average.
4. Fantastic.

POINTS: _____

I. My investments are successful mainly because:

1. God is always on my side.
2. I was in the right place at the right time.
3. When opportunities arose, I took advantage of them.
4. I carefully planned them to work out that way.

POINTS: _____

J. I have a high-yielding certificate of deposit that is about to mature, and interest rates have dropped so much that I feel compelled to invest in something with a higher yield. The most likely place I will invest the money is:

1. U.S. Savings Bond.
2. A short-term bond.
3. A long-term bond.
4. A stock fund.

POINTS: _____

TOTAL SCORE:

How to score yourself:

10–16 points:	You are a conservative investor who feels uncomfortable taking any risk.
17–29 points:	You are a moderate investor who feels comfortable taking moderate risks.
30–40 points:	You are an aggressive investor who is willing to take high risks in search of high returns.

If you are a hard-core money conservative, you should resist the temptation to put much in riskier investments even though they may sound promising. Keep the Investment Risk Pyramid in mind, though. You still don't want to have all your assets in only the safest bets.

If you are a moderate-risk investor, put more of your money in the middle and top sectors of the Investment Risk Pyramid as long as you carefully gauge the level of the risk you're taking.

For high-risk investors, which would be only a few Squirrels, allocate more of your money to the apex of the pyramid, but don't neglect the pyramid base. You should be careful not to become so enthusiastic about an investing idea that you put too much of your capital at risk in something that goes bust.

Wherever you are on the risk spectrum, keep in mind that dealing with your personal finances in general, and investing in particular, is not only about maximizing the amount of dollars in your pocket. Finding your financial comfort is also important so that you feel psychologically secure about the decisions you're making. It's no use becoming rich if you die from the stress of attaining your money—or never enjoy what money can bring you. Hopefully, you can ease up on the most extreme of your Squirrel habits of saving or even hoarding, and give yourself the pleasure of your much deserved little indulgences.

Landing on Your Feet—Investing in Real Estate

Many Squirrels are attracted to owning real estate. They like seeing what they own in a very real physical sense. A building has a presence, it stands on land, and it can be rented or sold. There are aspects of the real estate business that are risky, and these are not for you. However, let me direct you to what you may well want to invest in and feel safer about: a way for you Squirrels to increase your chestnut securely!

Real Options for You:

You may want to investigate worthwhile investments called REITs, especially if you're in any way interested in real estate. REIT is an acronym for real estate investment trusts, and they come in three primary types: equity, mortgage, and hybrid. REITs are publicly traded stocks that invest in office buildings, apartment complexes, industrial facilities, shopping centers, and other commercial spaces. Under current law, they do not pay taxes at the corporate level as long as they distribute at least 90 percent of their earnings to shareholders in the form of dividends each year. Shareholders then pay taxes on the dividends as regular income. In some cases, a portion of the dividends may be considered a return of capital for tax purposes and therefore is not taxed.

Here's what you should know about the three types:

Equity REITs: These trusts buy properties, fix them up, collect rents, and sometimes sell the properties at a profit. Equity REIT share prices reflect the general direction of real estate values. These REITs can provide some protection against inflation because they usually include rent escalator clauses in their contracts with tenants so that price increases can be passed along in the form of higher rents.

Some equity REITs buy different kinds of properties across the country. Others specialize in a particular type of real estate. For example, several REITs, including Healthcare Realty Trust and Health Care Property Investors, focus on health care facilities, while others, like Apartment Investment and Management Company, concentrate on apartment buildings. (See Resources at the end of this chapter for their vital information.) Others buy properties in only one region of the country; for example, Washington REIT buys properties in the Washington, D.C., market, while Weingarten Realty Investors specializes in shopping centers. (See Resources for details.)

Mortgage REITs: This type of REIT originates or buys mortgages on commercial properties. Buying these has an upside and a downside: Mortgage REITs offer yields of about 6 to 10 percent—much more than the 4 to 7 percent paid by equity REITs. But mortgage REITs offer little capital appreciation potential. If mortgages get into trouble or default, share prices can plunge. Some examples of prominent mortgage REITS include Annaly Mortgage Management and Thornburg Mortgage.

Hybrid REITs: As you might guess, these REITs combine equity and mortgage holdings. Hybrid trusts pay yields of 6 to 9 percent and offer some appreciation potential.

Okay. I know as a Squirrel you're thinking, "What does this all mean in terms of dollars?" and, "Why shouldn't I continue to keep my money in a savings account?" Let the numbers do the talking in this very simple example:

If you have $10,000 in a savings account earning 1 percent or even a half of 1 percent, in a year you have $100 or $50 in interest. Take the same $10,000 and put it in a real estate investment trust earning 7 percent, and you've brought in $700. After taxes, that $50 would become $35 or so, while your $700 would leave you $450 or so. Which would you rather have? And the value of a REIT can grow and produce more income as the company raises its dividends, especially if you invest in one of good quality. With a savings account, there's minimal possibility of growth.

A REIT payout is taxed like regular income at your income tax bracket, but if you own a high-dividend-paying non-REIT, like a utility or bank stock yielding 5 percent, and the dividend is taxed at 15 percent today, you get to keep more of the income than you would from a low-yielding savings or money market account. Stocks today give you the tax advantage of investing in higher-yielding vehicles—you get to keep 85 percent of dividends as opposed to 50 percent of savings account interest. You're better off, both in terms of paying lower taxes and having growth potential, investing in conservative income-oriented stocks.

Overcoming Your Fear of Getting Good Advice

Squirrels can benefit from working with good financial advisors. I know your quirk about not seeking advice because you're not sure whom to trust. Why do you need an advisor? This is the best reason: If you have a lot of money in CDs and it's earning 2 percent or less, hire a well-trained, objective financial advisor to get you out of your hole of dread. It's well worth it. You will blossom when you find a trusted advisor who can motivate you to invest and help you overcome your fears with sensible strategies and basic knowledge.

Why Do I Need a Planner?

You need a planner to clarify your goals of making some of your money grow. Think about the many aspects of your financial picture, past, present, and especially future. Now you want to enhance that vague goal of "making your money grow." You need an overall strategy that ties together the various financial threads in your life—this is where a planner's services may be invaluable. If you have a long-term goal, such as building a retirement nest egg or saving enough to buy a business, a planner can get you on the right path. But even if you don't have a major goal, a well-designed plan that helps you save and invest more wisely can improve your financial future.

Who Is This Planner and What Should I Know About Him or Her?

For a Squirrel, the ideal financial planner would know everything about budgeting, investments, taxes, insurance, credit, real estate, employee benefits, estate planning, retirement, college financing, and every aspect of your specific financial interests. You want this planner to help you figure out where you are now and how best to attain your goals. Finally, you want to be sure that the planner is advising you objectively and not recommending an investment just because he or she earns a commission from it.

Such planners do exist, but you have to do a little homework. Anyone can call him- or herself a planner, since there are no federal, state, or local laws that establish legitimate qualifications. However, there are several associations and organizations that grant credentials signifying a planner's level of education. (See Resources at the end of this chapter for the groups to call to check this.) Once you've gotten a list of names and established your planner's expertise, set up a face-to-face interview. You want to meet the person who will be advising you about your money to get a good sense of his or her personality and approach to planning. The checklist for choosing a financial planner, which follows on page 310, helps you gather and evaluate information about the planners you interview.

How Do Planners Charge?

Squirrels always ask me: "How do I talk to a planner?" or, "How much will I have to pay for these services?" Let me start with what I know might make you resist seeing a planner: the cost. In theory, planners have an ethical obligation to hold your financial interests above their own, but the incentive structure—their selling you products, such as an insurance policy or a mutual fund where they make a commission on the sale—can make that approach more difficult to adhere to. I want to encourage you to get financial advice to grow your money, so you'd do best to check out the planners who charge on a fee-only basis.

This is easy for you: Some professional planners assess your situation for a fee, set in advance based on time spent with you, a flat dollar amount, or a percentage of the assets they manage. Usually, such planners offer a no-cost, no-obligation initial consultation to explore your financial needs. They provide advice on how to implement their recommendations, but they don't collect a nickel in commissions if you take their suggestion. The advantage of this arrangement, of course, is that the planner has no vested interest in having you buy one product over another because they don't stand to gain from any specific recommendation.

These planners tend to suggest no-load mutual funds or low-load life insurance policies that you probably would never hear about from a commission-oriented planner. The largest association of fee-only planners is the National Association of Personal Financial Advisors (NAPFA), which will supply a list of fee-only planners near you. (See Appendix for details.)

Okay, now that you know you can feel more secure with a fee-only planner, what do you need to know about the person and how he or she transacts business? These ten questions will get you off to a good start:

1. *What services do you provide?* Most planners will help you assemble a comprehensive plan, while others specialize in particular areas of finance. The services you should expect include cash management and budgeting; education funding; estate planning; investment review and planning; life, health, and property/casualty insurance review; retirement planning; goal and objective setting; and tax planning. Ask about each service specifically.

2. *Can you show me a sample financial plan that you've done for someone who is generally in my income bracket?* Your planner should be pleased to show you a plan you can expect to be presented with after the information-gathering and planning process is complete. The planner can easily block out any names on a sample plan to not reveal confidential information.

3. *Who will I deal with on a day-to-day basis?* In larger planning firms, you might see the chief planner only at the beginning and end of the planning process and work with his or her associates along the way. If that's how they operate, ask to meet

the staff who will work on your account, and be sure to ask about their qualifications.

4. *Do you work with other professionals if my planning process takes us into areas in which you're not an expert?* A good planner should have access to a network of top accountants, lawyers, insurance specialists, and investment pros to fall back on. And a good planner doesn't hesitate to call on other experts to answer a question if necessary.

5. *Will your advice include specific product recommendations, or will you suggest only generic product categories?* Most planners will name a particular stock or mutual fund, for example. Others will advise that you keep 50 percent of your assets in stocks, 30 percent in bonds, and 20 percent in cash, leaving you to determine which stocks, bonds, and cash instruments are appropriate.

6. *Will you spend time to explain your reason for recommending a specific product and how it suits my goals, my risk tolerance, and my circumstances? And how, for example, do you plan to monitor a recommended mutual fund or insurance product once I've bought it?* It's really important for you to feel comfortable knowing that the planner makes an effort to ensure you understand the strategy and products recommended to you, and that they will continue to monitor the performance of those products.

7. *After you've delivered my plan, how will you follow up to ensure that it's implemented?* A good planner makes sure that you don't just file away the comprehensive plan you've set up and never put it into action! Not only should the plan be implemented, but it should also be reviewed and revised as conditions in your life, tax laws, or the investment environment shift.

8. *Will you have direct access to my money?* Some planners want *discretionary control* of their clients' funds, which allows planners to invest as they see fit. Be extremely careful about agreeing to this arrangement, which is fraught with potential for fraud and malfeasance. If you do agree to it, make sure that

the planner is bonded. This insurance will cover you in case he or she dips in inappropriately.

9. *What professional licenses and designations have you earned? Are you a registered investment advisor with the securities regulator in my state?* Planners should hold a certificate or degree that makes them a CFA, CFP, ChFC, CPA, or a PFS. Determine whether the planner is licensed to sell securities, which include stocks, bonds, partnerships, and mutual funds. If the planner wants to sell disability, life, and property/casualty insurance, as well as fixed or variable annuities, he or she needs a license to sell insurance products. Also find out the planner's educational background. If he or she started out as a lawyer, insurance agent, or some other specialist, it will most likely affect the advice you'll receive.

Also, all planners who provide investment advice should be registered with either the SEC or your state. If registered with the SEC, the planner is required to show you Part Two of his or her Form ADV or a brochure containing the same information. Disclosure requirements for state-registered advisors vary, so check with your state's securities department to find out what's required in your state. The North American Securities Administrators Association (NASAA) will provide you will more information. (Details on contacting them in the Appendix.)

And, finally,

10. *Have you ever been cited by a professional or governmental organization for disciplinary reasons?* Even if the planner says that he or she has never been in trouble, you can check with the state attorney general's office, the state securities office, and the state societies of financial planning organizations. (See Appendix for information on these offices.)

These questions cover the most important bases but you should also take a look at the Checklist for Choosing a Financial Planner that I've included on the following pages:

Checklist for Choosing a Financial Planner

Tough Questions to Ask

What is your educational background?
- ☐ College degree
  Area of study: _____
- ☐ Graduate degree
  Area of study: _____

What are your financial planning credentials/designations and affiliations?

- ☐ NAPFA-Registered Financial Advisor
  (60 hours continuing education every 2 years)
- ☐ Certified Financial Planner (CFP)
  (30 hours continuing education every 2 years)
- ☐ Chartered Financial Consultant (ChFC)
  (30 hours continuing education every 2 years)
- ☐ Certified Public Accountant/Personal Financial Specialist
  (CPA/PFS)
  (60 points every 3 years)
- ☐ Financial Planning Association (FPA)
  (continuing education not required)
- ☐ Other: _____
  _____

How long have you been offering financial planning services?
- ☐ Less than 2 years
- ☐ 2–5 years
- ☐ 6–10 years
- ☐ More than 10 years

Do you have clients who might be willing to speak with me about your services?
- ☐ Yes   ☐ No
- ☐ If no, explain: _____

Will you provide me with references from other professionals?
☐ Yes   ☐ No
☐ If no, explain: _____

Have you ever been cited by a professional or regulatory govern-
ing body for disciplinary reasons?
☐ Yes   ☐ No
☐ If yes, explain: _____

Describe your financial planning work experience or attach your
résumé.

_____

_____

_____

_____

_____

_____

BUSINESS PRACTICE
How many clients do you work with?

_____

Are you currently engaged in any other business, either as a sole pro-
prietor, partner, officer, employee, trustee, agent, or otherwise? (Ex-
clude non-investment-related activities that are exclusively charitable,
civic, religious, or fraternal and arc recognized as tax-exempt.)
☐ Yes   ☐ No
☐ If yes, explain: _____

Will you or an associate of yours work with me?
☐ I will
☐ An associate will
☐ We have a team approach

If an associate will be my primary contact, complete the questions in
the Background and Experience section for each associate as well.

Will you sign the Fiduciary Oath below?
☐ Yes   ☐ No

FIDUCIARY OATH

The advisor shall exercise his/her best efforts to act in good faith and in the best interests of the client. The advisor shall provide written disclosure to the client prior to the engagement of the advisor, and thereafter throughout the term of the engagement, of any conflicts of interest which will or reasonably may compromise the impartiality or independence of the advisor.

The advisor, or any party in which the advisor has a financial interest, does not receive any compensation or other remuneration that is contingent on any client's purchase or sale of a financial product. The advisor does not receive a fee or other compensation from another party based on the referral of a client or the client's business.

Do you have a business continuity plan?
   ☐ Yes   ☐ No
   ☐ If no, explain: _____

COMPENSATION

Financial planning costs include what a client pays in fees and commissions. Comparison between advisors requires full information about potential total costs. It is important to have this information before entering into any agreement.

How is your firm compensated and how is your compensation calculated?
   Fee-only (as calculated below)
   Hourly rate of $ _____ / hour
   Flat fee of $ _____
   Percentage _____% to _____% of _____
   Commissions only; from securities, insurance, and/or other products that clients buy from a firm with which you are associated.
   Fee and commissions (fee-based)
   Fee offset (charging a flat fee against which commissions are offset).
   If the commissions exceed the fee, is the balance credited to me?
      ☐ Yes   ☐ No

Do you have an agreement describing your compensation and services that will be provided in advance of the engagement?
      ☐ Yes   ☐ No

Do you have a minimum fee?
☐ Yes   ☐ No
☐ If so, explain: _____
_____
_____
_____

If you earn commissions, approximately what percentage of your firm's commission income comes from:

_____% Insurance products

_____% Annuities

_____% Mutual funds

_____% Limited partnerships

_____% Stocks and bonds

_____% Coins, tangibles, collectibles

_____% Other: _____

_____% Other: _____

100%

Does any member of your firm act as a general partner, participate in, or receive compensation from investments you may recommend to me?
☐ Yes   ☐ No

Do you receive referral fees from attorneys, accountants, insurance professionals, mortgage brokers, or others?
☐ Yes   ☐ No

Do you receive ongoing income from any of the mutual funds that you recommend in the form of 12(b)1 fees, trailing commissions, or other continuing payouts?
☐ Yes   ☐ No

Are there financial incentives for you to recommend certain financial products?
☐ Yes   ☐ No
☐ If so, explain: _____

SERVICES
Do you offer advice on (check all that apply):
- ☐ Goal setting
- ☐ Cash management and budgeting
- ☐ Tax planning
- ☐ Investment review and planning
- ☐ Estate planning
- ☐ Insurance needs in the area of life, disability, long-term care, health, and property/casualty
- ☐ Education funding
- ☐ Retirement planning
- ☐ Other: _____

Do you provide a comprehensive written analysis of my financial situation and recommendations?
    ☐ Yes   ☐ No

Does your financial planning service include recommendations for specific investments or investment products?
    ☐ Yes   ☐ No

Do you offer assistance with implementation of the plan?
    ☐ Yes   ☐ No

Do you offer continuous, ongoing advice regarding my financial affairs, including advice on non-investment-related financial issues?
    ☐ Yes   ☐ No

Do you take custody of, or have access to, my assets?
    ☐ Yes   ☐ No

If you were to provide me with ongoing investment advisory services, do you require discretionary trading authority over my investment accounts?
    ☐ Yes   ☐ No

REGULATORY COMPLIANCE
Federal and state laws require that, under most circumstances, individuals or firms holding themselves out to the public as providing investment advisory services are required to be registered with

either the U.S. Securities and Exchange Commission (SEC) or the regulatory agency of the state in which the individual/firm conducts business.

I (or my firm) is registered as an Investment Advisor:
  With the SEC
  With the state of _____

Please provide your Form ADV Part II or brochure being used in compliance with the Investment Advisors Act of 1940.
If not registered with either the SEC or any state, please indicate the allowable reason for nonregistration:

_____

_____

_____

Signature of planner: _____

Firm name: _____

Date: _____

*Reprinted by permission from the National Association of Personal Financial Advisors (NAPFA); www.napfa.org

Please Note:

A yes or no answer requiring explanation is not necessarily a cause for concern. We encourage you to give the advisor an opportunity to explain any response.

This form was created by the National Association of Personal Financial Advisors (NAPFA) to assist consumers in selecting a personal financial planner. It can be used as a checklist during an interview or sent to prospective planners as part of a preliminary screening. NAPFA recommends that individuals from at least two different firms be interviewed.

If a financial planner seems beyond your interest or scope, let me recommend another type of advisor that Squirrels can work with: investment management consultants.

Investment Management Consultants

This is a relatively new breed of investment advisor, who does not select stocks or bonds—he or she hires money managers to select and evaluate them, and evaluates the managers' performance based on the client's guidelines. When you find a sharp and honest consultant, he or she can provide you with high returns at relatively low risk by placing your assets with top money managers.

From a Squirrel's point of view, this might be a compatible match for your need for vigilance. Investment management consulting has become popular among clients, brokers, and money managers. The consultant constantly monitors many money managers possessing different investment styles and may recommend that you transfer assets from one manager to another if the manager's performance slips. The consultant, often associated with a brokerage firm, also performs all necessary record keeping and sends you statements quarterly.

A good investment management consultant will help you determine what kind of money manager best suits your needs. He or she will ask you to fill out a questionnaire listing your assets, liabilities, and investing experience. The consultant should then take you through an exercise that defines your risk tolerance and financial goals. (Turn to page 65, in the chapter on Strivers, and clarify your goals by filling out the form.) The consultant will then explain different money management styles and recommend several money managers who have superior records in each style. Some of the most common styles include blue chip growth, small-company growth, value, income, and international investments.

Good consultants favor money managers with strong long-term performance records so you will not have to shift your portfolio every few months or every year among the hottest managers. The consultants can also examine objectively money managers' performance claims.

Consultants work under a wrap-fee arrangement. If they charge a 3 percent annual fee, for instance, the consultant might get 1 percent of it and the money manager 2 percent. The money manager usually places his or her stock and bond trades through the consultant's brokerage firm, which generates commissions for the brokerage.

Now, from the money manager's point of view, dealing with consultants frees the manager to concentrate on choosing stocks and bonds, rather than marketing his investment services. If the money manager builds a good track record, consultants will beat a path to his door and flood the manager with new money. In addition, consultants must handle all client questions.

From the broker's point of view, he or she has no liability for recommending losing investments. The broker, if acting as a consultant, removes himself from the dangerous business of selling individual stocks, bonds, or mutual funds. If the money manager fails, the broker will advise you to fire him. In addition, the broker continues to earn annual consulting fees no matter which manager handles your money, as long as the broker keeps your account.

When choosing a consultant, watch for potential conflicts of interest. For example, if a money manager pays a finder's fee to a consultant, that arrangement must be disclosed in the manager's ADV form filed with the SEC. Also, determine how much of a consultant's clients' assets rest with the money manager. If he or she has placed too many customers with one manager, it may be difficult for the consultant to pull out if the manager's performance declines. Be sure to monitor the consultant, who in turn will be monitoring the money managers.

How to find a qualified investment management consultant? Your best bet is to locate one through major brokerage firms. To locate a Certified Investment Management Analyst, contact the Investment Management Consultants Association (see Appendix for details). They'll also provide you with a list of standards and rules.

FINALLY: POINTS TO REMEMBER FOR SQUIRRELS

You deserve to enjoy your money *now*. Let yourself understand that such pleasure will not lead you into disaster.

Don't let the past stop you from growing financially. Do your best to cope with any negative event or loss and finally move on.

Squirrels can benefit from the assistance of a good financial advisor. Learn what they can do for you and check them out thoroughly before signing up with one.

Increase your risk taking to allow your money to work harder for you.

Dealing with your personal finances in general, and investing in particular, is not only about maximizing the amount of dollars in your pocket. It's also about finding a certain financial comfort so you feel psychologically secure about the decisions you've made.

RESOURCES FOR SQUIRRELS

Books

Beating the Street: The Best-Selling Author of One Up on Wall Street *Shows You How to Pick Winning Stocks and Develop a Strategy for Mutual Funds,* by Peter Lynch (Simon & Schuster, 1230 Avenue of the Americas, New York, NY 10020; 212-698-7000; www.simonsays.com). This revised edition by the former manager of the Fidelity Magellan Fund provides notable investment advice.

Beyond the Grave: The Right Way and the Wrong Way of Leaving Money to Your Children (and Others), by Gerald M. Condon and Jeffrey L. Condon (HarperBusiness, 10 East 53rd Street, New York, NY 10022; 212-207-7583; www.harpercollins.com). This updated edition is an informative guide for estate planning.

The Complete Idiot's Guide to Buying Insurance and Annuities, by Brian H. Breuel (Alpha Books, 1633 Broadway, New York, NY 10019; 212-366-2000; http://us.penguingroup.com). A quick read, with some commonsense advice.

Missed Fortune 101: A Starter Kit to Becoming a Millionaire, by Douglas R. Andrew (Warner Business Books, 1271 Avenue of the Americas, New York, NY 10020; 800-759-0190; www.twbookmark.com). Presents a contrarian view on investing.

New Life Insurance Investment Advisor: Achieving Financial Security for You and Your Family Through Today's Insurance Products, by Ben Baldwin (McGraw-Hill, 1221 Avenue of the Americas, New York, NY 10020; 866-436-8502; www.mcgraw-hill.com). Helps you understand different types of insurance.

Organizations

American Council of Life Insurers (101 Constitution Avenue, NW, Washington, DC 20001; 202-624-2000; www.acli.com). A trade group of life insurance companies that lobbies on life insurance, long-term care insurance, disability income insurance, and retirement savings matters. The Web site has the following downloadable publications: *What You Should Know About Buying Life Insurance, Annuities: The Key to a Secure Retirement, Long-Term Care Insurance: Protection for Your Future, Disability Income Insurance: Protection for You and Your Family.*

Consumer Federation of America (1424 16th Street, NW, Suite 604, Washington, DC 20036; 202-387-6121; www.consumerfed.org). For a fee, this consumer-oriented group will help you evaluate life insurance policy proposals, decide whether to buy a cash value policy or term insurance, and determine if your existing cash value policy is worth keeping.

Insurance Information Institute (110 William Street, New York, NY 10038; 212-346-5500; www.iii.org). This group's Web site answers frequently asked questions about auto, home, and life insurance, as well as annuities, health insurance, and more. The life stages tool provides easy-to-use information on insurance and financial planning for different stages of your life. You can also request a free copy of various brochures, including the following: *Am I Covered?*, a guide to homeowners insurance, which also has information on flood insurance, earthquake insurance, and coverage for other natural disasters.

National Association of Insurance and Financial Advisors (2901 Telestar Court, Falls Church, VA 22042; 703-770-8100; www.naifa.org). This group educates the public about insurance and how to work with insurance agents and brokers and provides guidelines for making your decision about whom you should hire to advise you.

National Association of Investors Corporation (PO Box 220, Royal Oak, MI 48068; 877-275-6242; http://www.better-investing.org). If you don't want to choose stocks on your own, you have another option—starting an investment club or joining an existing one. Browse the Web site of NAIC, the trade group for investment clubs, for help getting started.

North American Securities Administrators Association (NASAA) (750 First Street, NE, Suite 1140, Washington, DC, 20002; 202-737-0900; www.nasaa.org). The umbrella group for state securities regulators. The Web site contains investor education, contact information for state regulators, and an investor-complaint center, among other things.

Real Estate Investment Trusts

Annaly Mortgage Management (1211 Avenue of the Americas, Suite 2902, New York, NY 10036; 212-696-0100; www. annaly.com). A real estate investment trust specializing in mortgage instruments, resulting in a high yield for shareholders.

Apartment Investment & Management Company (4582 S. Ulster Street Parkway, Suite 1100, Denver, CO 80237; 303-747-8101; www.aimco.com). A real estate investment trust that owns/operates multi-family properties in the United States.

Health Care Property Investors (3760 Kilroy Airport Way, Suite 300, Long Beach, CA, 90806; 562-733-5100; www.hcpi. com). An equity real estate investment trust that invests in health care facilities throughout the United States.

Healthcare Realty Trust (3310 West End Avenue, Suite 700, Nashville, TN 37203; 615-269-8175; www.healthcarerealty. com). A real estate investment trust that invests directly or through joint ventures in health care facilities.

Thornburg Mortgage (150 Washington Avenue, Suite 502, Santa Fe, NM 87501; 505-989-1900; www.thornburgmortgage.com). A real estate investment trust specializing in purchasing and originating adjustable-rate mortgage loans for single-family houses.

Washington Real Estate Investment Trust (6110 Executive Boulevard, Suite 800, Rockville, MD 20852; 301-984-9400; www.writ.com). A real estate trust that owns office buildings, shopping centers, apartment buildings, and industrial distribution centers in the Washington, D.C., metropolitan area.

Weingarten Realty Investors (2600 Citadel Plaza Drive, Houston, TX 77292; 713-866-6000; www.weingarten.com). A real estate trust that acquires and develops shopping centers around the United States.

Web Sites

Aaii.com. The stock section of the American Association of Individual Investors' Web site has helpful articles on topics that beginning stock-pickers might find useful. AAII members can get additional materials.

Smartmoney.com/oneasset. Asset allocation system designed to help you see how different asset mixes may be appropriate for investors in different circumstances. Plug in your individual numbers and the site will give you its recommendations.

Yodlee.com. Visit this site to find a sampling of financial services companies that offer account aggregation services.

AFTERWORD

Now that you've reached the end of this book, I hope what you've learned about mastering your Money Type will truly and powerfully launch a prosperous new beginning. I've provided insights, information, and problem-solving tools about the six different financial personality types as I know them—and I ask that you take the material as it applies to you to improve your future. The thing is, I can't make changes for you and I can't take the first step toward making money work better for you.

If there's one truth I'd like you to take with you, it's that there's only an upside to mastering your Money Type. The only investment you have to make is in yourself. To get serious about money, always be aware of how your emotions set your behavior with money into action. Focus on your money strengths and, over time, learn how to control your money weaknesses before they get you into trouble. The result? You'll change from a "have not" into a "have" or "have more" as soon as you get serious about your financial future.

It's your money, so make the most of it. Thrive and enjoy—and, of course, make a great life for yourself. Please let me know how you're doing. If you have any questions about your Money Type, contact me at moneyanswers.com for further information and Money-Type mastering support.

It's up to you!

APPENDIX

Taking Action: Where to Find Further Help

It's not easy to take that first step to financial freedom. But you need not be afraid to ask for help. There's no shame, for example, in hiring experts to guide you through the process. After all, a brain surgeon isn't necessarily the person you'd want tuning your brakes, and I, for one, wouldn't want my car mechanic to tinker with my brain. The point is that it's impossible to know everything about everything, so know your limits and when to ask for help. It may be the best advice you've ever paid for.

Whether you choose to hire experts or go it alone—there are advantages and disadvantages to both—make sure you read, read, read. I can't stress that enough. Knowledge truly is power.

There are many books, trade organizations, Web sites, publications, and government agencies to consult. You'd be amazed at how useful your computer, telephone, and snail mail can be in your quest to learn. This Appendix contains resources that will be useful for every financial personality. The resources that are especially helpful for your specific Money Type can be found at the end of the relevant chapter.

Remember, these resources are a starting point—don't be afraid to keep going. Whether you're a Debt Desperado, an Ostrich, a Coaster, a High Roller, a Squirrel, or a Striver, standing still is probably the worst thing you can do. So don't delay. Take charge of your finances. In many cases, the answers are only a phone call or mouse click away.

Books

Charles Schwab's New Guide to Financial Independence: Practical Solutions for Busy People, by Charles Schwab (Three Rivers Press, 1745 Broadway, New York, NY 10019; 212-782-9000; www.randomhouse.com/crown/trp.html). This revised edition by investment authority Charles Schwab will help you define and set investment goals, prepare and act on an investment plan, prepare for your children's education, deal with market fluctuations, and plan for a comfortable retirement.

The Complete Idiot's Guide to Managing Your Money, by Robert K. Heady and Christy Heady (Alpha Books, 1633 Broadway, New York, NY 10019; 212-366-2000; http://us.penguingroup.com). Simple-to-follow money management basics and loaded with tips to save and make money.

The Everything Personal Finance Book: Manage, Budget, Save, and Invest Your Money Wisely, by Peter J. Sander (Adams Media Corporation, 57 Littlefield Street, Avon, MA 02322; 508-427-7100; www.adamsmedia.com). Helps you choose the best investing options, consolidate and reduce debt, plan for retirement, and save money on your taxes.

Everything You Need to Know About Money and Investing: A Financial Expert Answers the 1,001 Most Frequently Asked Questions, by Sarah Young Fisher and Carol Turkington (Prentice Hall, One Lake Street, Upper Saddle River, NJ 07458; 201-236-7000; http://vig.prenhall.com/home). The Q&A format makes this book user-friendly. Topics include: financial planning, budgeting and debt reduction, insurance, saving for college and retirement, real estate, and taxes.

The Four Pillars of Investing: Lessons for Building a Winning Portfolio, by William J. Bernstein (McGraw-Hill, 1221 Avenue of the Americas, New York, NY 10020; 866-436-8502; www.mcgraw-hill.com). Offers practical advice and is easy to understand.

The Intelligent Investor, revised edition, by Benjamin Graham (updated with new commentary by Jason Zweig). (HarperBusiness, 10 East 53rd Street, New York, NY 10022; 212-207-7583; www.harpercollins.com). First published in 1949, this book has been updated to take into account the 1990s and early-twenty-first-century market trends.

J. K. Lasser's Your Income Tax (John Wiley & Sons, 111 River St., Hoboken, NJ 07030; 201-748-6000; www.wiley.com). Everything you need to know to file your tax return.

Only Investment Guide You'll Ever Need, by Andrew Tobias (Harcourt Trade Publishers, 525 B Street, Suite 1900, San Diego, CA 92101; 619-231-6616; www.harcourtbooks.com). This updated classic touches on every aspect of personal finance.

A Random Walk Down Wall Street: Completely Revised and Updated Eighth Edition, by Burton G. Malkiel (W.W. Norton, 500 Fifth Avenue, New York, NY 10110; 212-354-5500; www.wwnorton.com). A good starting point for novice investors. This classic book is rich in history, information, and advice.

Retire on Less Than You Think: The New York Times Guide to Planning Your Financial Future, by Fred Brock (Henry Holt, 115 West 18th Street, New York, NY 10011; 212-886-9200; www.henryholt.com). This book by Fred Brock of the *New York Times* helps you in your goal of attaining a secure retirement.

The Retirement Savings Time Bomb: And How to Defuse It, by Ed Slott (Viking, 1633 Broadway, New York, NY 10019;

212-366-2000; http://us.penguingroup.com). This book teaches readers how to retain as much of their retirement savings as possible in their own pockets instead of the IRS's.

Rich Dad Poor Dad: What the Rich Teach Their Kids About Money—That the Poor and Middle Class Do Not!, by Robert T. Kiyosaki with Sharon L. Lechter, CPA (Warner Business Books, 1271 Avenue of the Americas, New York, NY 10020; www.richdad.com or www.twbookmark.com). In this classic bestseller, Kiyosaki and Lechter present a unique perspective on how to accumulate wealth, both in real estate and in other ways.

The Right Way to Hire Financial Help: A Complete Guide to Choosing and Managing Brokers, Financial Planners, Insurance Agents, Lawyers, Tax Preparers, Bankers, and Real Estate Agents, second edition, by Charles A. Jaffe (MIT Press, Five Cambridge Center, Cambridge, MA 02142; 617-253-5646; http://mitpress.mit.edu). Takes readers through the basics of hiring and managing brokers, financial planners, insurance agents, lawyers, tax preparers, bankers, and real estate agents.

Publications

Barron's (Dow Jones & Co., One World Financial Center, 200 Liberty Street, New York, NY 10281; 800-369-2834; http://online.barrons.com). Provides information about investing and the market. The Web site has free tools, including an economic calendar and listings of stocks, mutual funds, options, and futures.

Business Week (McGraw-Hill; 1221 Avenue of the Americas, New York, NY 10020; 866-436-8502; www.businessweek.com). Although it focuses more on the economy and business strategy, *Business Week* also has columns about Wall Street and personal investing.

Forbes (60 Fifth Avenue, New York, NY 10011; 212-620-2200; 800-888-9896; www.forbes.com). Known for its acerbic and witty style. Check out the Web site for timely and well-written articles on topics such as estate planning, investing strategies, and retirement, as well as special guides on mutual funds, exchange-traded funds, and international investing.

Fortune (Time & Life Building, 1271 Avenue of the Americas, New York, NY 10020; 212-522-1212; 800-541-1000; www. fortune.com). A business magazine with extensive coverage of Wall Street and stock selection. *Fortune* also publishes extensive lists and rankings of companies, stocks, and more.

Kiplinger's Personal Finance Magazine (1729 H Street NW, Washington, DC 20006; 800-544-0155; www.kiplinger.com). You can subscribe to the paid publication or visit the Web site for articles related to investing. You'll also find tools to help you make financial decisions.

Money (Time & Life Building, 1271 Avenue of the Americas, New York, NY 10020; 212-522-1212; 800-541-1000; www. money.cnn.com). Brings financial planning ideas to average Americans, including advice and news on investing, taxes, retirement, and other topics in personal finance. The Web site has several useful calculators and a "Money 101" course.

SmartMoney (1755 Broadway, 2nd Floor; New York, NY 10019; 800-444-4204; www.smartmoney.com). Look on the Web site for articles about the economy, small business, personal finance, and much more, including sophisticated investing articles.

Wall Street Journal (Dow Jones & Co., One World Financial Center, 200 Liberty Street, New York, NY 10281; 800-369-2834; www.wsj.com). In addition to breaking stories, the paper does a good job of explaining trends and talking about the market in easy-to-understand terms.

Federal and State Government Agencies

Board of Governors of the Federal Reserve System (20th and Constitution Avenue NW, Washington, DC 20551; 202-452-3000; www.federalreserve.gov). Everything you need to know about U.S. monetary policy. The Web site has special links devoted to consumer information and education. In the consumer section, you can find information on banking, mortgages, credit, personal finance, identity theft, and leasing. The education section has tons of information on consumer banking, consumer protection, economics, homes and mortgages, interest rates, loans and credit, and more.

Centers for Medicare and Medicaid Services (7500 Security Boulevard, Baltimore, MD 21244; 877-267-2323; www.cms.hhs.gov). A federal agency that oversees the Medicare and Medicaid health insurance system. Check out the consumer section of the Web site for questions you might have about Medicare.

Federal Trade Commission (600 Pennsylvania Avenue NW, Washington, DC 20580; 877-FTC-HELP; www.ftc.gov). Offers many helpful brochures in the consumer section of the Web site, on topics such as identity theft, investments, privacy, and credit. You can also lodge fraud complaints.

Internal Revenue Service (800-829-1040; www.irs.gov). Contains a wealth of information and forms. Use the Web site to find your local office for personal, face-to-face tax help.

Labor Department, Pension and Welfare Benefits Administration (200 Constitution Avenue NW, Washington, DC 20210; 866-4-USA-DOL; www.dol.gov). Sets rules for and oversees all employee benefits programs. Can explain your rights under federal law.

National Association of Insurance Commissioners (2301 McGee Street, Suite 800, Kansas City, MO 64108; 816-842-3600; www.naic.org). The organization of state insurance regulators as well as regulators from the District of Columbia and the four U.S. territories. From the Web site, consumers can view complaints, licensing, and financial information about a particular insurance company. You can also lodge a complaint online with your state insurance department. You can request a free copy of the following publications: *Buyer's Guides to Fixed Deferred Annuities, Guide to Fixed Deferred Annuities with Appendix for Equity-Indexed Annuities, Choosing a Medigap Policy, Consumer's Guide to Auto Insurance, Consumer's Guide to Home Insurance, Life Insurance Buyer's Guide, Life Insurance Buyer's Guide with Appendix, A Shopper's Guide to Cancer Insurance,* and *A Shopper's Guide to Long-Term Care Insurance.*

National Association of Securities Dealers, Inc. (1735 K Street NW, Washington, DC 20006; 202-728-8000; www.nasd.com). Regulatory body that focuses heavily on investor protection and education. On the group's Web site, consumers can read about scams and complicated products. Consumers can also file a complaint against their broker or brokerage firm and check the professional background, registration and license status, and disciplinary history of their broker.

North American Securities Administrators Association (750 First Street NE, Suite 1140, Washington, DC 20002; 202-737-0900; www.nasaa.org). The umbrella group for state securities regulators. The Web site contains investor education, contact information for state regulators, and an investor complaint center, among other things.

Securities and Exchange Commission (Office of Investor Education and Assistance, 450 Fifth Street NW, Washington, DC 20549; 202-942-7040; www.sec.gov). Agency charged with protecting investors and maintaining fair markets. The investor information section of the SEC's Web site has many calculators and online articles written in easy-to-understand language.

Social Security Administration (Office of Public Inquiries, Windsor Park Building, 6401 Security Boulevard, Baltimore, MD 21235; 800-772-1213; www.ssa.gov). Provides information about your Social Security benefits.

U.S. Department of Education (400 Maryland Avenue SW, Washington, DC 20202; 800-872-5327; www.ed.gov). Everything you need to know about finding and financing college as well as loan consolidation and servicing.

Organizations

AARP (601 E. Street NW, Washington, DC 20049; 888-687-2277; www.aarp.org). Trade group for those nearing retirement and the retired, with lots of resources on every aspect of planning for and enjoying retirement.

Accreditation Council for Accountancy and Taxation (1010 North Fairfax Street, Alexandria, VA 22314; 888-289-7763; www.acatcredentials.org). Accredits specialists in accounting and taxation who serve the financial needs of individuals and small businesses. ACAT also oversees the examinations and standards for Accredited Tax Preparers and Accredited Tax Advisors.

American Arbitration Association (335 Madison Avenue, Floor 10, New York, NY 10017; 212-716-5800; www.adr.org). Will supply you with an arbitrator if you need to settle a dispute with a financial advisor. Has branches in most states. Offers a number of brochures, which can be downloaded free from its Web site, including one on resolving employment disputes and one on resolving commercial financial disputes.

American Association of Individual Investors (625 North Michigan Avenue, Chicago, IL 60611; 800-428-2244; www.aaii.com). A nonprofit organization that provides education and tools designed to help individuals manage their finances effectively and profitably. The Web site has a host of information on various investing topics. Members can also attend local and national events.

American Bankers Association (1120 Connecticut Avenue NW, Washington, DC 20036; 1-800-BANKERS; www.aba.com).

Represents commercial banks in legislative and regulatory activities and legal action. Also educates the public about banking. The consumer section of the group's Web site has information about identity theft, predatory lending, and other fraudulent activities, as well as materials about budgeting, credit, and saving.

American Bar Association (321 North Clark Street, Chicago, IL 60610; 312-988-5000; www.abanet.org). The main trade association for U.S. lawyers. Offers a consumers' guide to legal help and a primer on how courts work.

American Financial Services Association (919 Eighteenth Street NW, Washington, DC 20006; 202-296-5544; www.american finsvcs.com). Represents companies that lend to consumers and educates the public about credit and budgeting issues. Offers educational material to the public at www.afsaef.org. From that site, consumers can request a plethora of publications ranging from personal loans to bankruptcy and view a list of phone numbers for fighting credit fraud.

American Institute of Certified Public Accountants (1211 Avenue of the Americas, New York, NY 10036; 212-596-6200; www.aicpa.org). Represents and maintains standards for CPAs. Visit http://pfp.aicpa.org, for help finding a tax-oriented accountant or an accountant who provides financial planning services. You can also call 888-999-9256.

American Insurance Association (1130 Connecticut Avenue NW, Suite 1000, Washington, DC 20036; 202-828-7100; www. aiadc.org). Represents property/casualty insurance companies in lobbying on insurance-related issues. Educates the public about insurance issues.

American Savings Education Council (2121 K Street NW, Suite 600, Washington, DC 20037; 202-659-0670; www.asec.org). Undertakes initiatives to raise public awareness about what is needed to ensure long-term personal financial independence.

America's Community Bankers (900 Nineteenth Street NW, Suite 400, Washington, DC 20006; 202-857-3100; www.americas communitybankers.com). Trade group of community banks. The Web site has useful calculators related to mortgages, personal debt, retirement, and more. Also has information on mutual funds, annuities, ATM safety, and avoiding telemarketing scams.

Association for Conflict Resolution (1015 18th Street NW, Suite 1150, Washington, DC 20036; 202-464-9700; www. acrnet.org). A group of people interested in alternative dispute resolution techniques. Can help you find a mediator in your area.

Association of Financial Guaranty Insurers (139 Lancaster Street, Albany, NY 12210; 518-449-4698; www.afgi.org). Represents insurance companies that insure municipal bonds against default.

Bond Market Association (360 Madison Avenue, New York, NY 10017; 646-637-9200; www.bondmarkets.com). This trade association's Web site contains useful articles related to investing in bonds as well as helpful links to other organizations, educational materials, and market information.

Certified Financial Planner Board of Standards (1670 Broadway, Suite 600, Denver, CO 80202; 303-830-7500; www.cfp. net). Administers certified financial planner examinations and licenses individuals to use the CFP designation. You can contact the CFP board to check if a planner is certified, has been disciplined by the board, or to lodge a complaint. You can also request a free financial planning resource kit.

CFA Institute (560 Ray C. Hunt Drive, Charlottesville, VA 22903; 800-247-8132; http://www.cfainstitute.org). Formerly known as the Association for Investment Management and Research. Confers the Chartered Financial Analyst (CFA) designation on those who have passed a series of examinations related to investment management. The group's Web site contains information about the CFA, and educational pieces such as "Choosing a Financial Advisor," "Defining Your Investment Objectives," and "12 Common Mistakes Investors Make."

Chartered Property Casualty Underwriters Society (720 Providence Road, Malvern, PA 19355; 800-932-2728; www.cpcu society.org). The society is a professional association of agents and other insurance professionals selling property and casualty insurance and risk management services. The society publishes several newsletters about developments in the property/casualty field. You can search the Web site to find an agent or broker by location or for pertinent articles and links to other insurance-related sites.

Consumer Bankers Association (1000 Wilson Boulevard, Suite 2500, Arlington, VA 22209-3912; 703-276-1750; www.cba net.org). Organization that provides education and research and also lobbies on issues related to retail banking.

Council of Better Business Bureaus (4200 Wilson Boulevard, Suite 800, Arlington, VA 22203; 703-276-0100; www.bbb.org). The national organization for local Better Business Bureaus offers publications on how to avoid fraud.

Credit Union National Association (5710 Mineral Point Road, Madison, WI 53705; 800-356-9655; www.cuna.org). Trade association for credit unions. The Web site has personal finance tips, educational materials, and calculators.

Employee Benefit Research Institute (2121 K Street NW, Suite 600, Washington, DC 20037; 202-659-0670; www.ebri.org). Public policy research organization devoted to employee benefit programs.

Employers Council on Flexible Compensation (927 15th Street NW, Suite 1000, Washington, DC 20005; 202-659-4300; www. ecfc.org). Nonprofit trade association that studies and promotes use of defined contribution plans, 401(k) plans, cafeteria plans, and other employee benefit offerings.

Fannie Mae (3900 Wisconsin Avenue NW, Washington, DC 20016; 202-752-7000; www.fanniemae.com). Private, shareholder-owned company that provides financial products and services that help allow people of all income levels to buy homes. Web site offers consumers information, tools, and worksheets related to buying a home and mortgages. You can also search for a counselor to help you with a reverse mortgage or read about the product in *Money from Home: A Consumer's Guide to Reverse Mortgage Options,* which is available in PDF format.

Financial Accounting Standards Board (401 Merritt 7, PO Box 5116, Norwalk, CT 06856; 203-847-0700; www.fasb.org). Sets financial reporting standards for private-sector organizations. Its sister organization, Governmental Accounting Standards Board, sets standards for state and local governments.

Financial Planning Association (4100 East Mississippi Avenue, Suite 400, Denver, CO 80246; 800-322-4237; www.fpanet. org). Visitors can use the group's Web site to find a financial planner. They can also ask general financial planning questions and access calculators, articles, brochures, and checklists.

Freddie Mac (8200 Jones Branch Drive, McLean, VA 22102; 703-903-2000; www.freddiemac.com). A shareholder-owned corporation chartered by Congress to create a continuous flow of funds to mortgage lenders. The group's Web site takes you through the ABCs of preparing for home ownership, buying a house, and mortgages. Site also has calculators and worksheets to help you throughout the process.

Futures Industry Association (2001 Pennsylvania Avenue NW, Suite 600, Washington, DC 20006; 202-466-5460; www.futures industry.org). Represents brokerage firms and brokers that deal in futures, and lobbies on issues related to the futures industry.

Identity Theft Resource Center (PO Box 26833, San Diego, CA 92196; 858-693-7935; www.idtheftcenter.org). Helping people prevent and recover from identity theft.

Institute of Business and Finance (7911 Herschel Avenue, Suite 201, La Jolla, CA 92037; 800-848-2029; www.icfs.com). This organization grants the Certified Fund Specialist (CFS) designation. CFSs are skilled at helping you assemble a mutual fund portfolio that is appropriate for your needs. The institute also sponsors several other board-certified designations in other areas of personal finance.

Investment Company Institute (1401 H Street NW, Washington, DC 20005; 202-326-5800; www.ici.org). Trade association for the mutual fund industry. The Web site provides key statistics and educational pieces about various facets of the industry from the basics of investing in mutual funds to college planning to retirement planning.

Investment Counsel Association of America (1050 17th Street NW, Suite 725, Washington, DC 20036; 202-293-4222; www.icaa.org). Professional organization of independent investment counsel firms that manage the assets of individuals, pension plans, trusts, and nonprofit institutions, such as foundations. Offers a free membership directory for those who are looking for an investment counselor.

Investment Management Consultants Association (5619 DTC Parkway, Suite 500, Greenwood Village, CO 80111; 303-770-3377; www.imca.org). The professional group for consultants who find and monitor the performance of money managers on behalf of individual and institutional investors. The group sponsors the Web site www.investmenthelp.org, where you can search for a certified investment management analyst in your area. That site also has financial calculators on home financing, investments, retirement, leasing, and more.

Investment Program Association (1140 Connecticut Avenue NW, Suite 1040, Washington, DC 20036; 202-775-9750; www.ipa-dc.org). Trade association that represents investors in non-traded investment programs such as partnerships, nontraded real estate investment trusts, and limited liability companies.

Investor Responsibility Research Center (1350 Connecticut Avenue NW, Suite 700, Washington, DC 20036; 202-833-0700; www.irrc.org). Publishes impartial reports and analyses on contemporary business and public policy issues for corporations and institutional investors that vote proxies independently.

Mutual Fund Education Alliance (100 NW Englewood Road, Suite 130, Kansas City, MO 64118; 816-454-9422; www.mfea.com). An educational group composed mostly of no-load mutual funds. Consumers can obtain free educational materials on topics such as asset planning, saving for college, and saving for retirement. They can also find financial calculators, asset allocation models, and learn the basics of mutual fund investing.

National Association of Enrolled Agents (1120 Connecticut Avenue NW, Suite 460, Washington, DC 20036; 202-822-6232; www.naea.org). A group of enrolled agents—people who have demonstrated technical competence in the field of taxation and can represent you before the IRS. Use the Web site to find names of enrolled agents in your area.

National Association of Personal Financial Advisors (3250 North Arlington Heights Road, Suite 109, Arlington Heights, IL 60004; 800-366-2732; www.napfa.org). This association represents financial planners who work for fees only and collect no commissions from the sale of products. Consumers can get referrals to fee-only planners via the group's Web site.

National Association of Realtors (430 North Michigan Avenue, Chicago, IL 60611; 800-874-6500; www.realtor.org). Trade association for Realtors. The consumer-oriented Web site, www.realtor.com, includes tools such as a home affordability calculator and how to figure the best mortgage for your situation. Can help you find a Realtor in your area.

National Association of Women Business Owners (8405 Greensboro Drive, Suite 800, McLean, VA 22102; 800-55-NAWBO; www.nawbo.org). Provides technical assistance, management training, and business and economic information to women business owners through national meetings and local chapters, and represents members in legislative and lobbying efforts.

National Consumers League (1701 K Street NW, Suite 1200, Washington, DC 20006; 202-835-3323; www.nclnet.org). Offers free brochures on how to avoid fraud. Consumers can also report fraudulent activity through the National Fraud Information Center at 800-876-7060 or online at www.fraud.org.

National Endowment for Financial Education (5299 DTC Boulevard, Suite 1300, Greenwood Village, CO 80111; 303-741-6333; www.nefe.org). Nonprofit foundation dedicated to educating Americans about personal finance and helping them make appropriate decisions to reach financial goals. Resource center has many educational brochures on retirement, life-changing situations, and raising a money-smart child. Also offers a guidebook to help late savers prepare for retirement and a "Wealth Care Kit" with worksheets and checklists for dealing with insurance, investments, taxes, retirement, and estate planning.

National Senior Citizens Law Center (1101 14th Street NW, Suite 400, Washington, DC 20005; 202-289-6976; www.nsclc. org). Specializes in litigation, research, lobbying, and training lawyers on issues of concern to retired persons. Use the Web site to find an elder care attorney and other useful links.

National Society of Accountants (1010 North Fairfax Street, Alexandria, VA 22314; 800-966-6679; www.nsacct.org). Can help you find a professional to meet your personal and small-business needs in accounting services, audits, tax preparation, taxpayer representation, financial and estate planning, and management services.

Pension Benefit Guaranty Corporation (1200 K Street NW, Washington, DC 20005; 202-326-4000; www.pbgc.gov). Federal agency that insures defined benefit pension plan payments to pensioners in case the pension plans are unable to fulfill their obligations. The Web site has a retirement planning section with useful links. Publishes various newsletters on pension-related issues.

Pension Rights Center (1350 Connecticut Avenue NW, Suite 206, Washington, DC 20036; 202-296-3776; www.pensionrights. org). Consumer group that helps educate the public about pension issues. Offers resources to people having trouble with their pensions.

Privacy Rights Clearinghouse (3100 5th Avenue, Suite B, San Diego, CA 92103; 619-298-3396; www.privacyrights.org). A nonprofit consumer education program established in 1992, it works to educate consumers about informational privacy issues and their legal privacy rights. Has a hotline for consumers to report privacy abuses and request information. Also provides fact sheets, in English and Spanish, on topics including Internet privacy, wireless communications, junk mail, medical information, and identity theft.

Profit Sharing/401(k) Council of America (20 North Wacker Drive, Suite 3700, Chicago, IL 60606; 312-419-1863; www. psca.org). Has articles and tools related to retirement planning.

Securities Industry Association (120 Broadway, New York, NY 10271; 212-608-1500; www.sia.com). Represents securities brokers and dealers, underwriters, and investment bankers in lobbying Congress on issues of concern to the industry. Educates the public about the securities industry.

Society of Financial Service Professionals (270 South Bryn Mawr Avenue, Bryn Mawr, PA 19010; 610-526-2500; www.financial pro.org). Will refer you to a credentialed financial service professional in your area that specializes in services such as financial planning, estate planning, retirement counseling, and asset management. You can also download such articles as "General

Financial Planning," "Choosing a Financial Planner," "Buying Insurance," and "Life-Stage Information."

U.S. Chamber of Commerce (1615 H Street NW, Washington, DC 20062; 202-659-6000; www.uschamber.com). Represents the business community's views on business, the economy, and other issues at the federal, state, and local level. Sponsors educational programs. Provides special help to small businesses.

Web Sites

Agingwithdignity.com. Includes a template for a living will that meets legal requirements in most states and the District of Columbia.

Bankrate.com. This handy site allows users to compare rates for a host of products, including CDs, money markets, mortgages, and home equity loans. The site also has numerous articles on a variety of topics ranging from personal finance to real estate to auto loans and credit cards.

Bloomberg.com. Provides news, commentary, and more.

Bond information (www.bondsonline.com; www.investingin bonds.com; www.nasdbondinfo.com). These sites contain much valuable information about bonds, including tools, news, and calculators.

Cardweb.com. Site helps you find a credit card that's right for you, such as ones with a low or no annual fee or ones that offer frequent flyer miles or other rewards.

Credit monitoring (www.annualcreditreport.com). This Web site is a centralized service where consumers can request annual credit reports. The site was created by the three national consumer credit reporting agencies, Equifax, Experian, and Trans Union (www.equifax.com; www.experian.com; www.transunion.com). Visit the agencies' individual Web sites for more information on credit, understanding your report, and other educational materials.

Domania.com. Site allows users to check rates, see if they qualify for a mortgage, and get advice on buying, selling, or owning a home. You can also get an estimate of your home's value and use the site's tools to determine whether or not to refinance.

Financeware.com. Helps you find a financial advisor. You can also experiment with a trial version of the company's software.

Financial Education Clearinghouse (www.nefe.org/amexecon fund). A joint effort between American Express and the National Endowment for Financial Education. Offers a wide range of curricula, self-study programs, and Web site resources. Topics include banking, budgeting, credit management, estate planning, insurance, risk management, savings, and taxes.

Financialengines.com. For a fee this site will create an investment strategy and provide advice and monitoring services.

Financiallearning.com. This site is a gold mine of information for people looking to learn about financial matters. Has numerous calculators on budgeting, estate planning, retirement planning, and taxes, as well as articles on topics ranging from health care to life insurance to retirement to college planning to making smart investments.

Financial-planning.com. Covers the financial planning industry and the latest trends in financial planning.

Firstgov.com. The U.S. government's official Web portal. Everything you need to know about government-related services.

H&R Block (www.hrblock.com). Site has a tax estimator, a withholding calculator, online tax programs, and other tax- and investment-related articles.

Hoovers.com. Searchable database of more than 12,000 company profiles. Some information is free to the public, while other data is subscription-based.

Insurance.com. Can help you figure out your insurance needs and do a price comparison for you.

Investools.com. A comprehensive investment Web site with tools and information to help you pick stocks, bonds, and mutual funds, whether you are a novice or experienced investor.

Investopedia.com. A treasure trove of information, from articles on investments to calculators to a dictionary of terms and tutorials.

Investors.com. The online version of *Investor's Business Daily.* You can read articles for free, use various investing tools, and sign up for workshops in your area.

Investorsleague.com. A free stock market simulation sponsored by the League of American Investors. Register online and receive a $100,000 twenty-stock virtual portfolio.

jklasser.com. J. K. Lasser's Year-Round Tax Strategies. Covers the main areas of tax planning, including deductions and the latest tax news. You can also submit your questions to a tax expert.

Kelley Blue Book (www.kbb.com). Site allows you to compare new and used car prices and to research models. Provides buying and selling advice and an online payment calculator.

Leadfusion.com. Site offers a plethora of calculators and tools on topics such as home loans, savings, investments, and life insurance. Spanish-speaking consumers can also use the tools with ease.

Lipperweb.com. Can help you find and track mutual fund performance.

Microsoft Money (www.microsoft.com/money). A simple program designed to track your income, expenses, and net worth; keep your checkbook; and pay your bills electronically.

Moneycentral.msn.com. Filled to the brim with market news, tools, planners, articles, and useful links.

Morningstar.com. Offers news and analyses on markets, stocks, and mutual funds, for individual investors. In addition to data, investors can get information on a host of topics including retirement savings, college planning, and taxes. Investors can also take online seminars and read articles pertaining to new products and trends.

The Motley Fool (www.fool.com). Site contains news, articles, discussions, and many more educational items to help individual investors.

National Association of Automobile Dealers (www.nada.com). New and used prices for cars, motorcycles, boats, etc.

Project for Financial Independence (http://www.consultaplanner. org). View the Web site to see if you qualify for pro bono financial planning assistance. You can also access personal finance articles, brochures, and tools provided by the Project for Financial Independence's six sponsoring organizations, which include the American Institute of Certified Public Accountants and Financial Planning Association.

Retirement Planning (http://retireplan.about.com). All about retirement planning. Full of informative articles and useful calculators.

Quicken.com. This site is a wealth of information for do-it-yourselfers. Consumers can sign up for a free newsletter, or they can use the online debt-reduction planner, savings calculator, and loan calculator. The site also offers insurance quotes, product demos, tax tips, a bill pay option, and much more.

Savingsbonds.gov. Web site of the U.S. Treasury that answers frequently asked questions and includes a "Savings Bond Earnings Report" telling you what your bonds are earning.

Standardandpoors.com. Provides market data, mutual fund data, research, and more.

Stocksearchintl.com. A resource to help you determine the value of your old stock and bond certificates and holdings in companies that have been merged out of existence.

Taxcut.com. Offers products and resources to help you do your taxes.

Tax Sites (http://taxsites.com). An online index of tax and accounting Web sites throughout the United States.

360 Degrees of Financial Literacy (www.360financialliteracy. org). The American Institute of Certified Public Accountants sponsors this educational site, which is full of useful information about financial planning during various life stages. The site also has articles and tools related to owning a business, education planning, estate planning, government benefits, investment planning, personal finance, protection planning, retirement planning, and tax planning.

Turbotax.com. Takes you through a tax preparation exercise using a series of questions and answers. Provides valuable advice and planning tips in preparing your tax strategy and returns.

See, there's more information out there than you thought, right? Guess what? There's even more. Now that you have a general idea of where to go, take a look at the ideas for your specific Money Type found in each chapter's Financial Path and the concluding Resources sections. You may also want to peruse the other Money Types as well, just to see if there are any other resources that strike your fancy. Happy hunting!

INDEX